Nig ght Photography

THE E

AMMONITE PRESS

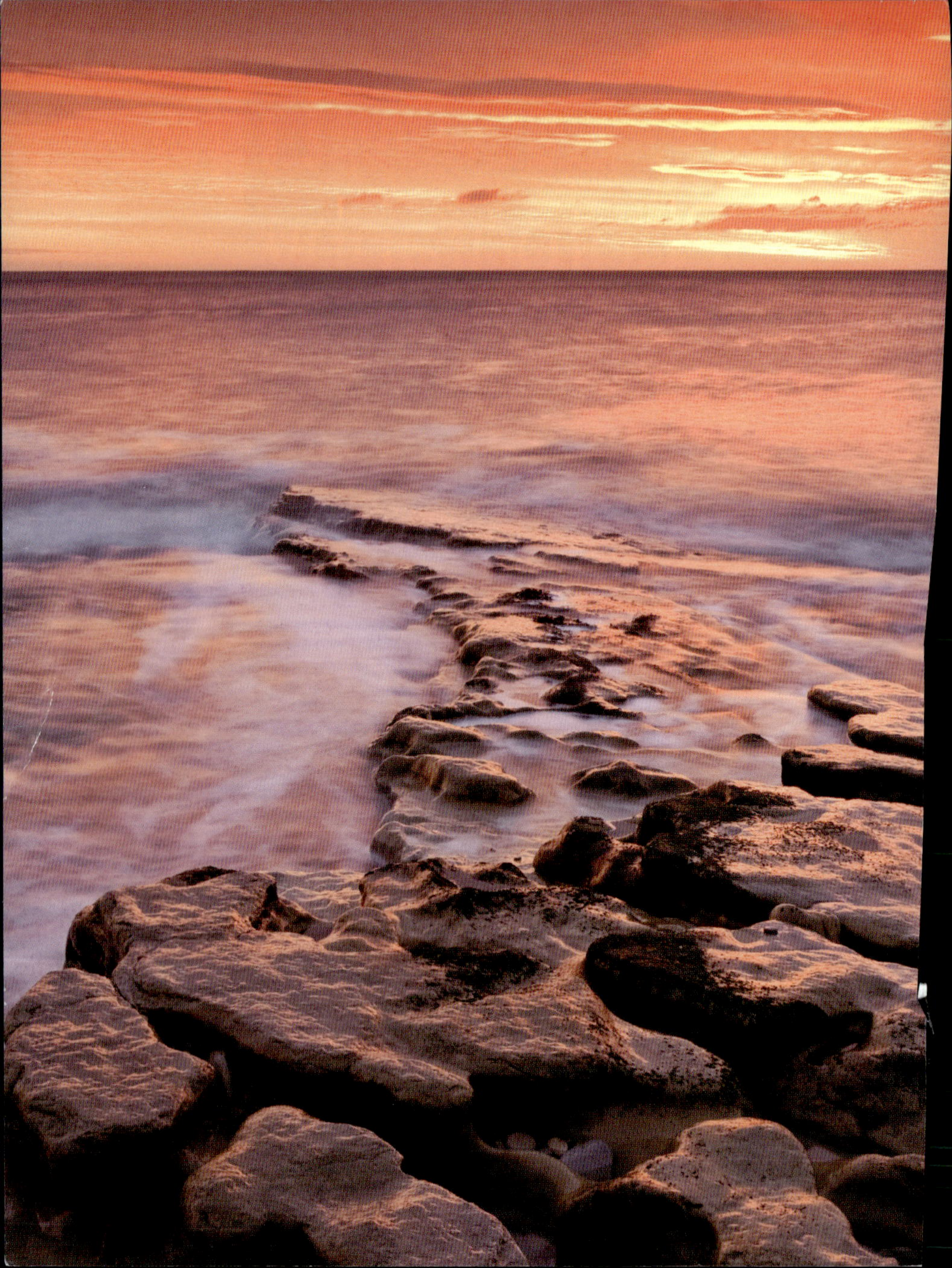

Night & Low Light Photography

THE EXPANDED GUIDE

David Taylor

AMMONITE
PRESS

First published 2012 by
Ammonite Press
an imprint of AE Publications Ltd
166 High Street, Lewes, East Sussex, BN7 1XU, United Kingdom

ISBN 978-1-90770-861-9

A catalog record for this book is available from the British Library.

Editor: Chris Gatcum
Series Editor: Richard Wiles
Design: Richard Dewing Associates

Typeset in Frutiger
Color reproduction by GMC Reprographics
Printed and bound in China by Hing Yip Printing Co. Ltd

(Page 2)
Sunrise over the "Wherry," northeast England.

CONTENTS

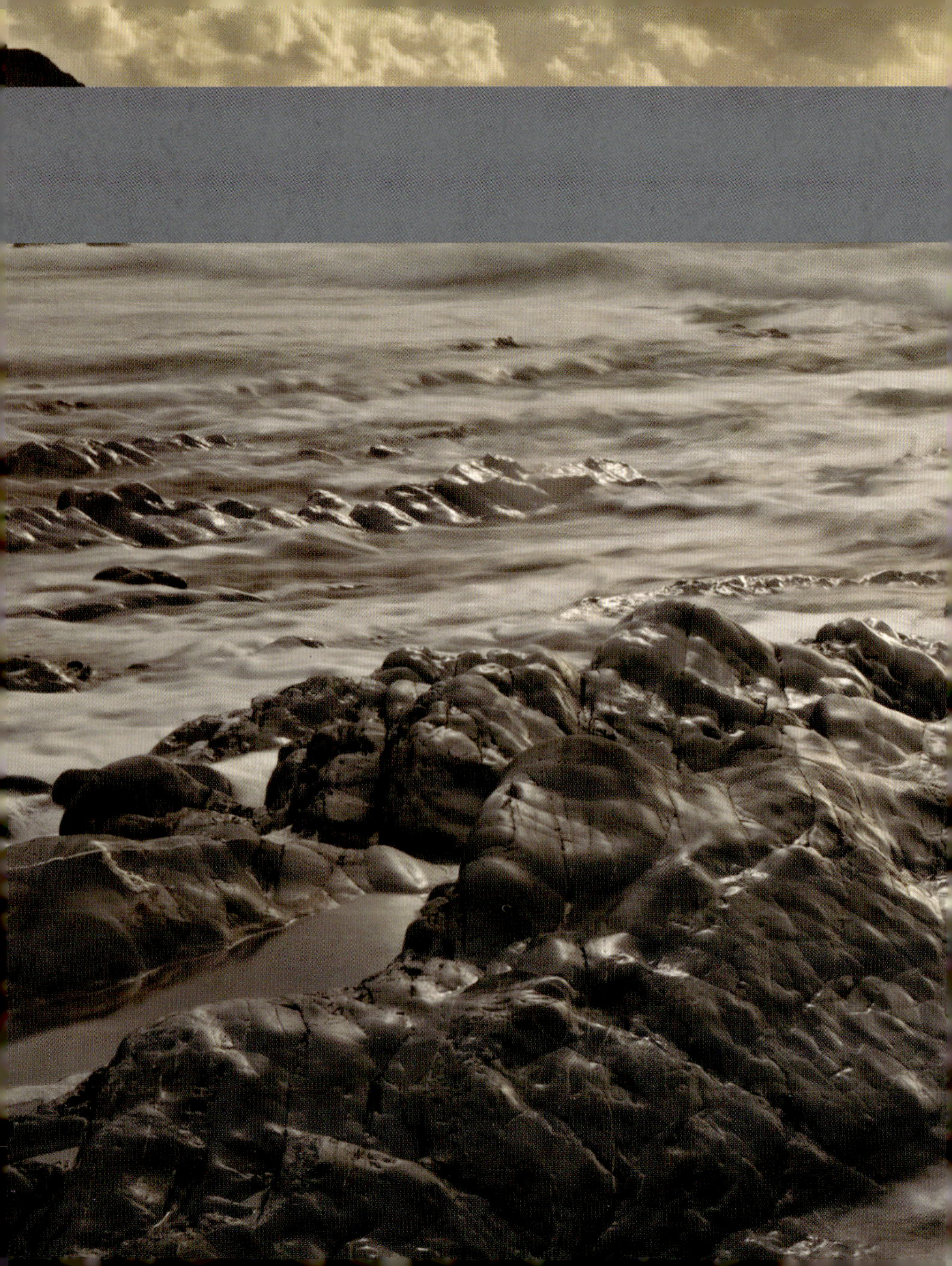

CHAPTER 1 LIGHT

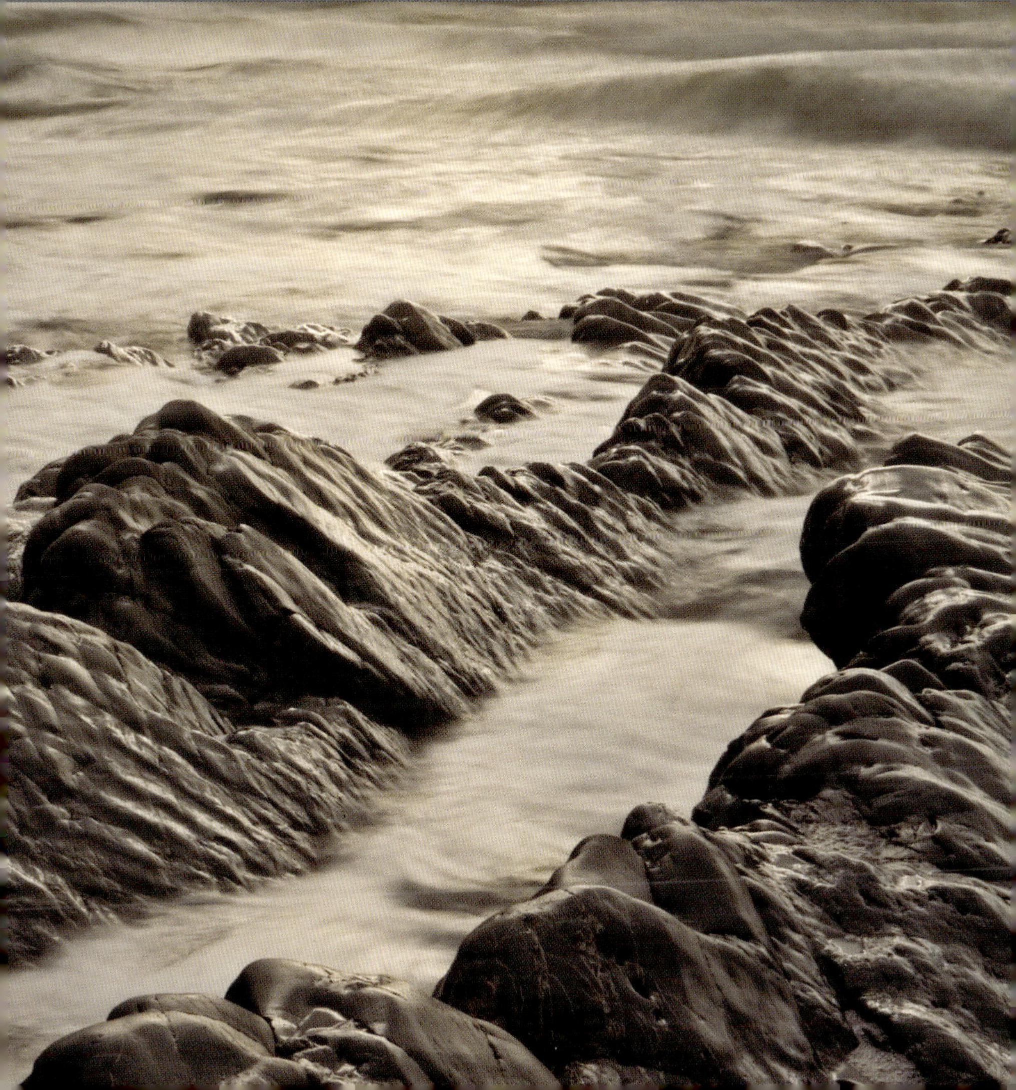

Light

Photography is the art of capturing light. However, this doesn't mean that photography should only be about sunny days. Working in low light is arguably a more interesting way of recording the world around you.

In the modern world there is always light. Even on the darkest night, light pollution can add a subtle glow to the sky, and where there is light, there can be photography. Working in low light is arguably easier now than it has ever been: sensor technology is improving all the time and techniques that were once impossible are now achievable with relative ease.

Over the next seven chapters we'll be exploring how to work and photograph in low light, starting with a look at light itself, and how its various qualities will affect the way in which your subjects are recorded. We'll also look at the seasons and how your location affects when and where you'll encounter low light.

Low light photography is a subject that I find endlessly fascinating. The world is changed when light levels drop, becoming more magical and mysterious. Hopefully, by the time you reach the end of this book, you'll share my enthusiasm.

Canon EOS 7D, 70–200mm lens (at 135mm), 1/20 sec. at f/4, ISO 6400

CAT
This image was shot handheld in low light using ISO 6400 and an image-stabilized lens. It's not a great shot, but it's sharp and would have been impossible to record without a modern digital camera system.

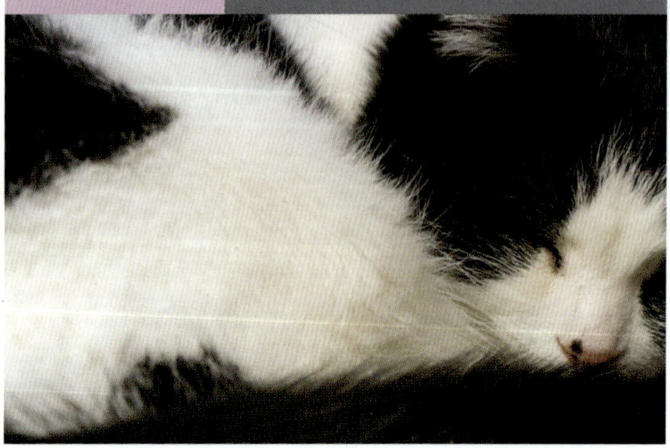

DAY OR NIGHT? *(Opposite)*
Superficially, this looks like a typical daytime scene, but it was actually shot at night: the light bursting from behind the trees is the moon. With the right exposure, photography can turn night into day.

Canon EOS 7D, 17–40mm lens (at 35mm), 2 min. at f/4, ISO 100

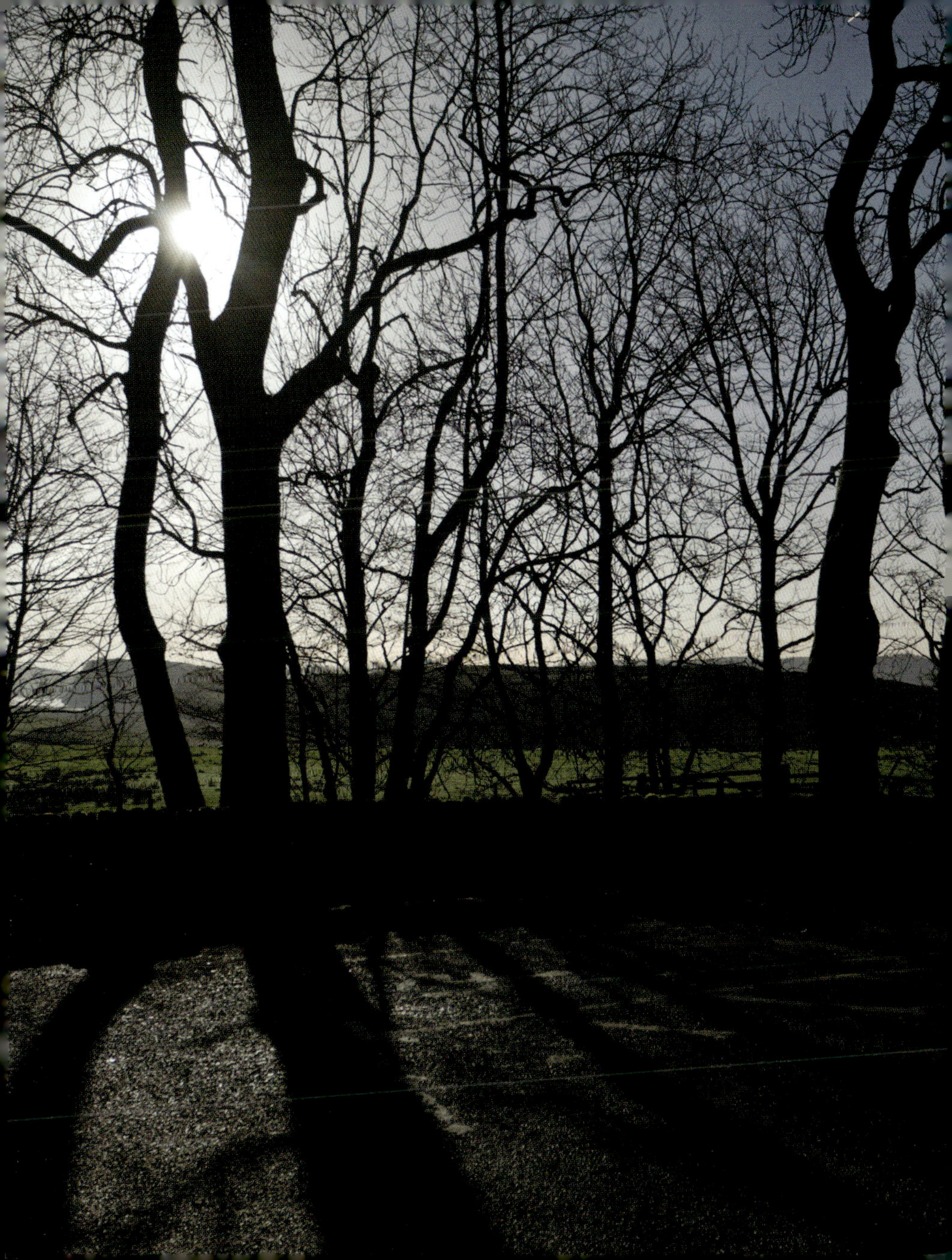

Lighting direction

Light is needed to make a photograph. However, the success or otherwise of an image often depends on the direction of the light.

Frontal lighting

Frontal lighting will illuminate your subject when the light source is directly behind your camera (or on top of your camera, as it is with flash). This type of lighting will evenly illuminate your subject, and it is easy to obtain a good exposure. However, frontal light tends to flatten texture and reduce a subject's sense of form. Also, if you're shooting with the sun (or other light source) behind you, keeping your own shadow out of the picture can be problematic, particularly when you are shooting with a wide-angle lens.

Side lighting

As the name suggests, side lighting is light that falls across the image space. Unlike frontal lighting, side lighting reveals texture and form, which is why landscape photographers often work at the ends of the day: when the sun is low, shadows can reveal dips and mounds in terrain that might otherwise seem perfectly flat.

Side lighting does have its drawbacks, though. Three-dimensional subjects can be brightly lit on one side, and in deep shadow on the other, resulting in high contrast that can make it difficult to obtain the correct exposure. As you will see in chapter 3, using filters and reflectors are two ways of combating this.

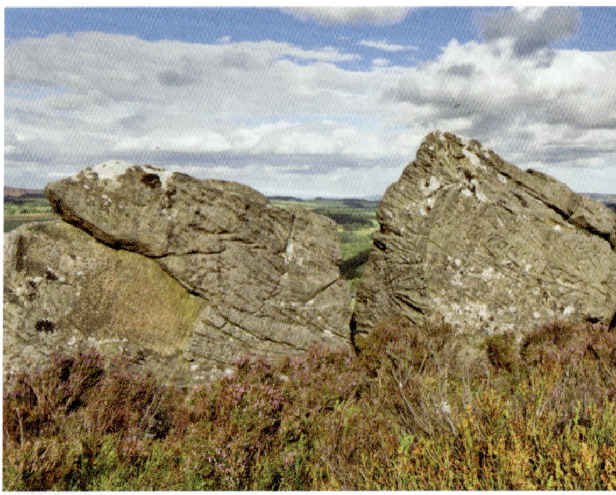

FRONT LIGHTING
The sun was behind me when this image was created. For me, it's not successful because the interesting texture of the rocks has been lost. I should have waited until later in the day, so that the sun was in a more favorable position.

Canon EOS 7D, 10–22mm lens (at 15mm), 1/25 sec. at f/11, ISO 320

Backlighting

Unsurprisingly, backlighting is the direct opposite of front lighting. The light in this instance will be behind your subject, pointing directly toward the camera. This means that contrast will be very high and it's likely that your subject will be in silhouette. Backlit scenes can look very dramatic, and the shadows will be projected toward the camera, as seen in the image at the start of this chapter.

If you don't want your chosen subject to be in silhouette, a backlit scene will require the use of either a reflector or additional lighting such as flash. Backlighting with a fill-in light is particularly effective when shooting portraits, as your subject's hair will be lit from behind (producing a halo effect). Perhaps more importantly, your subject will not be squinting in the light, so should be able to hold a more natural facial expression.

Flare

Lens flare is non-image forming light that occurs when rays of light from a strong point light source enter a lens and are reflected around inside the lens before reaching the sensor. This causes streaks and colored blobs as well as a reduction in contrast across an image, and is most likely to occur when shooting using side and backlighting.

A lens hood can help reduce flare caused by side lighting, but these are difficult to use with filters so my personal preference is not to use them. Instead, if flare from side lighting might be a problem, and my camera is on a tripod, I shield the lens with my body so that a shadow is cast across the front of the lens—the trick is not ending up in the image too! Flare from backlighting is more difficult to deal with, but keeping the glass elements of your lenses clean will help, as will keeping the light source hidden behind your subject.

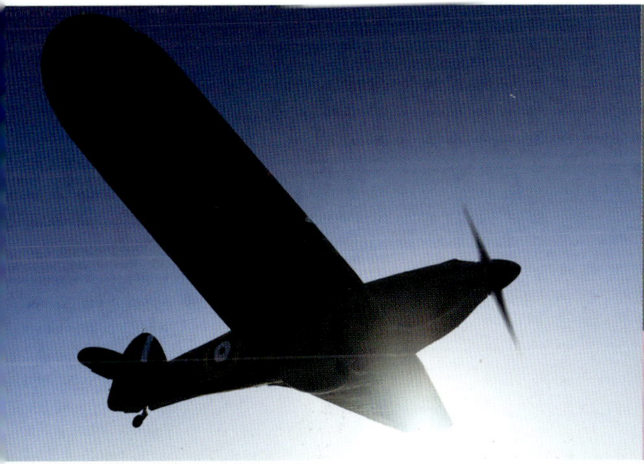

FLARE
Although flare is technically a blemish, in this instance I think it suits the subject.

Canon EOS 7D, 10–22mm lens (at 13mm), 1/1600 sec. at f/5.6, ISO 200

The qualities of light

Light can be soft or hard, and while some subjects will benefit from one, the other will not help them.

Hardness

Hard light is strongly directional and usually emanates from a point light source. Point light sources are those that are relatively small in comparison to the subject being lit: naked household bulbs and the sun when it is high in a cloudless sky, for example.

Hard lighting creates levels of high contrast with bright highlights and deep shadows. The edges of shadows are sharply defined with little or no shading from light to dark, and the closer a point light source is to your subject, the harder the shadows will be. One way to soften a point light source is to move your subject away from it, although this will also reduce the intensity and so requires longer exposures.

Hard light is generally unflattering for portraiture, although it can create a moody feel to photographs of men. In low light photography you will probably encounter hard lighting more frequently in urban environments than you will in the natural landscape.

HARD
This stone carving was lit from below with a point light source. As a result, the light is hard and contrast is high. However, this has helped to emphasize the texture of the stone.

Canon EOS 5D, 50mm lens, 1/50 sec. at f/3.2, ISO 800

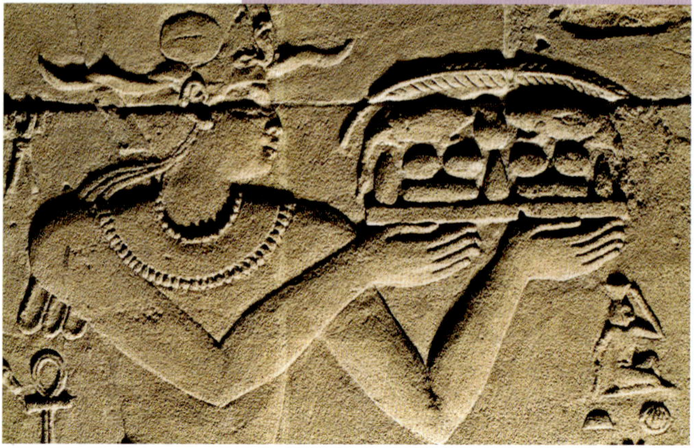

SOFT
This image was created on a wet, overcast day. This produced soft light that suits the subject.

Canon EOS 7D, 70–200mm lens (at 200mm), 1/200 sec. at f/4, ISO 320

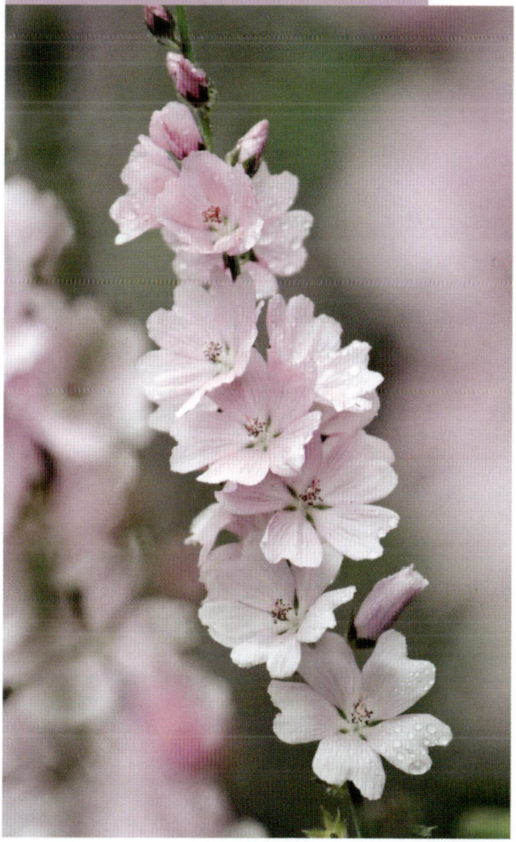

Soft light

A light that is relatively larger than the subject being lit will be soft. Soft lighting reduces contrast, as the light wraps around a subject, and shadows (if there are any) will be diffuse, with soft edges. Bright specular highlights are generally eliminated.

In the natural world, light from the sun is soft when it is scattered by cloud or mist. Shade is also an example of natural soft lighting—the light in shade comes from ambient light from the sky above.

Artificial light is generally hard, but fluorescent strip lighting is softer than domestic bulbs because the light emanates from a larger area. Shining a light source through a translucent white panel will soften it, as will reflecting the light. Lampshades are used in domestic interiors to make lighting more subtle and pleasant, even though the intensity of the light is reduced.

Soft light does not emphasize texture, and subjects can therefore look flat. Landscapes don't usually benefit from soft lighting, but it's an ideal light for portraiture and for subjects such as flowers.

Camera: Canon EOS 7D
Lens: 10–22mm lens (at 22mm)
Exposure: 1/125 sec. at f/9
ISO: 100

BACKLIGHTING

Translucent subjects (those that diffuse light as it passes through them) respond well to backlighting. Backlighting helps to define the shape and form of a translucent subject.

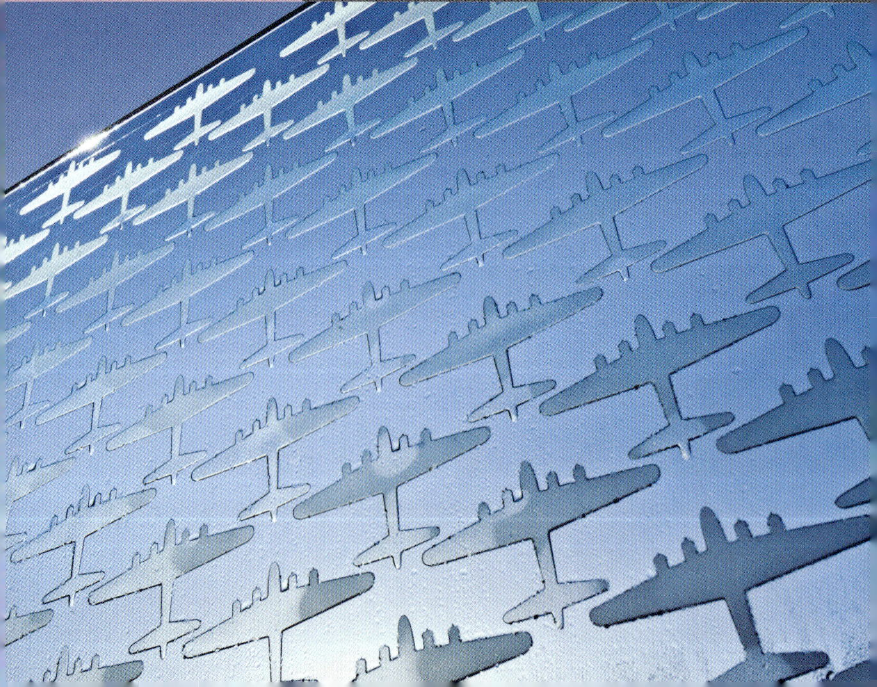

Camera: Pentax 67II
Lens: 200mm lens
Exposure: Unrecorded
ISO: 50 (Fuji Velvia)

In the landscape, side lighting is most often seen early in the morning or late in the afternoon when the sun is low in the sky. Side lighting at these times of day helps to define the textural quality of the landscape.

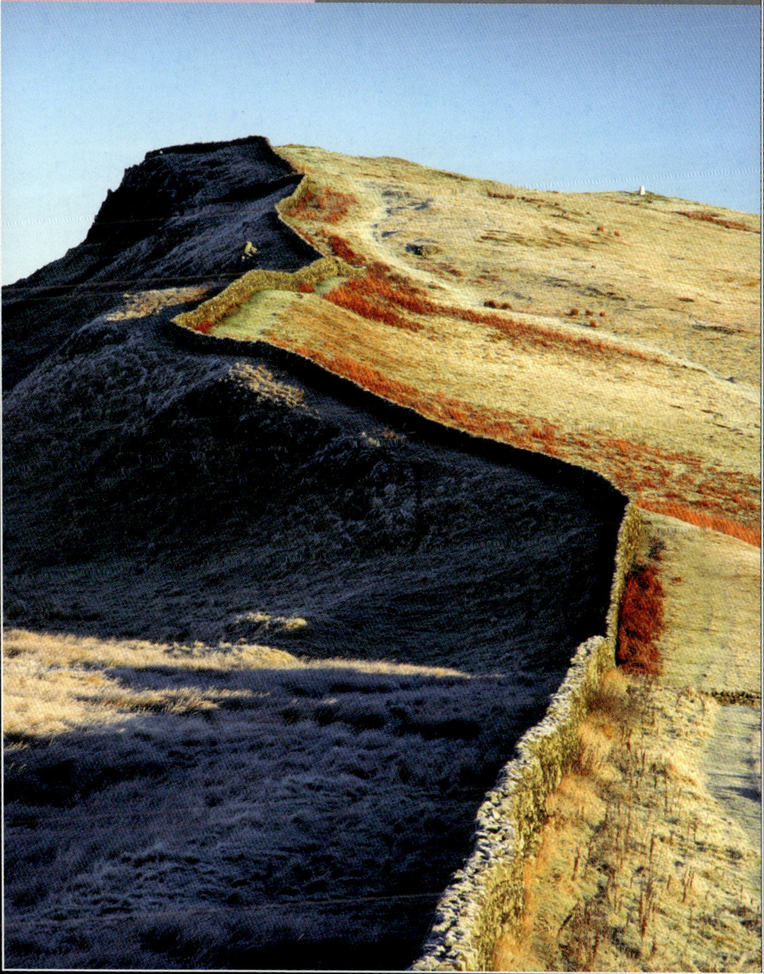

Color temperature

What we perceive as white light can be anything but that, as light often has a color bias that we don't notice. Cameras, being objective recording devices, are much more responsive to shifts in color.

Color bias

Visible light is a mix of different wavelengths, ranging from long wavelengths that correspond to red, across the spectrum of colors, to the shorter blue-violet wavelengths. Light that has a greater proportion of red wavelengths will be "warmer" in color; light with a preponderance of blue wavelengths will be "cooler." This variation in the color of light is known as color temperature which is measured in degrees Kelvin (K).

Somewhat counter-intuitively, the lower the color temperature of a light source, the warmer the light is. Candlelight has a color temperature of 1800K, for example, whereas the blue ambient light found in deep shade is approximately 7000K. Light that is neutral (with no color bias) is approximately 5500K, which is the color temperature of electronic flash and the light from the sun at midday.

White balance

It is possible to set your camera to neutralize the color bias of a particular light source by using the white balance facility. There are usually several ways to do this, with the simplest being to set your camera to Auto white balance (AWB). Set to AWB your camera will process an image so that it looks as though it was shot under a neutral light source.

Color temperature	
1800–2000K	Candlelight
2500K	Torchlight
2800K	Domestic lighting
3000K	Sunrise sunset
3400K	Tungsten lighting
3500K	Morning/afternoon sunlight
5000K–5500K	Midday sunlight
5500K	Electronic flash
6000–6500K	Overcast conditions
7000–8000K	Shade
10,000K	Clear blue sky

For slightly more control, most cameras offer a series of presets represented by different symbols. Although they vary subtly between cameras, the symbols for the various presets are shown below. Some cameras also let you set a Kelvin value, often in steps of 100–200K.

The greatest amount of control over color temperatures is achieved by setting a custom white balance. The mechanics of how to set a custom white balance vary from camera to camera, but it usually involves shooting an image of a white (or neutral gray) surface in the same light as your subject. The image should be entirely filled with this surface. Any other elements in the image could affect the accuracy of the result. Once this image has been written to the camera's memory card it can be selected as the custom white balance target from the relevant menu. The custom white balance preset should now be selected.

> ### Notes
> *Setting the correct white balance is important when shooting JPEG. Raw users can adjust white balance more easily in post-production.*
>
> *A custom white balance is only relevant for one particular lighting situation. If you move out of that situation it is likely that the custom white balance will no longer be relevant.*

AWB	Automatic White Balance
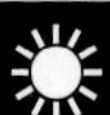	Daylight: Normal sunny conditions
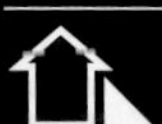	Shade: When shooting in shadow
	Cloudy: Adds warmth to an image on overcast days
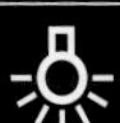	Tungsten: Incandescent domestic lighting
	White fluorescent lighting
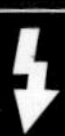	Flash
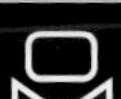	Custom white balance

Low light white balance

Some subjects benefit from corrected white balance, but there is no right or wrong answer to the subject. Some images plainly look wrong if corrected and this applies most strongly to those shot in low light. A good example is the warm light of sunrise; it could be neutralized, but this would reduce the atmosphere of the image. White balance is also very subjective. There is nothing inherently wrong with an image that is warmer or cooler than is strictly accurate, and color can be used to convey mood very effectively. Blues are associated with calmness, emotional detachment, and melancholy, for example, while reds are dangerous and exciting, but also romantic and lively.

Before digital there was film. Color film was available as either daylight or tungsten balanced, with any further color correction achieved through the use of filters. I regularly used daylight-balanced film such as Fuji Velvia, but I would not filter the film at all when shooting low light scenes and simply accept the resulting color cast. This habit is still ingrained and my digital camera is usually set to a daylight preset (unless I'm shooting under a strongly-colored light source, such as domestic lighting). Because I shoot Raw I can alter the color temperature in post-production, but I often find that little adjustment is needed. This is my way of shooting, but there's nothing wrong with finding your own solution.

Canon EOS 7D, 70–200mm lens (at 160mm), 10 sec. at f/6.3, ISO 200

MIXED
The color temperature of artificial lighting can vary enormously. The streetlamps in the background are far warmer than the lighting in the foreground.

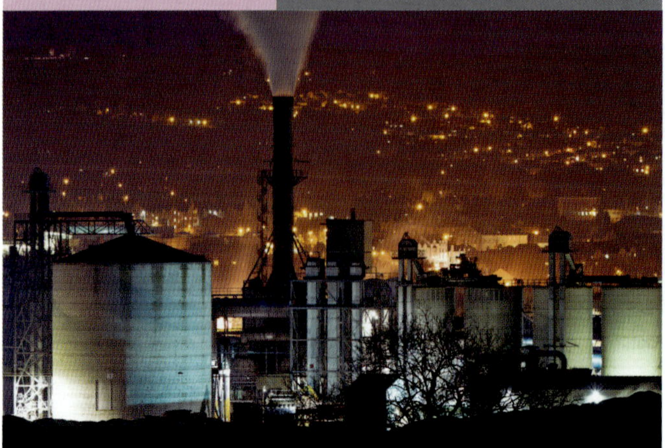

WHITE BALANCE
(Opposite)
These four images have been converted using different white balance presets in Adobe Lightroom:
Top left: Tungsten (2850K) *Top right:* Fluorescent (3800K) *Bottom left:* Daylight (5500K) *Bottom right:* Shade (7500K).
The Daylight preset is the closest match to the lighting conditions that the image was created in.

Canon EOS 7D, 50mm lens, 1/40 sec. at f/8, ISO 200

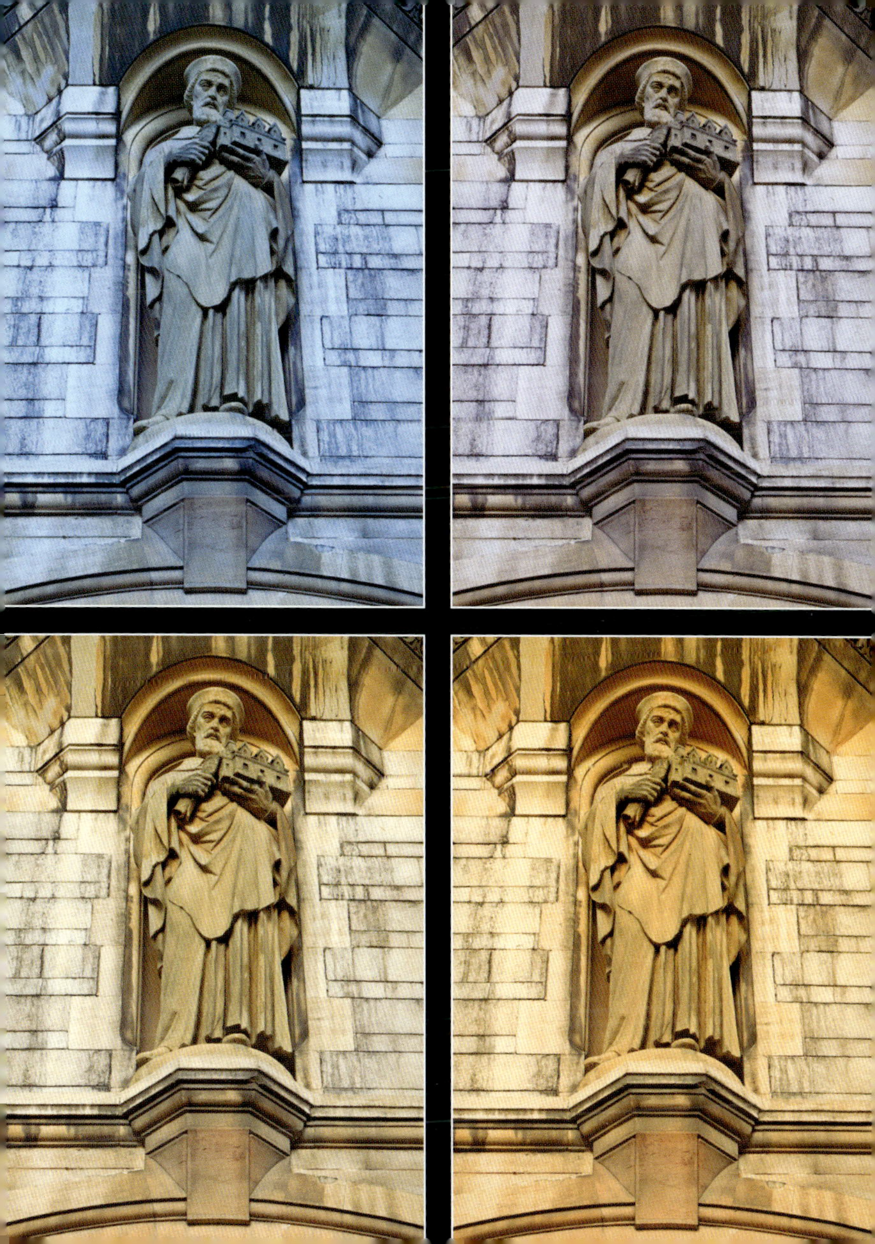

The seasons

Outdoors, the opportunity for low light shooting will vary throughout the year. Understanding how the seasons affect the length of night and day will help you prepare for low light photography sessions.

Looking in the right direction

The earth is tilted relative to its orbit around the sun. At the summer solstice (June 20–22) the North Pole is tilted toward the sun. The length of a day is at maximum in the northern hemisphere and is shortest in the southern hemisphere. Above the Arctic Circle the sun does not set and there is twenty-four hours of daylight; below the Antarctic Circle the sun does not rise and there is twenty-four hours of night. This is reversed at the winter solstice (December 20–22) when the South Pole points toward the sun.

Between these two extremes are the spring (March 20–22) and fall (September 20–22) equinoxes when day and night hours are equal in both hemispheres. At the equator the change of seasons has little effect on the length of day or night; the hours of both are roughly equal throughout the year.

The earth's axial tilt also affects the direction the sun rises and sets throughout the year. At

Tip

http://suncalc.net *is an excellent online tool for calculating the time and direction of sunrise and sunset.*

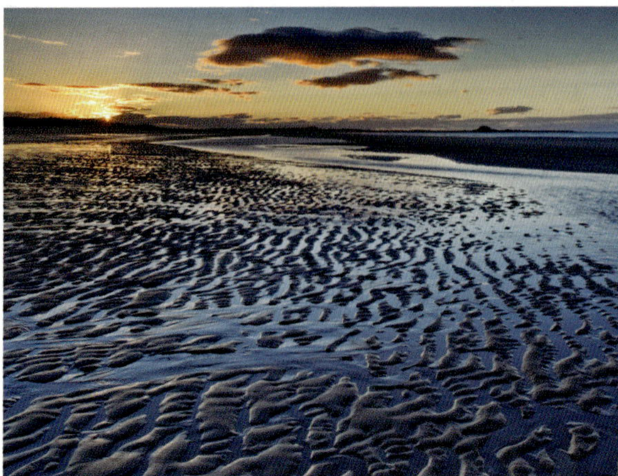

SUMMER

This image was recorded at 54° N, at the summer solstice. The length of day is at its longest and the sun sets at its most northerly.

Canon EOS 1Ds MkII, 17–40mm lens (at 30mm), 1/6 sec. at f/16, ISO 100

the December solstice 50° North and South (roughly the latitude of London and Rio Gallegos respectively) the sun rises in the southeast and sets in the southwest. At the two equinoxes it rises almost directly due east and sets due west. And then at the June solstice, the sun rises in the northeast and sets in the northwest.

Regardless of the time of year, the sun is always due south midway between sunrise and sunset (which may or may not be precisely 12.00pm, depending on your longitude and whether daylight saving is in operation).

Knowing the direction the sun rises and sets will help to make your low light photography trips more successful. This is particularly true for landscape photography, as landscape locations may work better in one season than another. If your subject is north facing and you want it to be directly lit at sunrise you need to be there close to the summer solstice. At the winter solstice, the sun will rise behind the subject and it will be in shadow (this could be a good opportunity to create a silhouette). A map and compass are invaluable tools to plan low light photography trips. Maps with contour lines that show the elevation of terrain are most useful: there is no point being at a location at sunrise if the sun doesn't appear for another hour because there's a hill in the way!

Note

The closer to the Arctic and Antarctic Circles you are, the further south and north the sun rises and sets at the winter and summer solstices respectively. The closer to the equator you are, the less far south and north.

Sunrise/sunset direction — **East/West**

Latitude	Nearest city (Northern/ Southern hemisphere)	Summer solstice		Winter solstice	
70°	Tromsø/–	–	–	–	–
60°	Oslo/–	35°	325°	140°	220°
50°	London/Rio Gallegos	49°	311°	128°	228°
40°	New York/Valdivia	58°	302°	120°	240°
30°	Austin/Porto Alegre	62°	298°	117°	243°
20°	Querétaro/Iquique	65°	295°	115°	244°
10°	Limon/Palmas	66°	293°	114°	246°
0°	Singapore/Quito	67°	293°	113°	247°

Sun height

The final factor affected by the time of year is the height that the sun rises in the sky during the day (with maximum elevation above the horizon occurring at midday). At the winter solstice, 50° N, the sun rises to a maximum elevation of no more than 16°, traveling in a very shallow arc from sunrise to sunset. In contrast, the sun rises to a maximum elevation of 63° at the summer solstice, and the arc the sun takes across the sky from sunrise to sunset is far greater. At the two equinoxes the sun rises to a maximum elevation of 40°, or roughly half way between the maximum heights of winter and summer. At 50° S the situation is reversed at the winter and summer solstices. The sun's maximum elevation does not vary at the equator and remains approximately 67° all year round.

Maximum sun elevation		**Northern/Southern hemisphere**			
Latitude	Nearest city (Northern/ Southern hemisphere)	Summer solstice		Winter solstice	
70°	Tromsø/–	43°	–	–	43°
60°	Oslo/–	53°	7°	7°	53°
50°	London/Rio Gallegos	63°	16°	16°	63°
40°	New York/Valdivia	73°	27°	27°	73°
30°	Austin/Porto Alegre	83°	37°	36°	83°
20°	Querétaro/Iquique	86°	47°	47°	86°
10°	Limon/Palmas	77°	57°	57°	77°
0°	Singapore/Quito	67°	67°	67°	67°

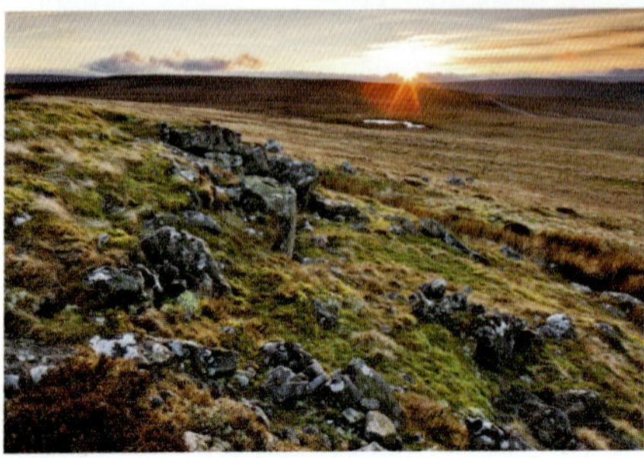

WINTER
This image was created at 54° N, at the winter solstice. The length of day is at its shortest and the sun sets at its most southerly.

Canon EOS 5D, 24mm lens, 1/4 sec. at f/16, ISO 100

Camera: Canon EOS 5D
Lens: 50mm lens
Exposure: 1 sec. at f/16
ISO: 100

As the equatorial regions vary so little over the year, it is easier to plan for your low light photography sessions.

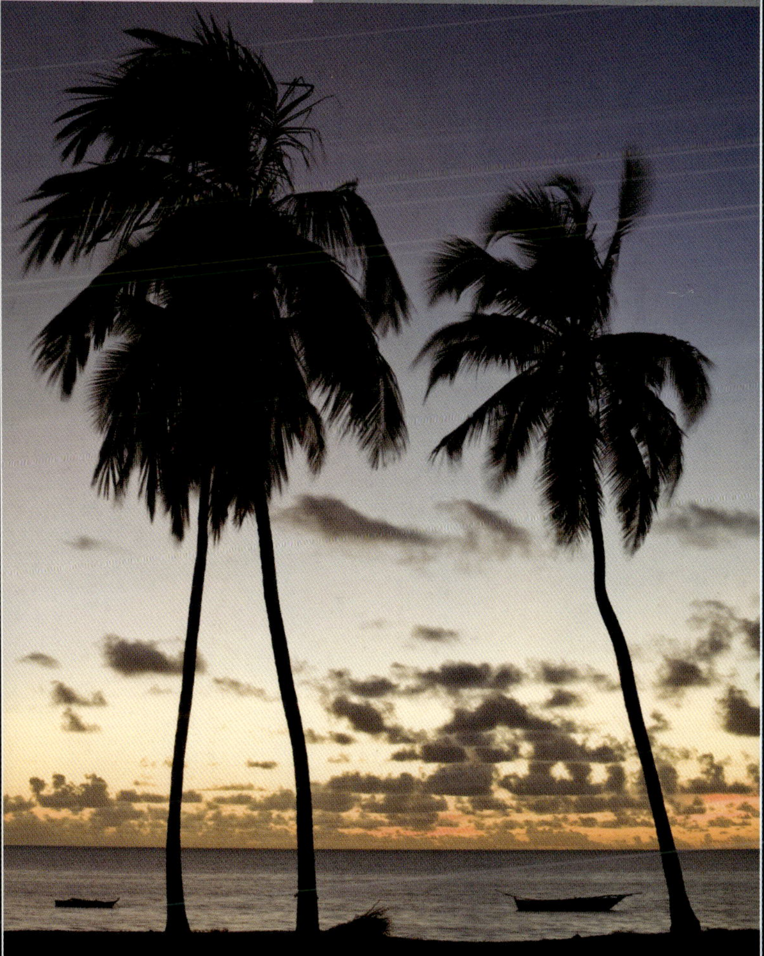

The golden hour

As previously mentioned, visible light is made up of different wavelengths, with red being longer and blue shorter. At sunrise and sunset, the sun's light travels more obliquely through the earth's atmosphere. All the visible wavelengths of light are scattered to some degree by atmospheric dust, reducing contrast and the overall intensity of light in comparison to midday. Blue wavelengths of light are scattered most, with the result that the sun's light looks redder the closer it is to the horizon. The period just after sunrise and before sunset is known as the "golden hour" for this reason. This warmth diminishes the higher the sun is in the sky, and by midday the sun's light is at its coolest in terms of color.

However, the golden hour isn't necessarily an exact hour. In winter, because the sun doesn't rise high in the sky all day, the sun's light is relatively warm in color from sunrise to sunset. The reverse is true in summer and the golden hour is shorter as the sun rises and sets at a steeper angle. At the equator, the golden hour can be incredibly brief, so careful planning is required to make the most of the warm light before it's lost and, rather ironically, before the heat is too high to work in comfortably.

Canon EOS 7D, 17–40mm lens (at 40mm), 3 sec. at f/11, ISO 100

DAWN
Pre-sunrise colors in a wintery northern England.

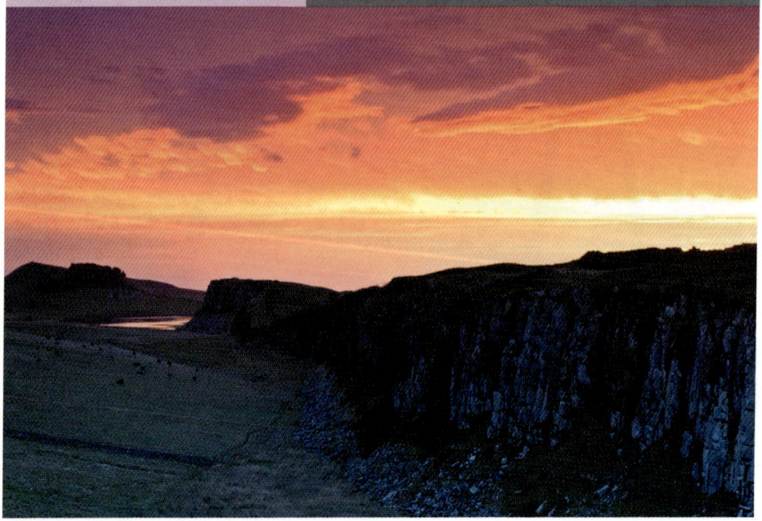

The reverse is true of the twilight hours. In summer the sun doesn't stray too far below the horizon, so twilight lasts for a relatively long period of time. In winter, twilight is far briefer and the period from absolute darkness to sunrise is shorter. One of the choices with urban twilight photography is whether to shoot in winter, at a respectable hour of the day but for less time, or to shoot in summer, for longer but late at night.

Color

The color of a sunrise or sunset depends on certain variables. The least interesting sunrises or sunsets occur when there is little or no cloud and no atmospheric haze. On these occasions the sun rises or falls with very little drama. Another bad time for sunrises or sunsets is when the sky is completely covered with cloud. However, sometimes all is not lost and occasionally when there's a break in the cloud, often just out of sight below the horizon, the results can be spectacular. The rule is not to give up until it's definitely too late. It's heartbreaking to have packed up your camera just before nature decides to put on a show.

When there is cloud in the sky—not too much, and not too little—the color of the sunset will reach its peak intensity once the sun is below the horizon. Sunsets are often more intensely colored and warmer than sunrises, as dust and pollution builds up during the day and these affect the color.

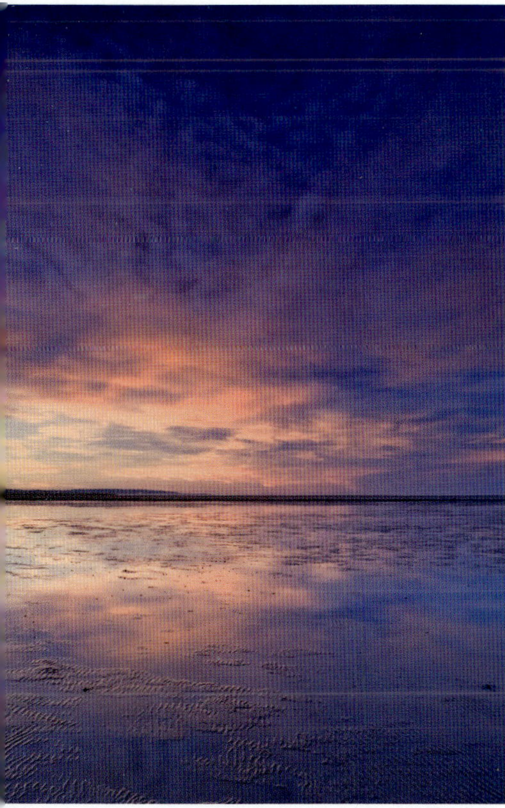

REFLECTIONS
Wet sand and still water readily reflect the colors of sunrise and sunset.

Canon EOS 5D, 24mm lens, 5 sec. at f/16, ISO 100

Keeping it cool

Color temperature can be used creatively. I have deliberately kept this image slightly blue (4800K) in overall color as that very effectively conveys a sense of a cold winter's morning. To me, the "correct" color temperature of 5800K used for the inset picture is "warmer" and far less atmospheric.

Camera: Canon EOS 7D
Lens: 70–200mm lens (at 170mm)
Exposure: 1/250 sec. at f/4
ISO: 400

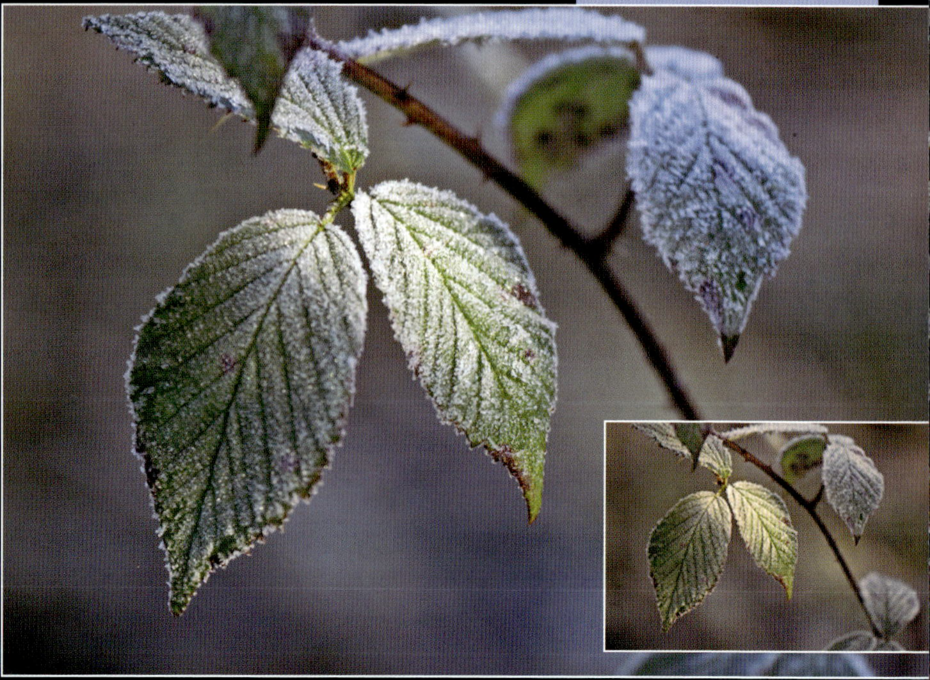

Raising the temperature

There are some subjects that appear far more attractive when a "warmer" approach is taken. Portraiture is one such subject, food is another. This cake, shot under tungsten lighting, looks distinctly less appealing in the "cooler" image (inset).

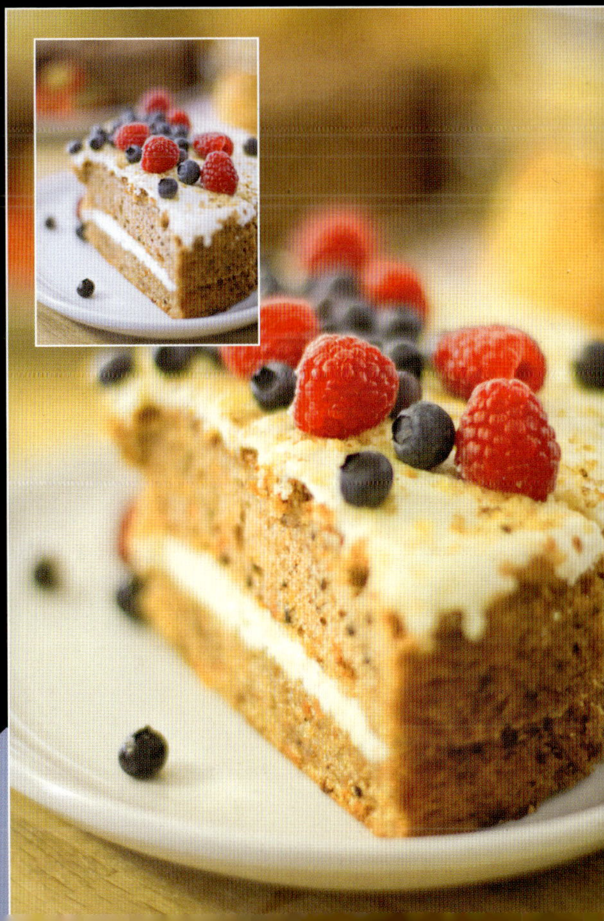

Camera: Canon EOS 7D
Lens: 50mm lens
Exposure: 1/100 sec. at f/1.4
ISO: 800

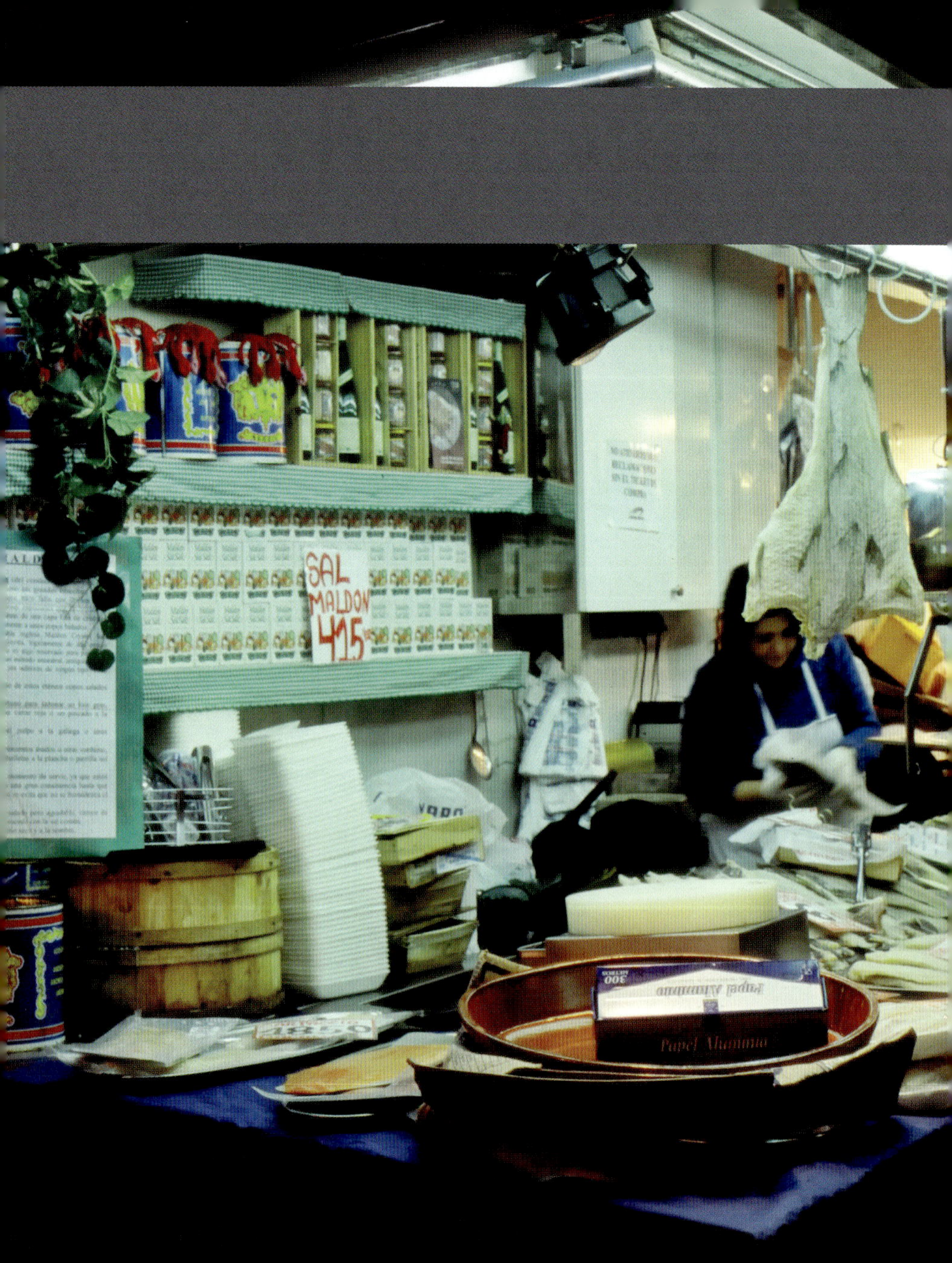
SAL
MALDON
415

CHAPTER 2 EXPOSURE

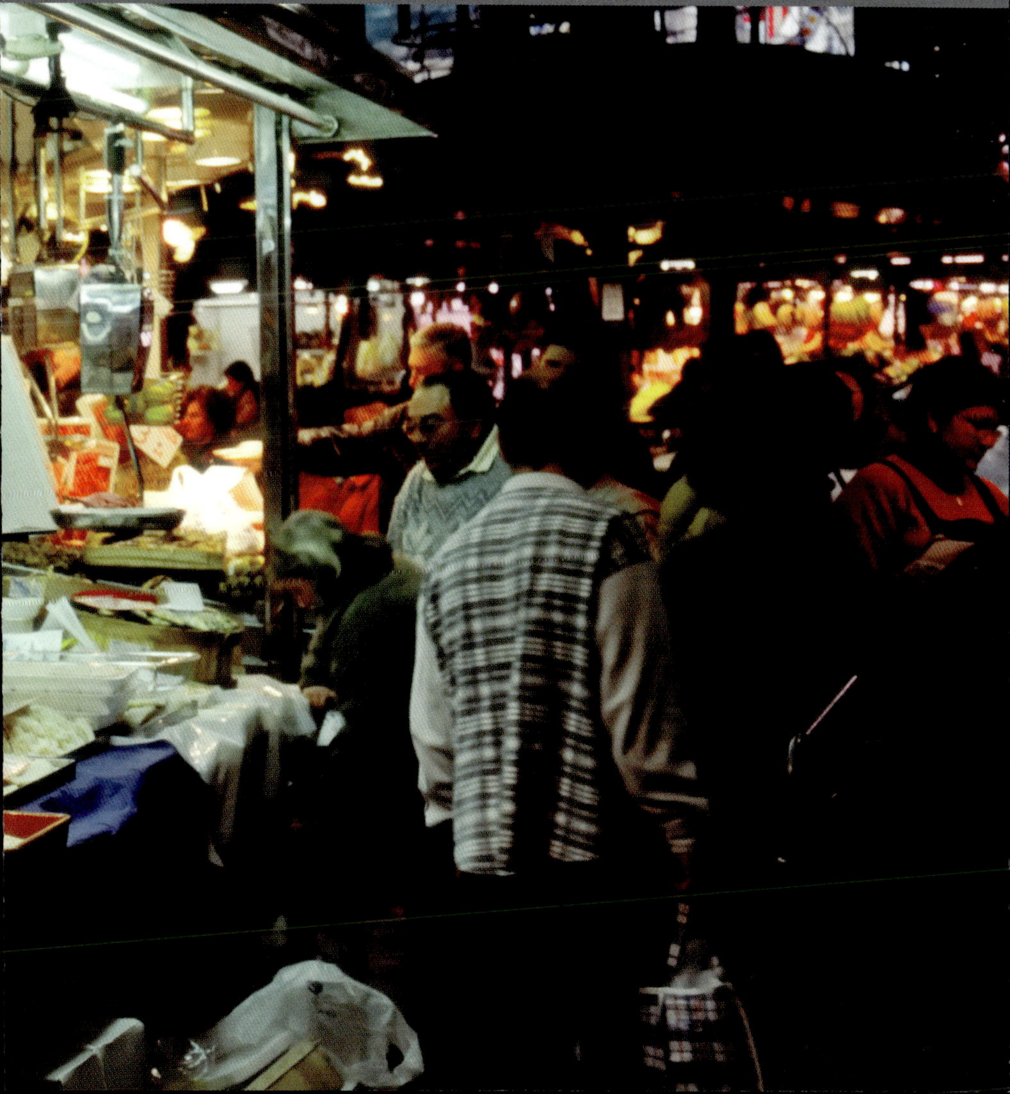

Exposure

To make an exposure is to allow light to fall in a controlled way onto a light-sensitive surface to form an image.

Controlling light

There are two ways in photography that you can control how much light reaches the sensor in your camera: the first is to vary the length of time that a light-tight shutter covering the sensor is open, and the second is to adjust the size of a variable aperture mounted within the lens.

Your camera has a range of shutter speeds, which are a measure of the length of time that the shutter is opened to make an exposure. The range available varies between camera models, but is typically between 1/4000 sec. to 30 seconds. In addition to this range of shutter speeds, some cameras also have a Bulb mode that locks the shutter open for as long as the shutter-release button is held down.

The shutter speed on a camera is varied by set amounts, such as 1/500 sec., 1/250 sec., 1/125 sec., 1/60 sec., and so on. The difference between these values is referred to as 1 "stop." When you increase the shutter speed by 1 stop (from 1/250 sec. to 1/500 sec., for example) you halve the amount of light that reaches the shutter. If you decrease the shutter speed by 1 stop (from 1/250 sec. to 1/125 sec.) you double the amount of light reaching the sensor.

SHUTTER SPEED
Very bright light sources require the use of fast shutter speeds or small apertures.

Canon EOS 7D, 10–22mm lens (at 16mm), 1/640 sec. at f/14, ISO 100

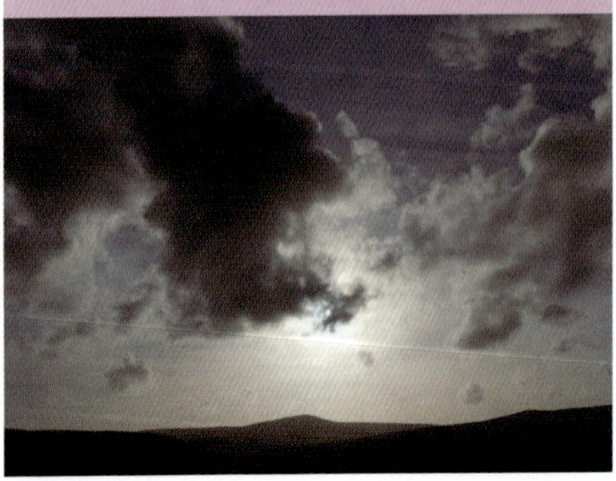

Note

Some cameras allow you to vary the shutter speed and aperture in ½ - or ⅓-stop increments: 1/160 sec. and 1/200 sec. are ⅓-stop increments between shutter speeds of 1/160 sec. and 1/250 sec., while f/9 and f/10 come between aperture settings of f/8 and f/11.

EXPOSURE *(Opposite)*
A well-exposed image is arguably one that appears "natural."

Canon EOS 1Ds, 70–200mm lens (at 70mm), 1/6 sec. at f/16, ISO 100

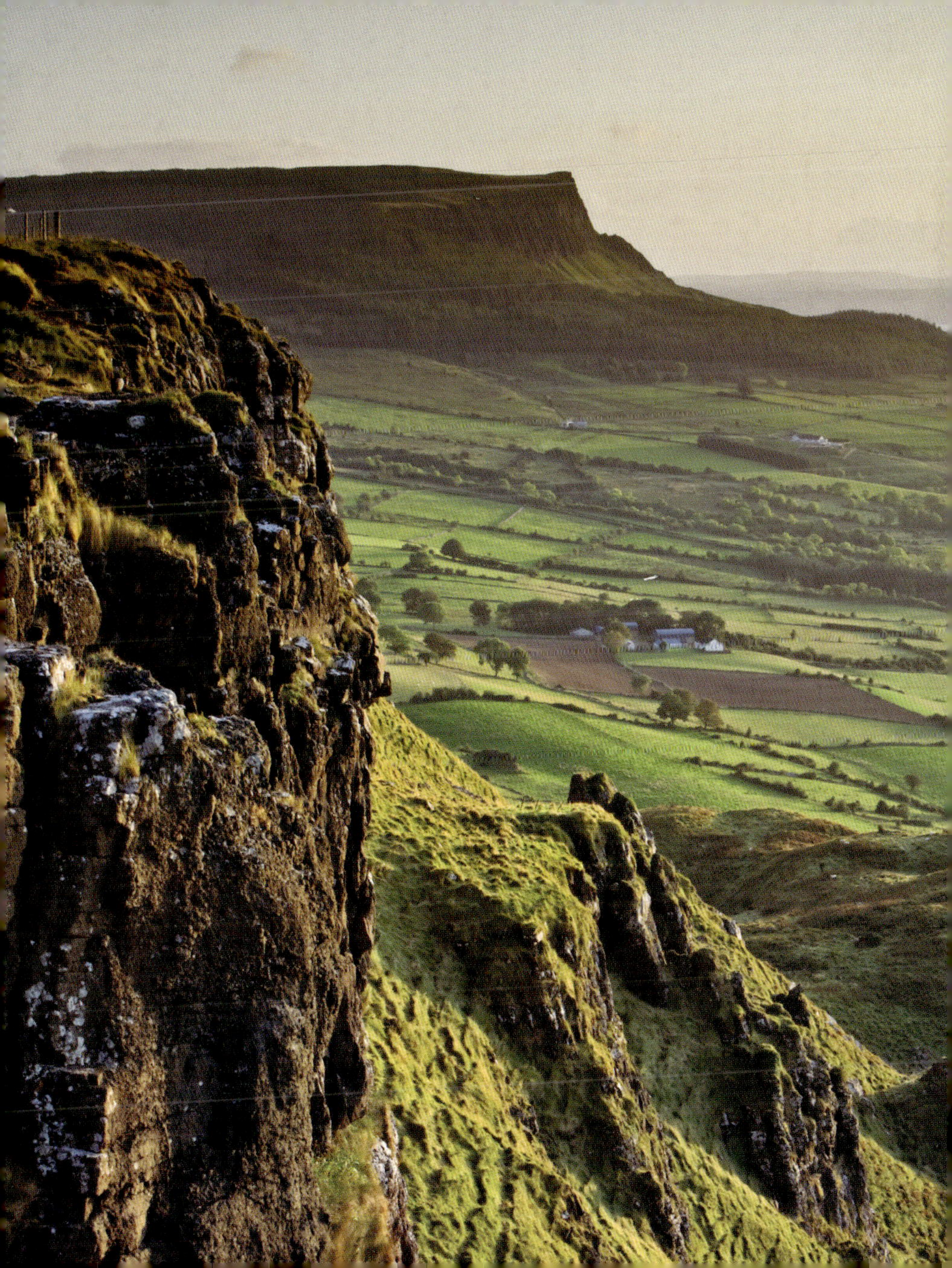

Within every camera lens is a variable iris known as the aperture. Like the iris in your eye it can be increased or decreased in size to take account of lower or higher light levels respectively. The size of a lens aperture is measured in f-stops, shown as f/ and a suffix number. A typical range of f-stops on a lens is f/2.8, f/4, f/5.6, f/8, f/11, and f/16. Counter-intuitively, the higher the number, the smaller the aperture: f/16 is a far smaller aperture than f/2.8, for example. The design of a lens will determine the maximum (largest) and minimum (smallest) apertures available.

When you decrease the size of the aperture by 1 stop (from f/5.6 to f/8, for example) you halve the amount of light that reaches the shutter. If you increase the aperture by 1 stop (from f/5.6 to f/4) you double the amount of light reaching the sensor.

Shutter speed/aperture relationship

The shutter speed and aperture are inextricably linked. If you alter one, the other must also be changed if you want the same amount of light to reach the sensor. If the shutter speed is increased (less light), then the aperture must be opened further (more light) to compensate. If the correct exposure for a scene is 1/500 sec. at f/8, for example, and you change the shutter speed to 1/1000 sec., the aperture must be set to f/5.6 to maintain the same exposure overall.

The following pages will explain why you would want to do that and illustrate the visual difference that altering the shutter speed and aperture makes.

Shutter speed

If your subject is static, the shutter speed doesn't matter at all—as long as the camera is stable during longer exposures. However, shutter speed does make a difference once there is movement in a scene. If your subject is particularly fast—a low jet screeching over your head, for example—you will need to use a fast shutter speed otherwise it will not be sharp in the final image. The slower your subject, the slower the shutter speed you can use to be

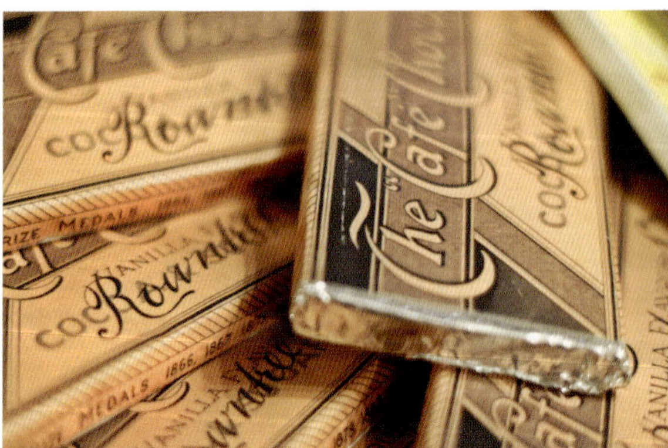

HANDHELD
In low light, larger apertures are often required to achieve a fast enough shutter speed to handhold the camera.

Canon EOS 7D, 50mm lens, 1/13 sec. at f/1.4, ISO 250

sure of a sharp result (see the table below for suggested shutter speeds for various subjects). Ironically, a moving subject frozen by the use of a fast shutter speed can look oddly static, and a small amount of blur can actually convey a sense of speed far more effectively than a pin-sharp image can.

The problem for low light photographers is that there is often not enough light to enable the use of fast shutter speeds (particularly if a small aperture is needed to increase depth of field). When the shutter speed is measured in seconds, minutes, or even hours, a moving subject will be blurred and potentially disappear entirely.

Suggested shutter speeds to freeze movement

Subject speed	*Subject filling frame*	*Subject half filling frame*
Person walking slowly	1/125 sec.	1/60 sec.
Person walking quickly	1/250 sec.	1/125 sec.
Waves	1/250 sec.	1/125 sec.
Person running	1/500 sec.	1/250 sec.
Person cycling	1/500 sec.	1/250 sec.
Galloping horse	1/1000 sec.	1/500 sec.
Car (on urban road)	1/500 sec.	1/250 sec.
Car (on freeway/motorway)	1/1000 sec.	1/500 sec.
Train	1/2000 sec.	1/1000 sec.
Fast jet plane	1/4000 sec.	1/2000 sec.

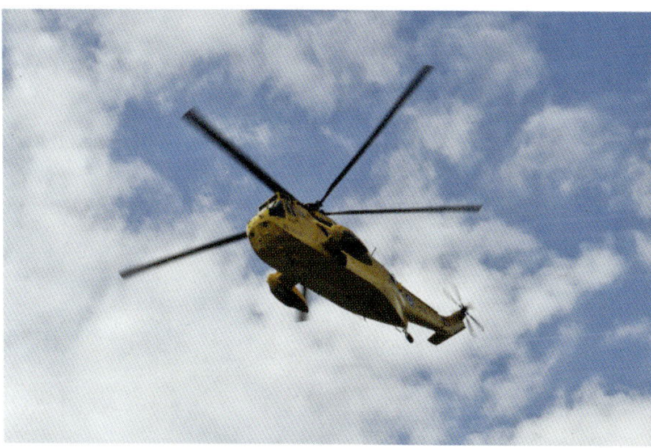

LANDING
Because this helicopter was hovering, the speed of forward movement wasn't that high. A shutter speed of 1/320 sec. was fast enough to guarantee it was sharp, although there is enough blur in the rotor blades to show that they were moving.

Canon EOS 1Ds MkII, 50mm lens, 1/320 sec. at f/11, ISO 100

> **Note**
> *The size of your subject in the frame, and its direction of travel, will also affect the shutter speed you need to use. The larger the subject is in the frame, the faster the shutter speed needed. Subjects traveling across the frame also require a faster shutter speed than those coming toward or going away from the camera.*

Suggested shutter speeds to blur movement

Waterfall	1/4 sec.
Waves (retaining detail)	1 sec.
Moving clouds	8 sec.
Waves (smoothed out)	15 sec.
Fireworks	30 sec.
Wind-blown foliage	30 sec.
Traffic trails	30–60 sec.
Waves (misty quality)	1–2 min.
Star trails	10+ min.

Slowly does it

When light levels are low, there are a few techniques that can be used to freeze action: increasing the ISO setting, using flash, and panning, are described elsewhere in this book. The other approach is to embrace low shutter speeds and the creative opportunities they offer. In fact, so interesting are the effects created by slow shutter speeds that some photographers (myself included) often used ND filters to deliberately extend exposure times. Techniques that use slow shutter speeds include blurring water, traffic, and star trails, as covered in later chapters.

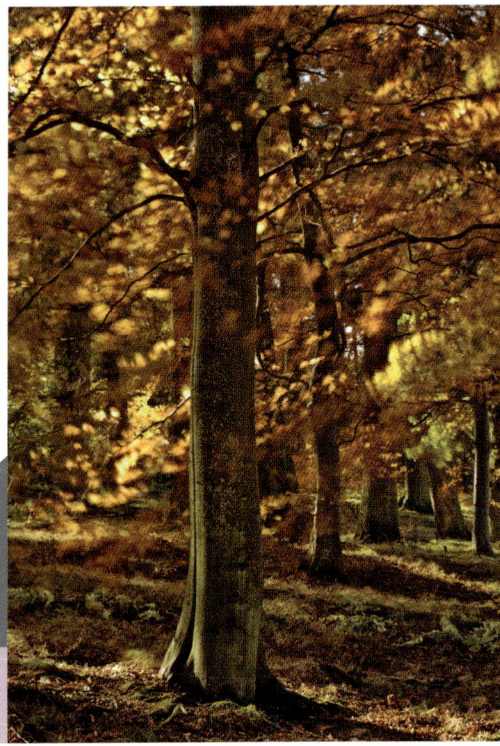

WIND
Using a slow shutter speed captured a sense of the breeze blowing through this wood far more effectively than a faster one would have done.

Canon EOS 5D, 100mm lens, 4 sec. at f/16, ISO 100

Aperture

The image from a lens is only truly pin-sharp at the point of focus. However, we can extend sharpness forward and backward from this point by using the aperture in the lens. The aperture also focuses light. The smaller the aperture, the greater the effect, and the further the zone of sharpness is extended. So, overall sharpness in an image will be greater at f/16 than it will be at f/2.8. The extent of this zone of sharpness is known as the "depth of field," which extends roughly twice as far back from the focus point than in front of it.

Depth of field is not just affected by the aperture—wide-angle lenses have a greater inherent depth of field at any given aperture than longer focal length lenses. The distance from the lens to the focus point also affects depth of field; the closer the focus point is to the lens, the less depth of field there is. This can be a particular problem when shooting macro, as very short focusing distances can mean that depth of field, even with small apertures, is virtually non-existent.

Hyperfocal distance

You'd be forgiven for thinking that shooting with the smallest aperture on your lens would be the way to achieve the sharpest image. It's certainly true that depth of field is at its greatest at the minimum aperture setting, but a lens is at its best optically when the aperture is roughly in the middle of the available range (usually f/8 or f/11). At smaller apertures lenses suffer from an optical effect known as "diffraction."

Note

Because compact cameras have such small focal length lenses, depth of field is always greater than an equivalent angle of view lens on a larger camera system.

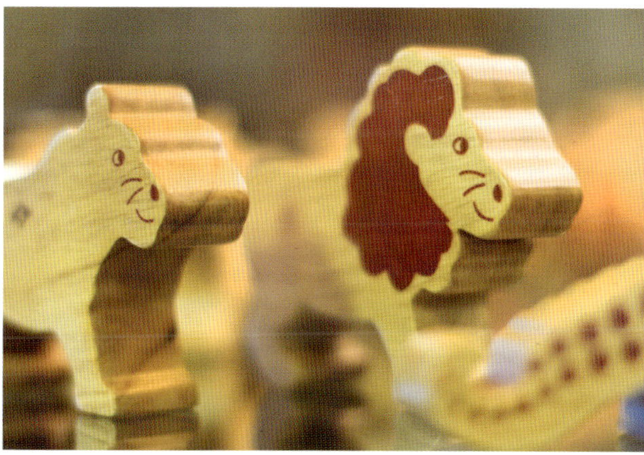

SOFT
With close focus and the use of a very large aperture, depth of field is reduced considerably.

Canon EOS 7D, 50mm lens, 1/25 sec. at f/1.6, ISO 800

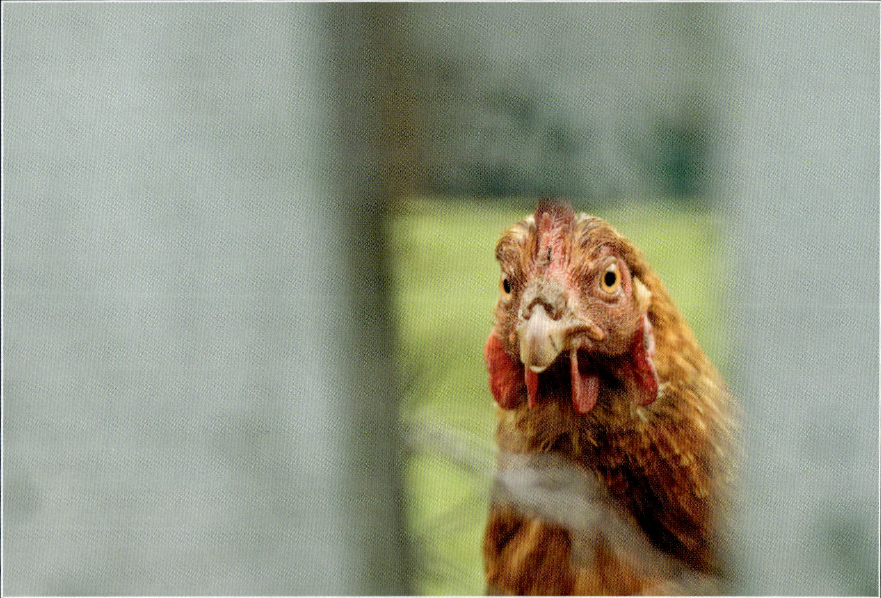

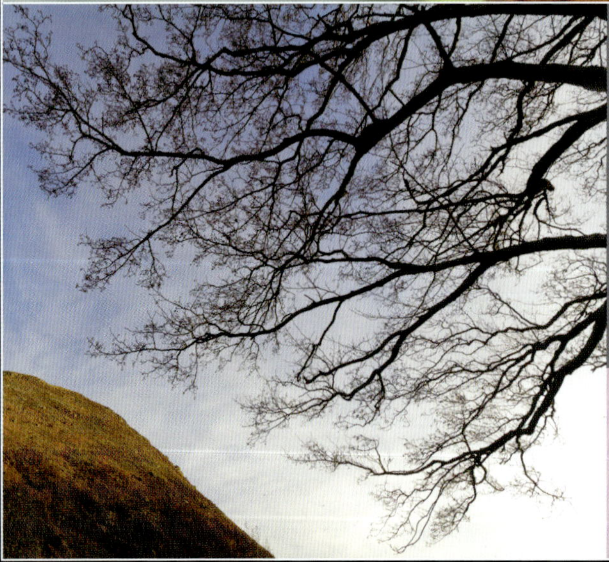

CHOICE

How much or how little depth of field to apply is one of the creative decisions you need to make in photography. We don't like to look at out-of-focus areas in an image, so a shallow depth of field can help direct the eye to a (sharp) subject. Conversely, front-to-back sharpness can unite elements in a scene, even if they are spatially far apart.

Top: **Canon EOS 7D, 50mm lens, 1/320 sec. at f/2.5, ISO 200**

Bottom: **Canon EOS 7D, 10–22mm lens (at 15mm), 1/8 sec. at f/10, ISO 200**

Diffraction is caused by light being scattered when it strikes the edges of the aperture blades, softening the resulting image. Diffraction happens at all apertures, but is most visible when smaller apertures are used. It is also more of a problem with smaller sensors, and is one of the reasons why compact digital cameras have relatively large maximum apertures compared to digital SLRs.

To minimize diffraction, the largest aperture that creates the right amount of depth of field should be used. This is achieved by setting the hyperfocal distance, which is the focus point at which a particular aperture's depth of field is maximized. When the hyperfocal distance is set, the image will be sharp from half that distance in front of the focus point to infinity behind it. When shooting in low light, careful use of larger apertures and setting the hyperfocal distance will keep shutter speeds lower.

Note

Diffraction is often visible at apertures smaller than f/11 on APS-C sensor cameras, but not until f/16 on full-frame cameras. However, the pixel density of a camera can also make a difference, so experimentation is recommended to determine the limits of your own camera.

Working smarter...

Apple iOS: *DOFMaster*

Android: *DOFMaster*

These apps by Don Fleming will help you calculate the hyperfocal distance for your lens and camera combination.

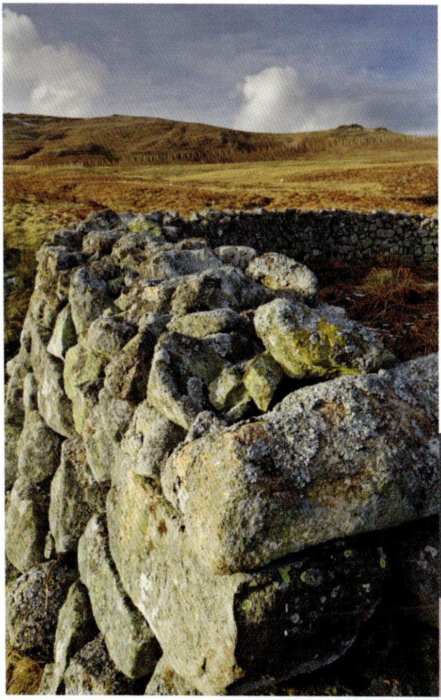

HYPERFOCAL DISTANCE

The hyperfocal distance for this scene was 2.8ft (0.85m) with an aperture of f/14. This gave me a depth of field that extended from 1.4ft (0.42m) to infinity.

Canon EOS 7D, 10–22mm (at 15mm), 1/4 sec. at f/14, ISO 100

Exposure and metering

"Metering" is the act of measuring how much light is required to create a photographic image. Your camera has an integral light meter, and understanding how it works will increase your photographic success rate.

Exposure meters

There are two types of light meter, incident and reflective. Incident light meters are small, handheld devices that measure the amount of light falling onto a scene. The meter in your camera is a reflective meter and this type of meter measures light that has been reflected from the scene in front of it.

Modern camera meters are generally very reliable. Fuzzy logic systems enable them to second-guess particular lighting situations to arrive at the required exposure. However, they are not infallible. A reflective meter assesses the world as a series of shades of gray. It assumes that the scene being metered reflects roughly 18% of the light that falls onto it. This 18% reflectivity equates to a matte mid-gray surface. In the cover of this book is an 18% gray card. It's not the most exciting color you'll ever see, but it's how an ordinary, every-day scene would look if all the tones in the scene were desaturated and then averaged out.

Ordinary, everyday scenes are all very well, but they aren't very inspiring and they are rarely encountered when shooting in low light. If there is a prevalence of dark or light tones in a scene, a reflective meter can be fooled into over- or underexposing respectively. In a predominantly light-toned scene—a snowman on a blanket of snow for instance—the camera meter would tend to underexpose, as the light tones would be pushed closer to the 18% gray ideal. Using the histogram on your camera is a very objective way to check exposure either before capture (in Live View), or afterward in image review. If the exposure needs correcting, exposure compensation can be used.

AVERAGE
This is the type of scene that reflective meters excel at. Dull isn't it?

Canon EOS 7D, 17–40mm lens (at 20mm), 1/30 sec. at f/13, ISO 100

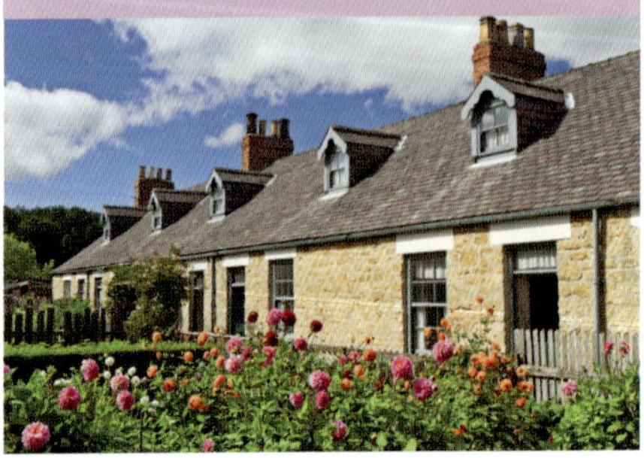

COMPENSATED *(Opposite)*
This image required "overexposure" because of the large areas of pale tone.

Canon EOS 7D, 17–40mm lens (at 22mm), 5 sec. at f/14, ISO 100

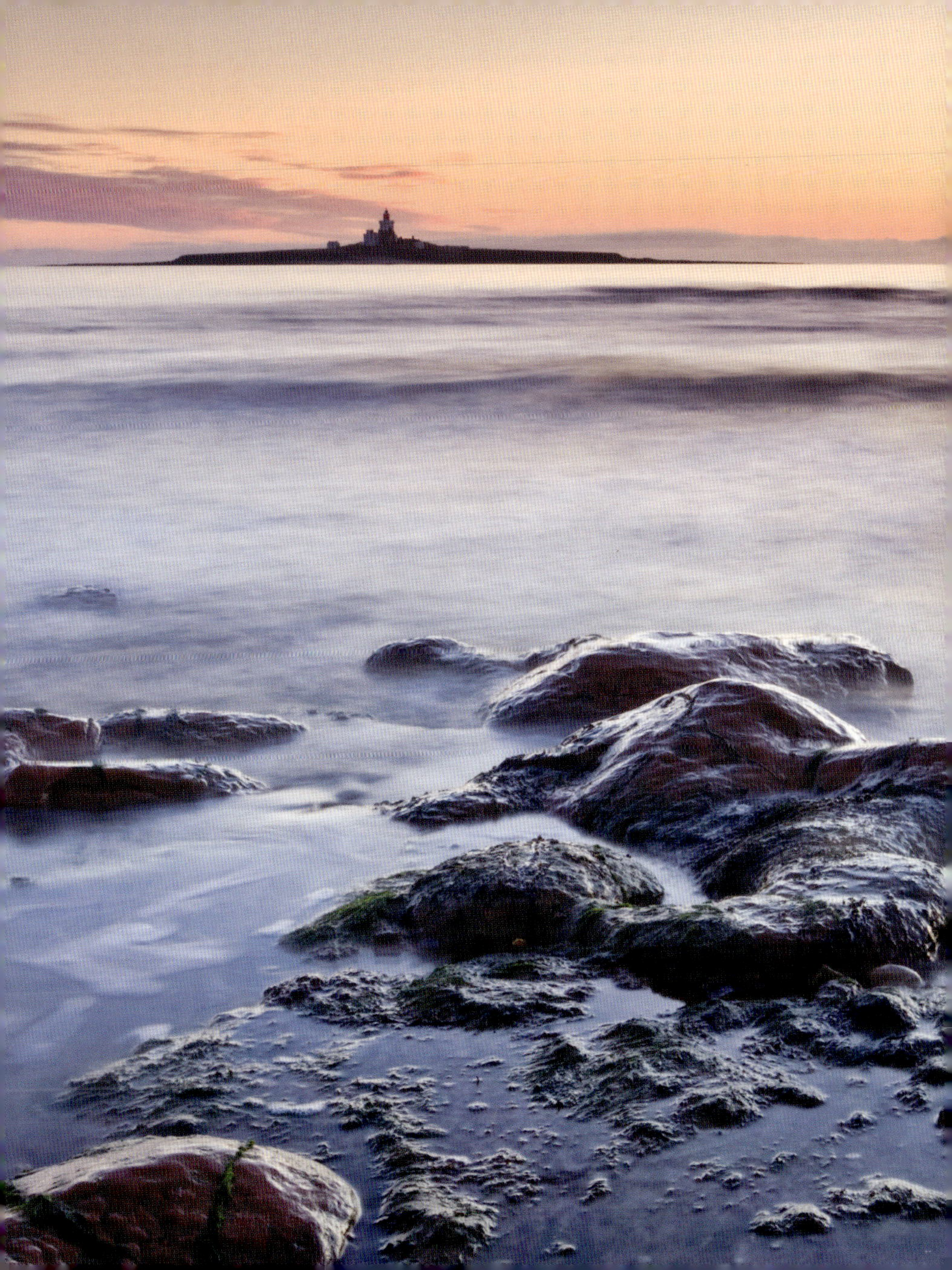

Camera meters

Cameras often have different metering modes, with the main difference between them being the proportion of the scene that is metered.

Evaluative, *Matrix*, or *Multipattern* metering are the terms used by different camera manufacturers to describe the general-purpose exposure metering mode that is usually the default setting on a digital camera. It works by dividing the image frame into a series of cells or zones, with the exposure for each zone measured separately. The final exposure is calculated by combining the results from the different zones, based on the camera "guessing" what sort of scene is being measured (a lighter top half would indicate that the scene was a landscape, for example). Evaluative metering is generally very accurate, but it can still be fooled, particularly when graduated ND filters are used.

Center-weighted metering has largely been superseded by evaluative metering, but it is still usually an option on most cameras. The entire scene is metered, but the exposure is biased toward the center of the image. The size of the bias varies between camera models, but is generally 60%. Center-weighted metering works well when your subject fills the center of the frame, but it is less accurate when the tonal range varies across the scene.

Spot metering measures a very small section of a scene, typically 1–5% of the image area. It is very useful to set the exposure for a particular area of an image, ignoring other elements such as bright light sources that may otherwise skew the exposure. When using your camera's spot meter, measure from parts of the scene that are a midtone, such as stone, grass, or blue sky.

> ***Working smarter...***
> Apple iOS: *Light Meter Free*
> Android: *Light Meter Tools*
> *Turn your smartphone into a handheld reflective exposure meter.*

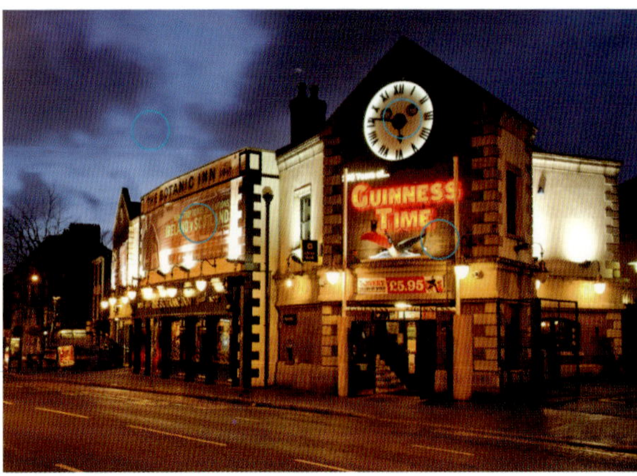

METERING
I was able to determine the correct exposure in this scene by taking a spot-meter reading from the midtone areas (circled).

Canon EOS 1Ds MkII, 17–40mm lens (at 40mm), 6 sec. at f/13, ISO 100

Exposure modes

Cameras often have specific automatic scene modes that make photography hassle free. However, using the modes below will give you more control over your image creation.

*Programmed Auto (or **P**)* is an automatic mode in which the camera chooses the aperture and shutter speed combination necessary for the correct exposure. Some models allow you to override these settings either by altering the aperture and shutter speed combination or by applying exposure compensation. Programmed Auto is a perfectly valid mode to use when you want to "point and shoot." However, the camera does not know anything about esthetics, so Programmed Auto may get in the way of your creative intentions for a shot.

Tip

Use exposure lock with spot metering to set the exposure and then recompose to make the image.

*Shutter Priority (**S** or **Tv**)* is a semi-automatic mode that allows you to set the shutter speed, with the camera setting the relevant aperture. This mode is particularly useful for action photography where specific shutter speeds are necessary to freeze movement.

*Aperture Priority (**A** or **Av**)* is also a semi-automatic mode, enabling you to set the aperture, while the camera sets the appropriate shutter speed. This mode is particularly useful when control over depth of field is important, such as in landscape photography.

*Manual (**M**)* is the mode that will give you the greatest control over the exposure, as you set both the shutter speed and aperture. Your camera will indicate whether the chosen combination is correct, but ultimately it is up to you to decide whether to take this advice.

MODE DIAL
Exposure modes are often chosen by turning a mode dial on the camera body.

Image © Canon

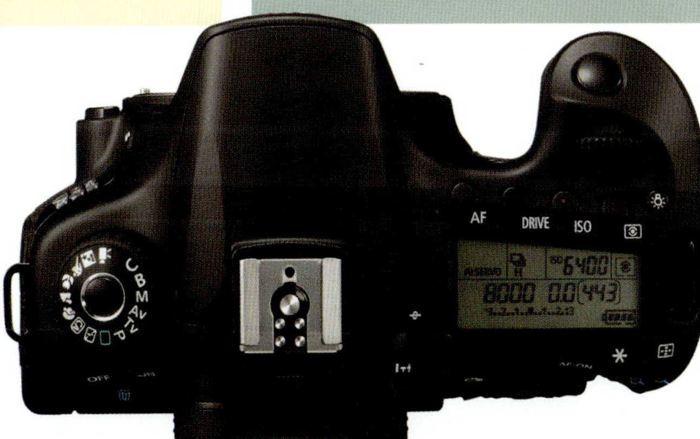

Exposure compensation

Although exposure meters on modern cameras are extremely sophisticated, there are occasions when you will need to step in to adjust the suggested exposure. The most direct way to do this is to shoot in Manual mode and set the shutter speed and aperture yourself. When shooting in semi-automatic modes, exposure is adjusted by using exposure compensation. The usual range of exposure compensation is ±3 stops (usually in ½- or ⅓-stop increments). Exposure compensation is often necessary when shooting in low light because low light scenes are by their very nature not composed of an "average" range of tones. Most cameras have an exposure compensation button that, when used in conjunction with a control wheel, allows you to add + (positive/more light) or – (negative/less light) compensation.

DIALLING IT IN
Some cameras, such as the Nikon P7100, use a dial (seen at the right of the camera's top plate) to set exposure compensation.
Image © Nikon

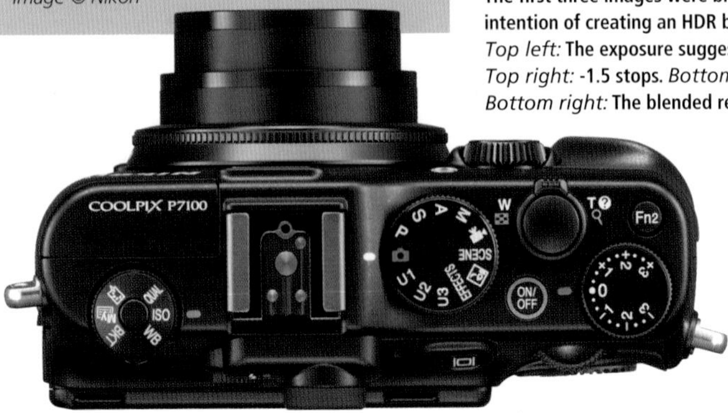

Bracketing

If you're unsure that the exposure you've set is correct, your camera's bracketing function will give you a safety net. Bracketing is the name given to shooting a sequence of shots, one at the correct exposure, one "underexposed," and one "overexposed." The order of the sequence can often be altered via a settings menu.

Bracketing can be achieved manually, but most cameras have an automatic bracketing (AEB) function. As with exposure compensation, bracketing is usually adjustable by ±3 stops in ½- or ⅓-stop increments. If you plan to create HDR imagery, AEB is the option to choose, as this will minimize contact with the camera during the shooting process.

> **Note**
> *Shooting in Manual mode will disable exposure compensation.*

BRACKETING *(Opposite)*
The first three images were bracketed with the intention of creating an HDR blend in post-production. *Top left:* **The exposure suggested by the camera.** *Top right:* **-1.5 stops.** *Bottom left:* **+1.5 stops.** *Bottom right:* **The blended result.**

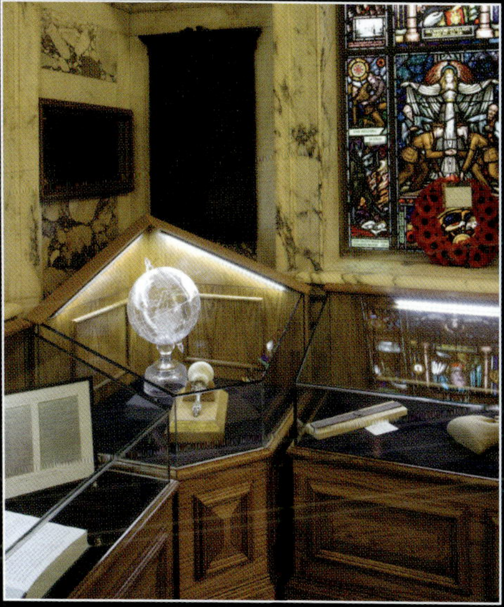
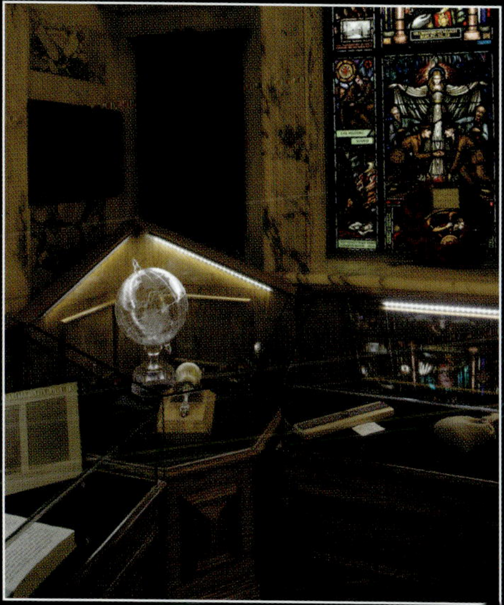
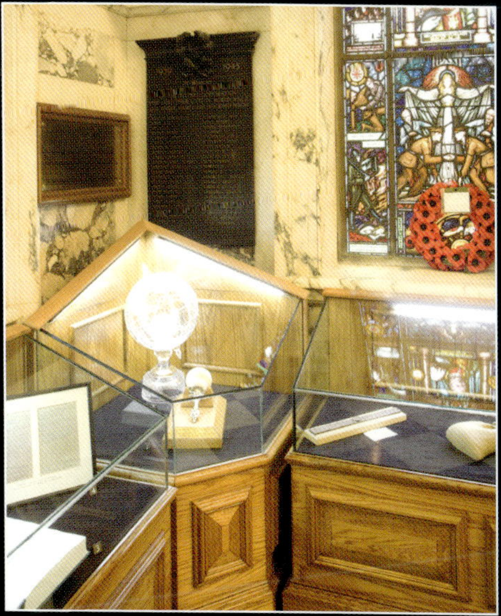
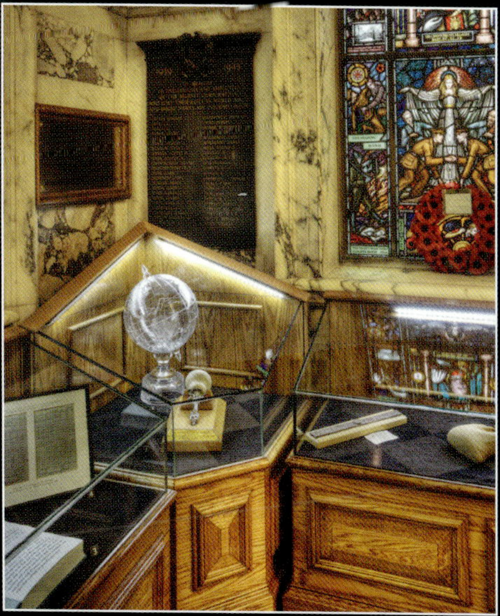

Dynamic range

A camera can only record a restricted range of luminance (brightness) levels, and it certainly cannot match the astonishing ability of our own eyes. The range of luminance levels that a camera can record is known as its "dynamic range," and different models of camera have different levels of dynamic range. As a general rule, the larger the sensor in a camera, the greater the dynamic range, so you would expect a full-frame digital SLR to have a greater dynamic range than a compact digital camera, for example.

Not all scenes have high levels of contrast. Mist reduces contrast so that shadows and bright highlights are virtually non-existent. Misty scenes are one subject that cameras can cope well with. However, other low-light scenes, such as pre-sunrise or post-sunset have very high levels of contrast: the image on the page opposite is a good example. Exposing to retain detail in the tree would have resulted in a grossly overexposed sky, that would have been white. With practise it gets easier to assess a scene and decide whether a compromise needs to be made in terms of where in the tonal range detail is lost. In high-contrast scenes it's generally more appealing to expose an image so that detail is retained in the highlights.

There are several methods that can be used to overcome the problem of dynamic range. Filters, particularly graduated NDs, are commonly used by landscape photographers to overcome the difference between a bright sky and an unlit foreground. Another method is to shoot a sequence of images using different exposures and to blend them, either as a succession of layers or as an HDR merge.

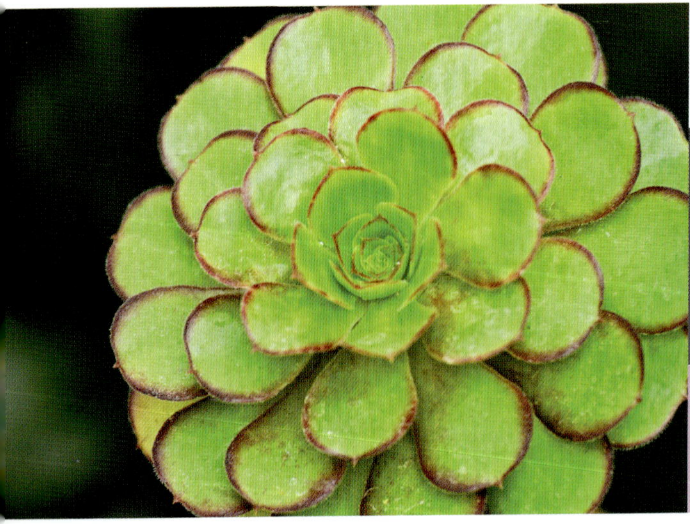

DETAILS
Low contrast suits delicate subjects such as flowers. I prefer working with these subjects when they're in shade or on overcast days.

Canon EOS 7D, 70–200mm lens (at 200mm), 1/2 sec. at f/5.6, ISO 100

Histograms

The histogram is a very useful tool for assessing the exposure of an image. A histogram is a graph showing (left to right) the range of tones in an image from black (shadows) to white (highlights). Vertically, the histogram shows how many pixels of a particular tone are in an image. Halfway across the histogram are tones that correspond to mid-gray. Subjects such as grass or stone roughly equate to mid-gray, so the histogram of a correctly exposed image of a rock face would peak in the middle.

There is no ideal shape for a histogram, although it is better to avoid clipping either edge if possible: once a pixel is either pure black or pure white there is effectively no image information there.

However, there is often little choice but to clip the histogram when shooting in low light. If you were to try to set the exposure so that something like the glow from a streetlamp didn't clip the histogram, the rest of the image would probably be grossly underexposed. In this instance it pays to worry less about the light and concentrate on exposing the rest of the scene correctly.

Some cameras show histograms in Live View. Live View histograms are particularly useful when assessing the effect of adding filters such as graduated NDs.

Note

One option when shooting JPEGs is to use a tool that controls an image's dynamic range (called Adaptive D-Lighting by Nikon and Auto Lighting Optimizer by Canon). These work by suppressing highlights and boosting shadows. It's a useful tool to have in high-contrast scenes, but it can cause visible noise in shadow areas.

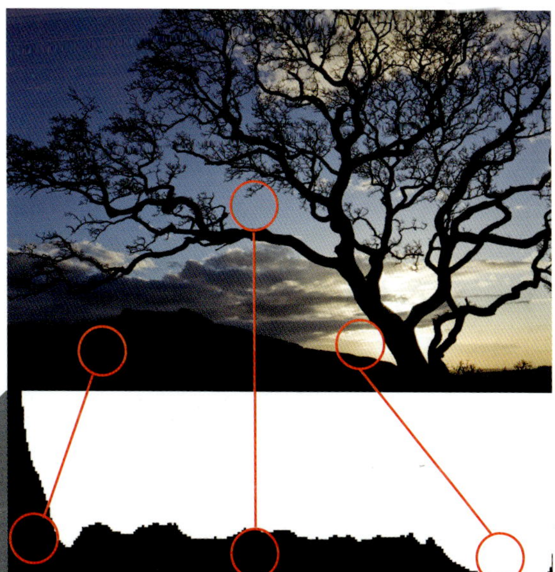

ASSESSING
With practise it becomes easier to see how the histogram corresponds to tones in an image.

Exposing to the right

Digital sensors capture more usable data in the lighter areas of an image than in the shadows. When shooting Raw files, a technique known as "exposing to the right" will help you maximize the amount of usable image data available for post-production, while reducing problems such as noise. Exposing to the right requires you to expose your image so that the histogram is skewed to the right (without clipping). This often means ignoring the "correct" exposure suggested by the camera and applying positive exposure compensation.

The results will look decidedly odd on your camera's LCD; an image exposed to the right will appear washed out and lacking in contrast. However, the image is easily normalized in post-production by increasing contrast and adjusting the exposure to suit.

Before exposing to the right, you need to set the picture style settings on your camera to "neutral," or similar. The histogram on the LCD is not generated directly from the Raw file but from a JPEG created using the currently selected picture style. This can affect the histogram and give you a false idea of the exposure.

EXPOSE TO THE RIGHT
The image on the left was "exposed to the right" and lacks contrast, but the shadow areas are noise free. The image to the right has been corrected by applying greater contrast.

Canon EOS 7D, 50mm lens, 1/400 sec. at f/1.6, ISO 200

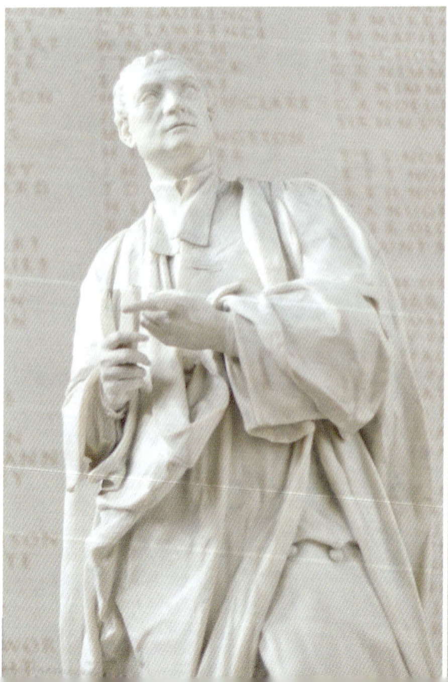

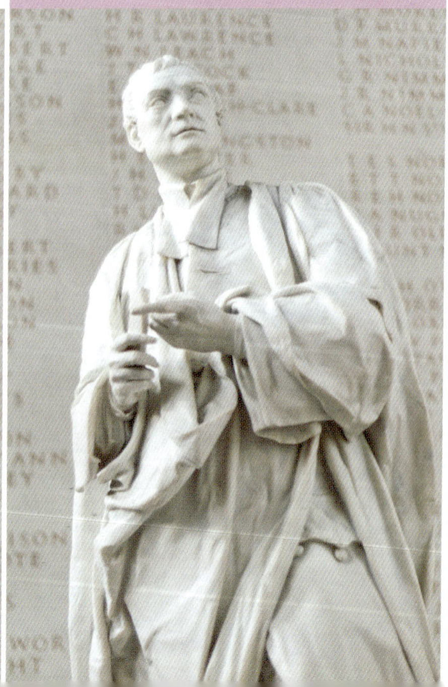

ISO

The range of usable shutter and aperture combinations can be controlled by altering the ISO settings on your camera.

ISO range

The term ISO was originally used to describe the sensitivity of film to light: the greater the sensitivity of a film, the higher the ISO value. Digital cameras also use ISO measurements and, as with film, the higher the value, the less light the sensor needs to create an image. In practical terms this means that shorter shutter speeds or smaller apertures are more readily usable.

As with aperture and shutter speed, ISO is measured in stops, and can frequently be set in ½- or ⅓-stop increments. The lowest ISO on a camera (also known as the base ISO) is usually ISO 100, although some cameras start as high as ISO 200. The highest ISO a camera is capable of also varies, and some cameras have the ability to almost see in the dark with ISO values in the hundreds of thousands.

However, there is a cost to using a high ISO setting. Sensors are designed to provide optimum quality at their base ISO, so as the ISO is increased, image quality decreases due to the intrusion of noise. Film users face a similar dilemma, as high ISO film is always far grainier than low ISO film. In photography there is often a compromise that needs to be made between the usability of the camera and image quality: a slightly noisy, but sharp image, is often better than a cleaner image with camera shake because the shutter speed was too low.

> **Note**
>
> *If your camera has an AUTO ISO setting it will change the ISO to suit the lighting conditions. This is useful if you're handholding your camera, but if it is on a tripod using the base ISO will maximize image quality.*

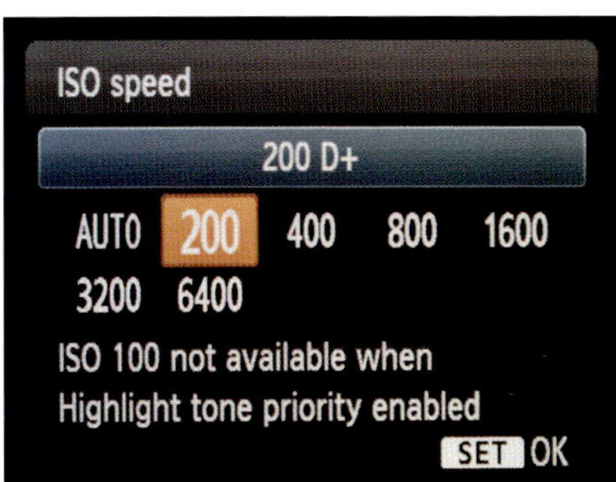

SETTINGS
The available ISO settings on a Canon EOS 1100D.

Noise

Digital noise is seen as random spots of color or variations in brightness in an image. Noise is caused by arbitrary signal fluctuations in a camera's electronics affecting the purity of the data used to create an image. Noise reduces fine detail images, making them look coarser. There are two types of digital noise; luminance and chroma. Esthetically, luminance noise is usually less objectionable than chroma, as luminance noise has a gritty look to it, rather like film grain (although less random). Chroma noise, however, results in color blotching that is particularly unwelcome in areas of even tone such as sky or on facial features: it is also the more difficult of the two to remove successfully.

Different cameras have different noise characteristics. More modern cameras typically have better noise suppression technology than older cameras, and it's also generally true that the larger the sensor in a camera, the better-controlled noise will be.

The noise characteristics of your own camera are something that will take experimentation to discover. This is done by making exposures at different ISO settings and viewing the resulting images at 100% on your computer's monitor. Once you have done that, you should have an idea of which ISO settings seriously compromise image quality and which are acceptable to you.

Note

Lightening an underexposed image will increase the noise in the image, particularly in the shadow areas.

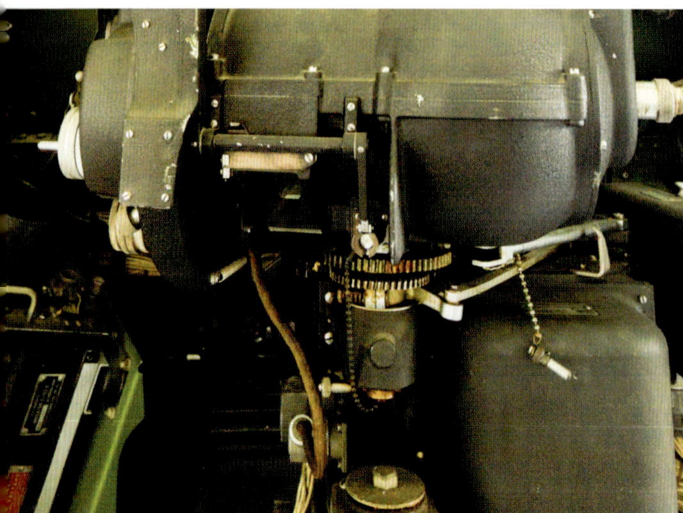

NOISE
This image was accidentally underexposed. In trying to lighten it in post-production I've increased the visible noise.

Canon EOS 7D, 10–22mm lens (at 10mm), 1/13 sec. at f/5.6, ISO 100

Long exposure noise

Long exposures also increase the presence of noise in an image, even at the base ISO. The longer a sensor is active, the hotter it gets and the greater the corruption of the image data. The very nature of a long exposure requires the sensor to be running continuously. To combat long exposure noise most cameras have a Long Exposure Noise Reduction facility. This function typically requires the same length of time as the original exposure, effectively doubling the time needed to shoot an image. If you need to shoot continuously using long exposures, it's better to switch Long Exposure Noise Reduction off.

Noise reduction

When a JPEG is processed in-camera, noise is usually reduced automatically, but Raw shooters will need to use noise reduction techniques in post-production. Most good Raw conversion software has a noise reduction facility, and software such as Adobe Photoshop allows the addition of third-party plug-ins such as Noise Ninja (which is also available as a standalone package). Noise reduction should be used sparingly though, as too much can obliterate detail and leave your images with an overly smooth, "plastic" appearance. This will be particularly noticeable on subjects that have a delicate texture, such as skin or stone.

Note

Long exposures can result in "hot pixels." These are random pixels in an image that are far brighter than they would normally be. They do not mean that your sensor is defective and are easily cloned out. Because they are so small you will probably need to be at 100% magnification to see them.

BEFORE AND AFTER
The image below on the left has had no noise reduction applied, the image on the right has.

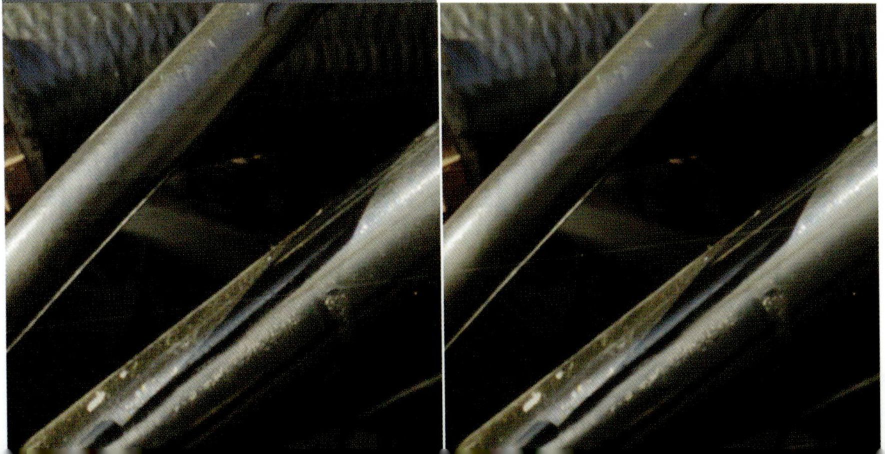

Exposure values

Imagine trying to make successful images without access to a working light meter—it sounds like a nightmarish situation. However, in a particular lighting situation, the light that's available to make an exposure will generally always be the same. For example, on a sunny day, with the aperture at f/16, the correct shutter speed at ISO 100 will be 1/100 sec. (or 1/125 sec. if this was the closest available shutter speed). This is known as the "Sunny 16" rule, which is basically saying that on a sunny day, with the subject in direct sunlight, the shutter speed will have the same value as the ISO setting when you use an aperture of f/16. So, if the ISO were increased to 200, the shutter speed would jump to 1/200 sec. as well, and so on. From this basic rule it's possible to work out the other shutter speed and aperture combinations that would also work on a sunny day.

Although you may think that the Sunny 16 rule has no place in a book on low light photography, the same underlying principal—that particular lighting situations will require the same basic exposure—still holds true. The grid on the page opposite shows a range of situations from very intense artificial lighting to ambient light from dim artificial lighting. For each situation there is a range of shutter speed and aperture combinations. In a particular situation, try setting the exposure manually using the relevant values from the table and then making your image. You may well find it more accurate than your camera's light meter.

SUNNY
This image was shot with a polarizing filter. Without it, the exposure would have been 1/125 sec. at f/16. With the polarizing filter the exposure needed to be adjusted to 1/30 sec. at f/16.

Canon EOS 7D, 17–40mm lens (at 30mm), 1/30 sec. at f/16, ISO 100

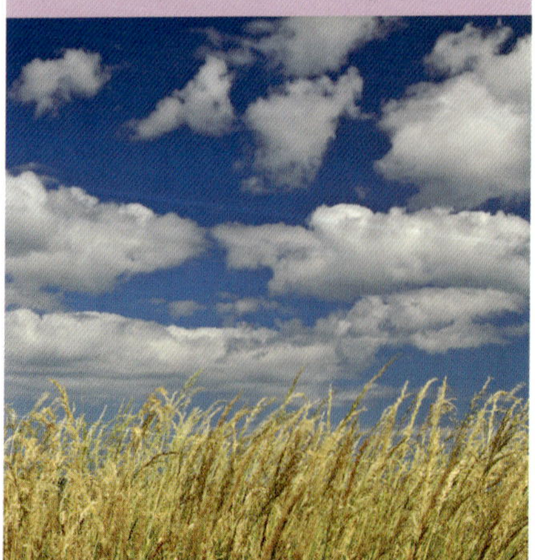

Note

If you're using filters, these must be taken into account when setting the exposure using this table. As an example, a polarizing filter at maximum strength will absorb 2 stops of light. So, with a polarizing filter fitted (and used at maximum strength), you would need to look at the EV value for the relevant lighting situation and then deduct 2 from that value.

Exposure settings at ISO 100

EV	*f/2.8*	*f/4*	*f/5.6*	*f/8*	*f/11*	*f/16*	
-1	15 sec.	30 sec.	1 min.	2 min.	4 min.	8 min.	Ambient light from dim artificial lighting
0	8 sec.	15 sec.	30 sec.	1 min.	2 min.	4 min.	Ambient light from artificial lighting
1	4 sec.	8 sec.	15 sec.	30 sec.	1 min.	2 min.	Cityscapes at night
2	2 sec.	4 sec.	8 sec.	15 sec.	30 sec.	1 min.	Eclipsed moon. Lightning
3	1 sec.	2 sec.	4 sec.	8 sec.	15 sec.	30 sec.	Fireworks. Traffic trails
4	1/2 sec.	1 sec.	2 sec.	4 sec.	8 sec.	15 sec.	Candle light. Floodlit buildings. Fairgrounds at night
5	1/4 sec.	1/2 sec.	1 sec.	2 sec.	4 sec.	8 sec.	Home interiors with average lighting
6	1/8 sec.	1/4 sec.	1/2 sec.	1 sec.	2 sec.	4 sec.	Home interiors with bright lighting
7	1/15 sec.	1/8 sec.	1/4 sec.	1/2 sec.	1 sec.	2 sec.	Deep woodland cover. Indoor sports events
8	1/30 sec.	1/15 sec.	1/8 sec.	1/4 sec.	1/2 sec.	1 sec.	Bright neon-lit urban areas. Bonfires
9	1/60 sec.	1/30 sec.	1/15 sec.	1/8 sec.	1/4 sec.	1/2 sec.	Ten minutes before sunrise or after sunset
10	1/125 sec.	1/60 sec.	1/30 sec.	1/15 sec.	1/8 sec.	1/4 sec.	Immediately before sunrise or after sunset
11	1/250 sec.	1/125 sec.	1/60 sec.	1/30 sec.	1/15 sec.	1/8 sec.	Sunsets. Deep shade
12	1/500 sec.	1/250 sec.	1/125 sec.	1/60 sec.	1/30 sec.	1/15 sec.	Heavily overcast daylight (no shadows). Open shade
13	1/1000 sec.	1/500 sec.	1/250 sec.	1/125 sec.	1/60 sec.	1/30 sec.	Bright overcast daylight (shadows just visible)
14	1/2000 sec.	1/1000 sec.	1/500 sec.	1/250 sec.	1/125 sec.	1/60 sec.	Weak sunlight. Full moon (very soft shadows)
15	1/4000 sec.	1/2000 sec.	1/1000 sec.	1/500 sec.	1/250 sec.	1/125 sec.	Bright or hazy sunny conditions (distinct shadows)
16	1/8000 sec.	1/4000 sec.	1/2000 sec.	1/1000 sec.	1/500 sec.	1/250 sec.	Brightly lit sand or snow (dark, hard-edged shadows)
17	1/16000 sec.	1/8000 sec.	1/4000 sec.	1/2000 sec.	1/1000 sec.	1/500 sec.	Very intense artificial lighting (very dark, hard-edged shadows)

High dynamic range

One method to overcome the limitations of a camera's dynamic range is to shoot HDR images. This technique requires some forethought when shooting, but it is a useful "get out of jail free" card.

Shooting for HDR

In the first instance, HDR requires you to shoot a sequence of exposures of the same scene. The typical number of images needed is three; one "correctly" exposed, another exposed for the shadow areas, and a third exposure to record detail in the highlights. The greater the contrast between the shadows and highlights, the greater the difference between the exposure settings of the images will need to be.

For low light photography, the big drawback with HDR is that ideally there should be no movement in the scene during the bracketing process. Outdoors this can be tricky, as wind-blown foliage or water movement will produce noticeable differences between shots, and in low light, this is likely if you need to use a slow shutter speed. You can minimize the time between shots by switching off Long Exposure Noise Reduction, and if wind is a problem, try and wait until there is a calm period before shooting your sequence.

Handholding your camera during the bracketing process introduces another potential source of movement. However, this doesn't mean that it is impossible to create an HDR image from handheld shots. Good HDR software will have a function to align a sequence of images, although this requires additional processing time.

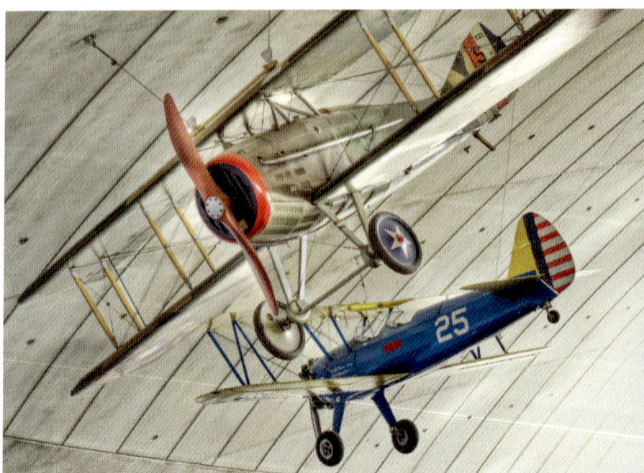

KEEPING STILL
This HDR image was created from three handheld exposures. To minimize movement between the shots I braced myself against a sturdy barrier.

Canon EOS 7D, 50mm lens, three shots at f/4, ISO 200

> **Notes**
>
> *It is possible to use one Raw image processed to produce different "exposures," but this is usually less successful than making three separate exposures at the time of capture.*
>
> *Although it is not a true HDR package, the Enfuse plug-in for Adobe Lightroom is useful for blending bracketed images.*

HDR Software

There is a thriving market for HDR software, with commercial packages fighting it out with open-source and freeware offerings. The latest versions of Adobe Photoshop and Photoshop Elements both have a facility to generate HDR images (though in the latter case, it's probably fairer to say that it's more of a pseudo-HDR effect). Alternatively, the Photomatix suite is a well-regarded standalone HDR package that has many adherents.

HDR imagery has a distinctive style that some like and others loathe. It's an intriguing new avenue in image-making that is fun to explore. Ultimately it's a personal choice as to whether it's a technique that will add to your pleasure of photography. Fortunately, most of the software mentioned above is available on a 30-day trial basis, so it won't cost anything to give it a go.

> **ESTHETICS**
>
> HDR imagery can appear "hyper-real" (or, less kindly, gaudy), so my personal preference is to use HDR for black-and-white images only.

Canon EOS 7D, 10–22mm lens (at 17mm), three shots at f/4, ISO 200

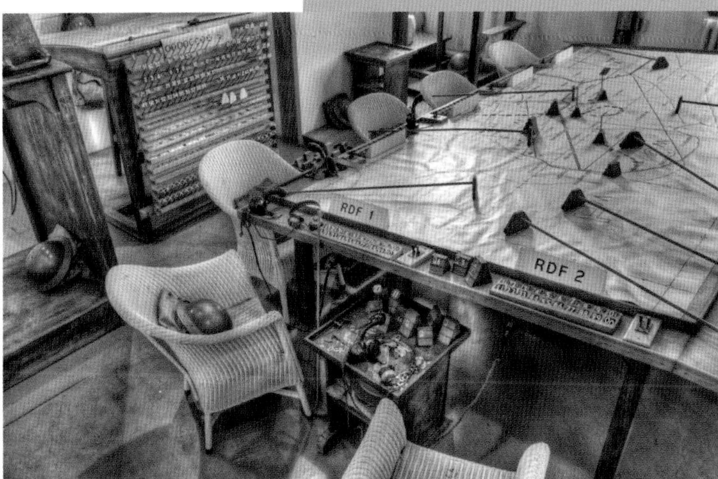

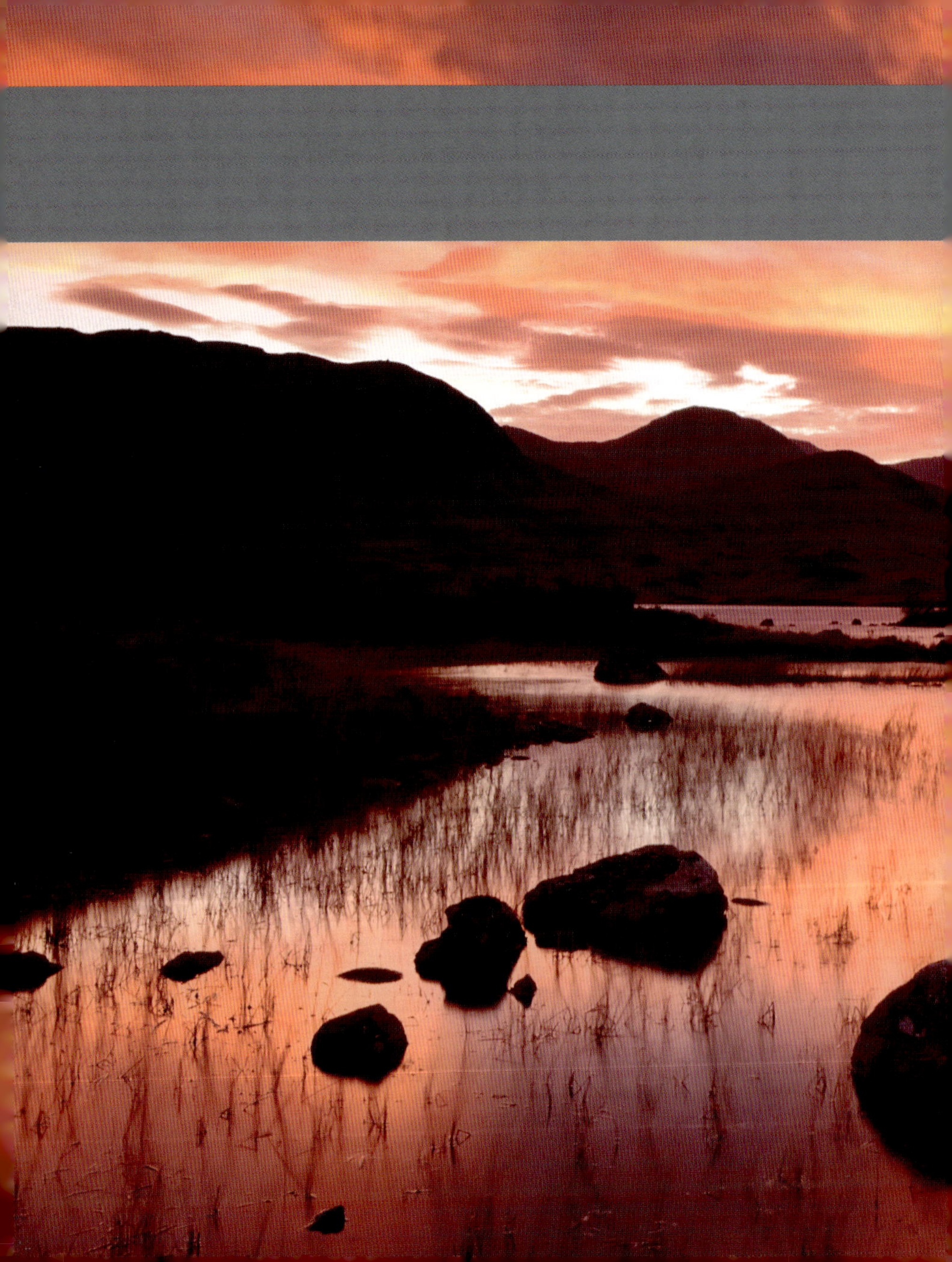

CHAPTER 3 EQUIPMENT

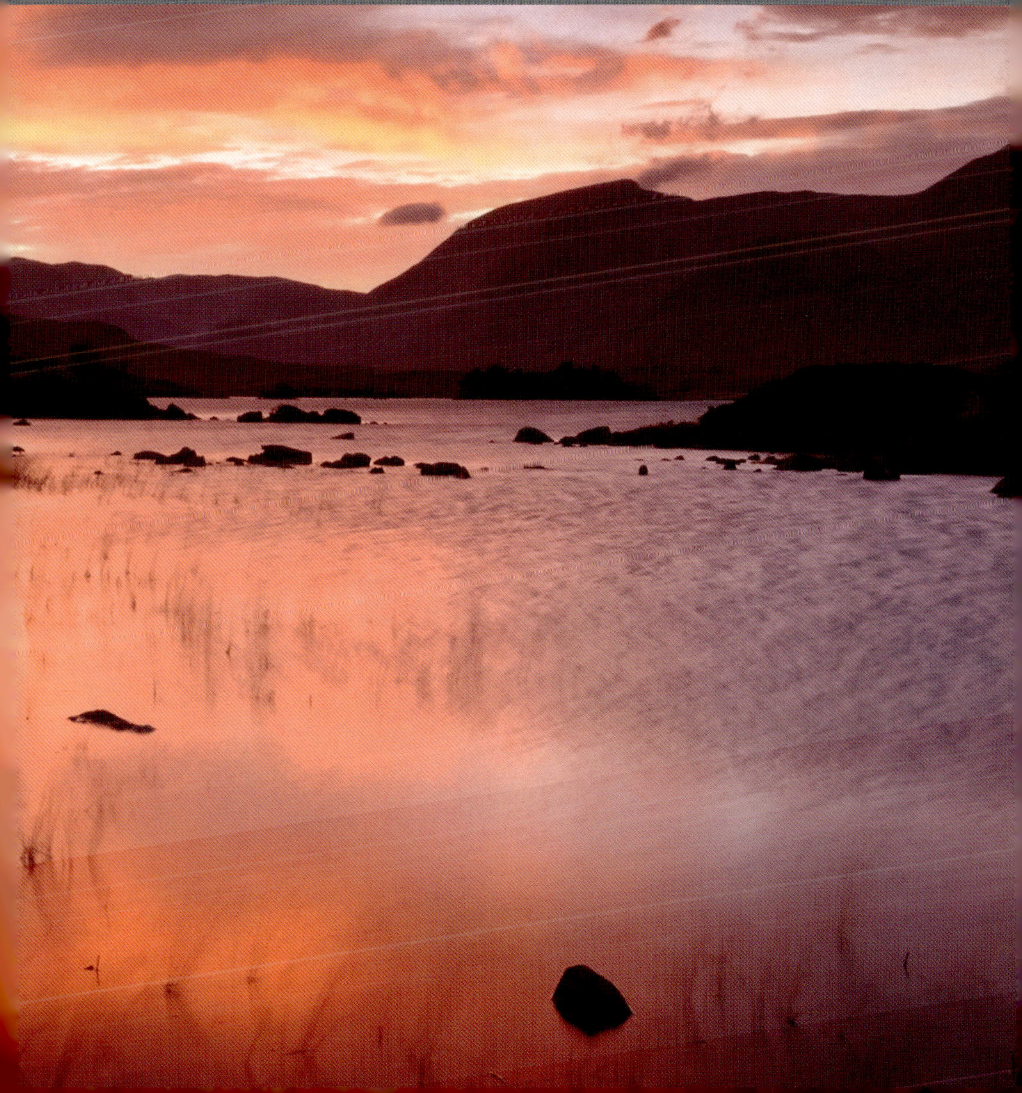

Cameras

Almost every camera can be persuaded to shoot in low light. However, you'll ultimately be more successful if you are using a system camera, such as a digital SLR.

System cameras

Low light photography can stretch a camera to the limits of its capabilities. System cameras, which are those that allow you to swap lenses and add additional equipment such as flashes, are far more capable than compact and phone cameras. This is mainly because the sensor in a system camera is far larger than the sensor found in a compact or phone camera, which means it will have a wider dynamic range and offer higher ISO settings without compromising image quality to the same extent.

System cameras also tend to allow you to use a greater range of apertures and shutter speed settings, as well as supporting Raw files. A Raw file is image data taken directly from the camera sensor without processing. This means you can tweak factors such as white balance in post-processing, without a loss of image quality. Shooting Raw involves a commitment in time, both in learning how to get the best out of Raw and in processing your files, but for the optimum image quality it is the best way to work.

The most familiar type of system camera is the Digital Single Lens Reflex (or DSLR) camera, which uses a reflex mirror and pentaprism to direct light from the lens to an optical viewfinder. Manufacturers such as Canon, Nikon, Olympus, Pentax, and Sony all produce digital SLR camera systems.

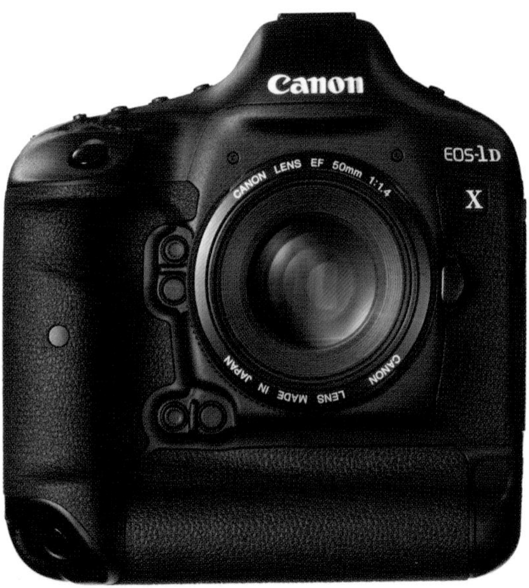

SYSTEM
Canon's EOS-1D X digital SLR camera.
Image © Canon

Now, however, mirrorless camera systems are gaining market share. These camera systems use LCDs or electronic viewfinders to display the image direct from the sensor. Mirrorless system cameras tend to be smaller and lighter than a traditional digital SLR, but without sacrificing image quality. Olympus and Panasonic were the first to market with the Micro Four Thirds system, but are now competing with Sony's NEX system and Fuji's new X-Pro1 rangefinder.

Compact cameras

There is no reason why you cannot use a compact camera for low light shooting. Indeed, many compact cameras have shooting modes designed specifically to help you in a variety of low light situations. The main drawback is that it is usually only possible to shoot using JPEG files. A JPEG is a processed file, so factors such as white balance and noise reduction are "baked" into the file by the camera. Although you can alter a JPEG in post-production, when compared to a Raw file, this can only be done in a very limited way if you are to avoid a serious reduction in image quality. There are a few high-end compact cameras that shoot Raw and allow a greater control over settings such as aperture and shutter speed, but these are generally few and far between.

One way in which a compact camera is very useful is as a "walkabout" camera. The size and weight of a compact means it is easy to keep in a jacket pocket or bag. This is ideal for a more spontaneous approach to photography, and ultimately, the best camera is the one you have with you when it's needed.

COMPACT
Fuji X10 compact digital camera.
Image © Fuji

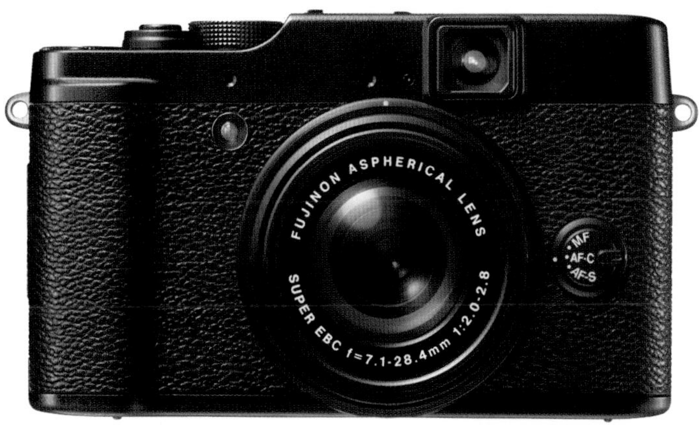

Lenses

In many respects the lens is the most important part of your camera system. No matter how sophisticated your camera is, the quality of the images you shoot will be determined primarily by the lens you use.

Focal length

The description of a lens will usually include its focal length (or if the lens is a zoom, the range of focal lengths covered). Focal length is a measurement of the distance from the optical center of the lens to the focal plane when a subject at infinity is in focus. The sensor is located at the focal plane, and this is often indicated by a symbol on the body of the camera *(see opposite)*.

The focal length of a lens affects its angle of view, which is the angular extent of an image projected by the lens onto the sensor. A lens with a short focal length has a wide angle of view (and so, unsurprisingly, is referred to as a wide-angle lens). Telephoto lenses with longer focal lengths have a narrower angle of view, but with a greater magnification, making your subject larger in the image.

The size of the sensor in a camera also affects the angle of view of the image recorded by the camera. On full-frame cameras, a 28mm wide-angle focal length has an angle of view of 75° whereas on an APS-C (or cropped-frame) camera, the angle of view is only 54° (making it far less wide). To achieve roughly the same angle of view on an APS-C camera, an 18mm focal length must be used instead.

The sensors in compact cameras are smaller still, which means an even wider focal length lens—sometimes 8mm or less—must be used to achieve an angle of view of 75°. To avoid

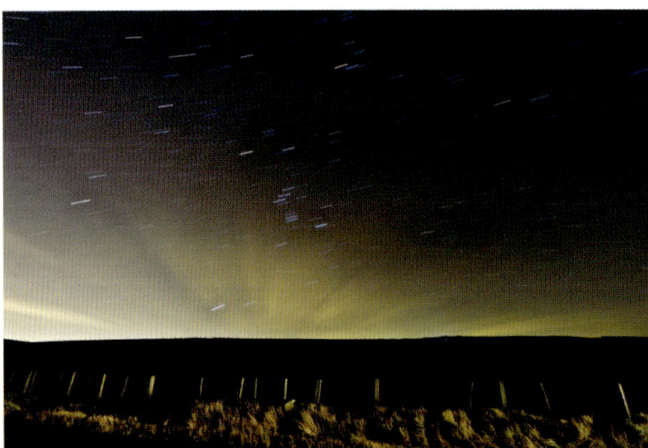

ULTRA-WIDE LENS
This star trail image was shot with a 10mm lens on an APS-C camera. This would be equivalent to using a 16mm focal length on a full-frame camera.

Canon EOS 7D, 10–22mm lens (at 10mm), 10 min. at f/4, ISO 200

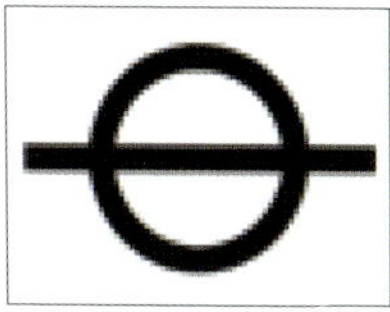

FOCAL LENGTH
The symbol used on a camera body to show the position of the sensor or film plane.

confusion, manufacturers often give the "35mm equivalent" focal length in a compact camera's specifications as a familiar reference point.

> **Note**
> *Full-frame cameras are so-called because the sensor size is equal to the dimensions of an image created on 35mm film.*

Prime lenses versus zoom lenses

Although digital SLR cameras can be bought "body only," most are sold as part of a bundle with a zoom lens or two. These zooms are usually good value, but are not the best that a manufacturer produces. One problem with them is the relatively small maximum aperture available (often f/4–f/5.6). For general use this is usually not too much of a drawback, but it can prove a problem when shooting in low light.

Camera autofocus systems also need a certain amount of light to maintain accuracy and responsiveness, so a lens with a small maximum aperture is at an immediate disadvantage in comparison to a lens with a large maximum aperture. Also, the larger the maximum aperture of your lens, the easier it will be for you to see details in the camera's viewfinder.

Unfortunately, zoom lenses with large maximum apertures are far heavier than standard kit lenses, and also more expensive. A compromise is to keep a prime lens or two in your camera bag.

A prime lens is a fixed focal length lens. They are generally relatively inexpensive and have the advantage of large maximum apertures. If you choose to buy a prime lens, think about the focal length you use most often on your zoom lens and look for an equivalent. I have 24mm and 50mm primes for landscape work, for example, but if I was a portrait photographer I'd probably consider an 80mm prime instead of a wide-angle lens. If I was a wildlife photographer, then a 200mm or 400mm prime lens would be in my bag.

SIZE
An advantage of prime lenses is their weight. Some, such as Panasonic's 18mm "pancake" lens, weigh almost nothing compared to a zoom lens.
Image © Panasonic

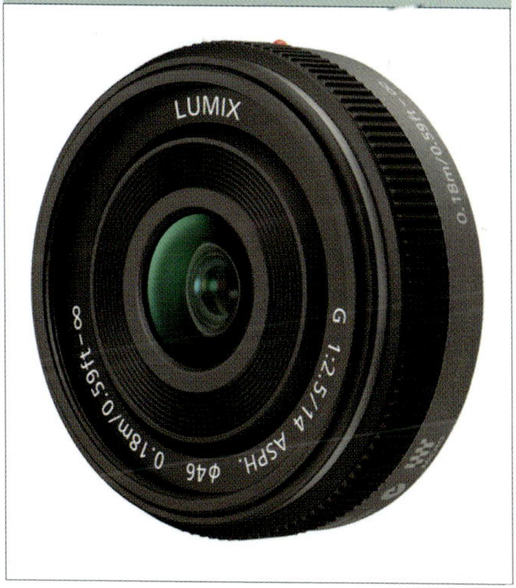

Lens problems

All lenses, no matter how expensive, will suffer from flaws as it's impossible to design the perfect lens. Certain techniques when shooting in low light can bring out the worst in a lens. Fortunately, many of these problems can be solved in-camera when shooting JPEG or in post-production when converting Raw files.

Vignetting

Shooting at maximum aperture can cause vignetting, an effect that causes the outer edges of an image to be subtly darker than the center. Wide-angle lenses are usually more prone to vignetting than telephotos. Although this is a defect of a lens, it can be used creatively to emphasize your subject if the subject is kept to the center of the image. Vignetting usually decreases rapidly as smaller apertures are used.

AXIAL CA
Red and green fringing caused by axial CA.

Canon EOS 7D, 50mm lens, 1/320 sec. at f/1.4, ISO 100

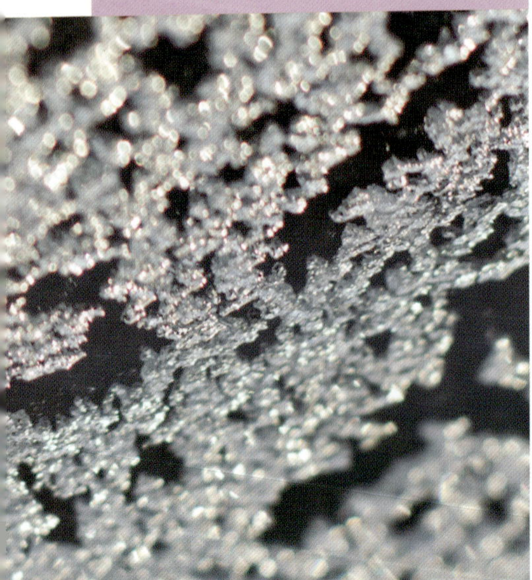

Chromatic aberration

Visible light is composed of a spectrum of wavelengths of electromagnetic radiation. The longest wavelength corresponds to the color we see as red, the shortest to blue/violet. A lens that cannot focus these different wavelengths to the same point will suffer from chromatic aberration (often shortened to CA). Chromatic aberration is seen as color fringing around the boundaries of light and dark areas of an image.

There are two types of chromatic aberration: axial and transverse. Axial CA is seen across the whole image when a lens is set to maximum aperture. Transverse CA is seen in the corners of images and is visible at all apertures. Transverse CA can be corrected relatively easily in post-production. Axial CA is more difficult to correct and can only be reduced by stopping the lens down to a smaller aperture setting.

> ***Note***
> *Some of the techniques featured later in this book require setting the lens focus to infinity. This is shown as ∞ on the lens focus ring.*

Avoiding the shakes

Handholding your camera when the light levels are low and shutter speeds are long introduces the risk of camera shake. This results in unsharp images characterized by directionality to the softness. The longer the lens, the more acute the problem becomes.

Posture is very important in reducing the risk of camera shake. Stand as upright as possible, keeping your feet shoulder-width apart. Tuck your elbows lightly against your body for support. Grip the camera firmly with one hand, and use your other hand to support the lens from below. Breathe in and then slowly out. Before breathing in again gently squeeze down on the camera's shutter-release button to take the shot. When shooting from a kneeling position, steady your upper body by resting your elbow on one knee.

Bracing your camera against makeshift supports, such as fence posts or streetlamps, can make a big difference to the stability of your camera. Walls also make useful supports. Use a cloth, or better still a beanbag, to rest your camera on and to protect its base from scratches.

A very cheap way to increase your camera's stability is to use a length of string. It needs to be roughly a foot longer than your height. Tie a loop at both ends. When you come to make your photo, put one loop around your foot, the other around the camera lens. Now pull the string taut. The tension in the string will keep your camera more steady than if you'd simply handheld it.

MOVEMENT

Camera shake has directionality—essentially the path taken by the camera during the exposure. The arrow shows the direction of the camera shake in this image.

Canon EOS 7D, 50mm lens, 1/30 sec. at f/8, ISO 200

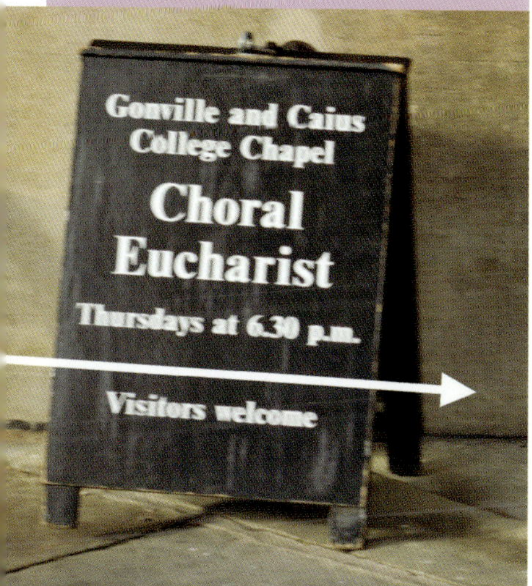

TIP

A good way to avoid camera shake is to use a shutter speed greater than the focal length of the lens. So, if you're using a 50mm lens, use a shutter speed of 1/50 sec. or faster; with a 200mm lens use 1/200 sec., and so on. Your camera's Auto or Program modes will try to achieve this automatically.

Image stabilization

Another way to avoid camera shake is to use a lens or camera with image stabilization. Image stabilization systems work by compensating for slight movements of a camera during an exposure. In practical terms, this enables you to handhold a camera at slower shutter speeds than normal without camera shake. The results vary from system to system, and from person to person, but 2–4 stops difference is usually possible.

There are currently two approaches to image stabilization. The first is lens-based (known as Optical Image Stabilization or OIS). Inside an OIS lens tiny gyroscopic sensors detect movement, which is cancelled out by the shifting of a floating lens element. The two main adherents to this approach are Canon and Nikon, with image stabilized lenses bearing the code IS (Canon's Image Stabilization) and VR (Nikon's Vibration Reduction). The main advantage with this stabilization option is that it is possible to see the stabilized image when looking through the viewfinder. A disadvantage is that image-stabilized lenses are expensive compared to equivalent non-stabilized versions.

The second approach to combating camera shake is to move the sensor inside the camera. Unsurprisingly, this is known as sensor-shift stabilization. The main adherents of this technology are Olympus, Pentax, and Sony. The big advantage of sensor-based stabilization is that it works with any lens that is attached to the camera. The main drawback is that the effect isn't visible when looking through a viewfinder (although it is visible when using Live View).

SONY A55
The Sony A55, equipped with Sony's sensor-based SteadyShot stabilization system.

Image © Sony

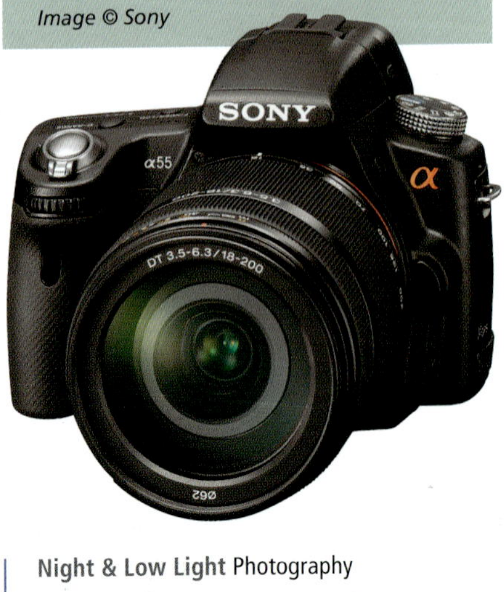

Notes

Image stabilization should always be switched off when your camera is mounted on a tripod.

Image stabilization isn't instant and it can take a second or more before full stabilization is achieved.

STEADY ON *(Opposite)*
Image stabilization is particularly useful on longer lenses. With a 180mm focal length and a 1/40 sec. shutter speed the image is very unsharp (top). However, with stabilization activated (in this case Canon's IS system), the result is far more acceptable (bottom), even though the same shutter speed is being used.

Canon EOS 7D, 70–200mm lens (at 180mm), 1/40 sec. at f/9, ISO 800

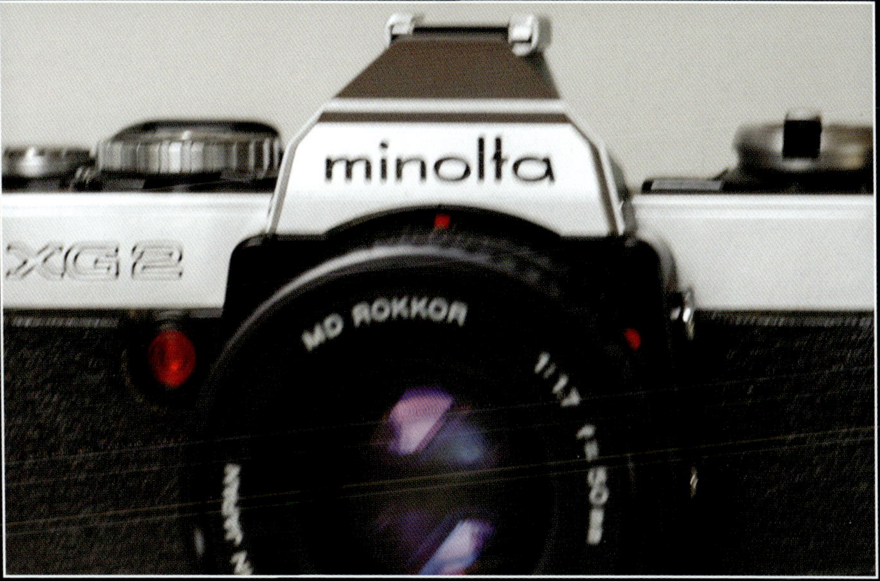
minolta
XG 2
MD ROKKOR
1:1.7 f=50mm

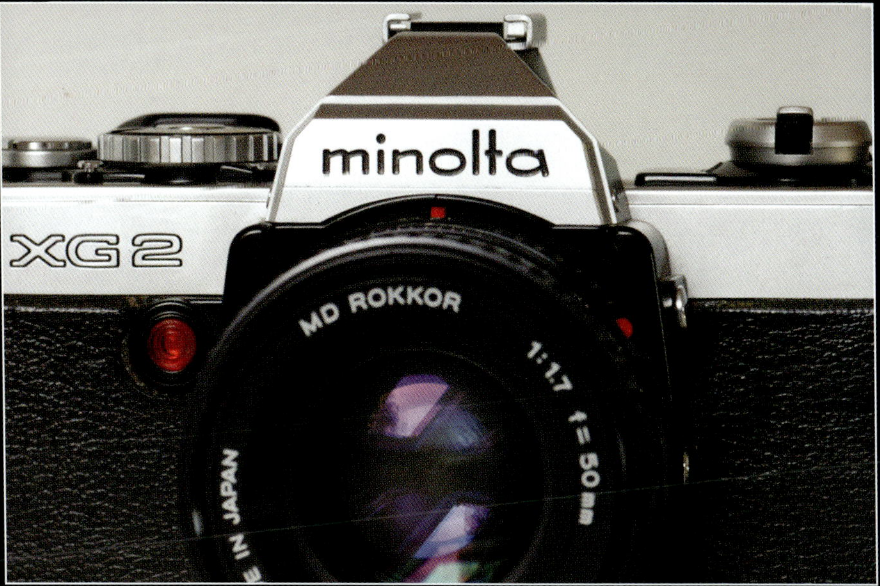
minolta
XG 2
MD ROKKOR
1:1.7 f=50mm
E IN JAPAN

Tripods

When light levels are low and shutter speeds are long, handholding a camera will result in unsharp images. This is when a tripod is an invaluable tool.

Choosing a tripod

A tripod has one job in life and that is to keep your camera steady during an exposure. There is an element of compromise to be made when choosing a tripod: you want one that will not be a burden to carry, but that is robust enough so that it is able to support your camera successfully. A good rule of thumb is that the heavier your camera equipment, the weightier your tripod will need to be.

The least expensive tripods tend to be made of cheaper materials such as plastic, which makes them light to carry, but less robust, and more liable to be blown over. Metal tripods are a little more expensive, but also stronger, and aluminum tripods generally offer a reasonable compromise between weight and cost. However, the best weight-to-strength material currently used to make tripods is carbon fiber,

> ***Tip***
>
> ***Metal tripods can be agony to hold when temperatures drop. To protect your hands, wrap foam insulation designed for pipes around one of the legs and use that to hold onto.***

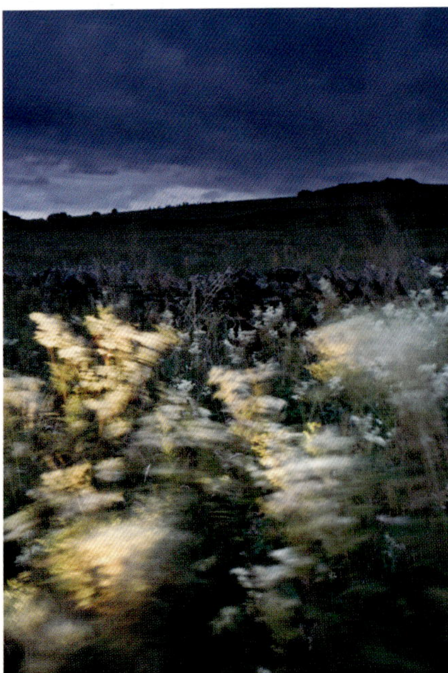

INVALUABLE
A tripod is vital for the low light photographer, and there are numerous techniques, such as painting with light, which would be impossible without one.

Canon EOS 1Ds MkII, 17–40mm lens (at 20mm), 5 sec. at f/9, ISO 200

which is an astonishingly rigid material given its weight. There is a catch however: carbon fiber tripods are often two to three times more expensive than an equivalent metal model. Choosing a tripod therefore involves weighing up your photographic needs with the amount you're prepared to pay.

COMBINATION
Benro A-169 tripod and B-0 ball-head.

Image © Benro

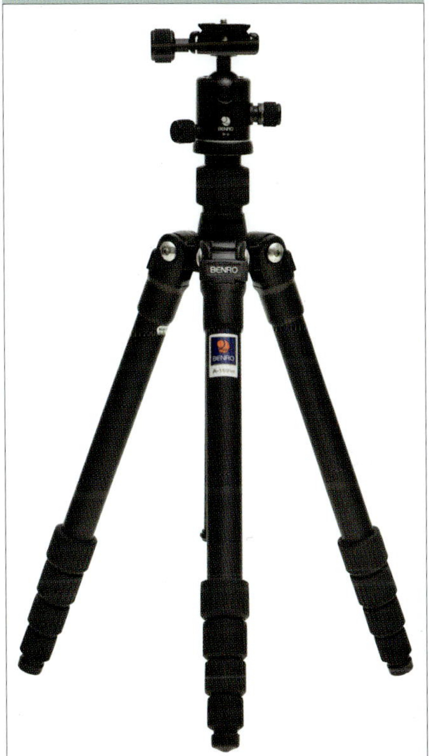

Tripod heads

Tripods either have a head already attached, or come without a head, requiring you to buy one separately. Although the latter type will ultimately prove more expensive, it does mean that you can mix and match the tripod and head to suit your own needs.

There are three main tripod head types, and each has strengths and weaknesses. The first, and most common, is the three-way head. This type of head can be moved and locked in any of the three axes. The second type of tripod head is the ball-head. As the name suggests, the head pivots on a ball that can be unlocked to move freely. Ball-heads have an excellent weight-to-strength ratio, so even a small ball-head can generally hold a heavy camera reasonably steadily. However, ball-heads can be fiddly to use and it's difficult to make fine adjustments. The third type of tripod head is the geared variety. These heads allow very precise adjustments in three axes. Unlike a three-way head, a geared head does not have to be locked into position, but the penalty that's exacted for this ease of use is weight: geared heads are typically far heavier than the other two types.

Regardless of the head design, a very useful feature to look for is a quick-release system. This will allow you to quickly attach and remove your camera from the tripod head, which saves considerable time and effort when setting up your camera system.

Good tripod technique

Even if you use a tripod, it is still possible to create unsharp images if your tripod technique is sloppy. For example, a tripod can wobble slightly if the legs are not extended evenly, so try to make sure that it isn't leaning before you attach your camera. Another cause of unsteadiness is use of the center column, which raises the center of gravity of your tripod, making it top heavy. To avoid this, make sure that you have extended the tripod legs to their maximum height before you consider using the center column.

The next problem area is you. No matter how careful you are you will cause a vibration in the camera-tripod combination every time you touch it. Use a cable release or the self-timer on your camera to reduce the risk of this happening. Don't move around during long exposures either, particularly if the ground is soft: this may cause the tripod to move or, in very low light, you could accidentally walk into or trip over the tripod.

The final potential cause of image softness when using a digital SLR is the camera itself. The reflex mirror swings upward when the shutter is fired, and this can result in slight vibration, even though the movement is damped. Most cameras have a mirror-lock facility, which allows you to lock the mirror up before making an exposure, which will reduce "mirror slap." Needless to say, mirrorless cameras and digital SLRs in Live View mode (when the mirror is already raised) will not suffer from this problem.

Long lenses can also cause a tripod to become slightly unstable. If you own a long lens that has a lens collar, always use that when attaching the camera to the tripod, rather than attaching the camera body itself.

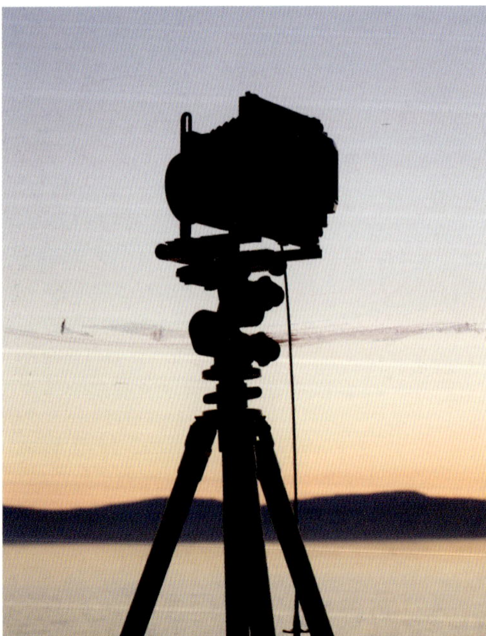

STAYING STILL
Once my tripod is set up I try to minimize my movements: nothing's worse than knocking the tripod and ruining a carefully composed shot.

Remote releases

The humble remote release is an often-overlooked item of equipment. The simplest variety is the cable-release that screws directly into the shutter button. There is no electronic signal and it's the mechanical act of pushing down the plunger on the cable release that fires the shutter. Most modern camera manufacturers no longer support the cable-release, with the exceptions of Fuji and Leica.

Most cameras today use proprietary remote releases, incompatible with rival systems. These remote releases are electronic devices that control the shutter by wire connection or infrared. Using a remote release means you can avoid touching your camera when it's mounted on a tripod. This all helps to reduce the risk of camera shake and knocking the camera. A vital feature to look out for when choosing a remote release is a shutter lock facility. This is used when employing Bulb mode and avoids the necessity of keeping a finger on the shutter button during the exposure.

The most sophisticated remote releases are those with programmable functions such as timer, timed Bulb, and an intervalometer. Intervalometers allow the shooting of multiple images over a regular period. This facility is particularly useful when shooting images for time-lapse movies or for star trail stacking.

THIRD–PARTY REMOTES
There is a number of third-party alternatives to an official camera manufacturer's remote control, offering varying levels of control.

Notes

A number of Nikon's digital SLRs have built-in intervalometers.

Some cameras have a Time function in addition to Bulb. When the camera is set to Time, pressing the shutter-release button once locks the shutter open. Pressing it again closes the shutter.

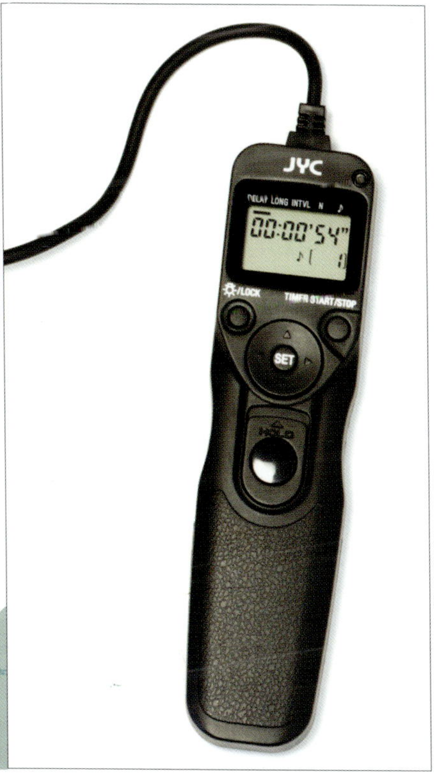

Filters

Despite the fact that imaging software is so advanced, there is still a place in the equipment bag for filters.

Filter types

A filter is a piece of glass, gelatin, or optical resin that affects the light passing through it in some way. This can be subtle, or, like the starburst filter described below, change the light in a way that is far from understated.

Filters are available either in a screw-in form that attaches to the filter thread on the front of a lens, or as part of a holder system. Screw-in filters are usually relatively inexpensive, but as there is no standard filter thread size you may find that you need to buy multiple filters of the same type if you have a collection of lenses with different filter thread diameters. A more elegant solution is to buy a filter for the largest thread size and then buy step-up rings so you can use the same filter on your smaller lenses.

The alternative is a filter holder, which is a slotted plastic device that clips to an adapter ring screwed to the front of a lens. The filters that fit into a holder are usually either square or rectangular, and there are currently three different sized systems on the market: 67mm (Cokin A); the 84/85mm (Cokin P); and 100mm (produced by a number of manufacturers including Cokin, Lee Filters, and Hitech). If you own a number of lenses you can use the same filters on each of them—all you need to buy is an appropriate (and inexpensive) adapter ring for each lens. Be careful to get the right size filter holder to start with though—the smaller systems are the least expensive, but they are also less compatible with wide-angle lenses as they can cause noticeable cut-off in the corners of the frame.

Notes

Filters degrade image quality slightly, so while it is possible to stack multiple filters in front of a lens, it is not advisable.

You can keep your filters clean using a dedicated soft cloth.

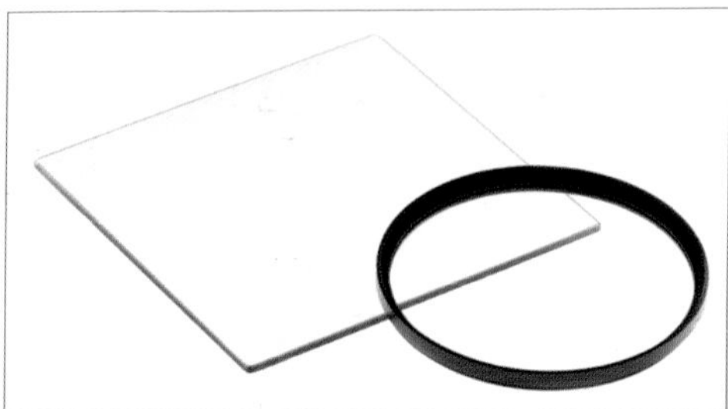

FILTERS
100mm square filter and 77mm screw-in filter.

Starburst (cross-screen) filters

Starburst filters are covered in a grid of finely etched lines that refract the light from point light sources. This produces distinctive colored lines radiating out from the light source: the number of lines is determined by the filter's grid pattern. There was a vogue for using starburst filters during the 1980s, but they are now seen as a touch passé. However, fashions come and go, and their day may yet come again.

Skylight and UV filters

Both of these filters absorb UV light, helping to reduce the effects of atmospheric haze and the coolness caused by UV light. Skylight filters have a slightly pink tint and so also subtly "warm" an image (they are available in two strengths, 1A and 1B, with 1B being warmer). UV and skylight filters do not affect exposure, and for this reason some photographers leave one attached to each of their lenses to protect the front element from damage. UV and skylight filters are particularly useful at high altitude where there is a greater concentration of UV light.

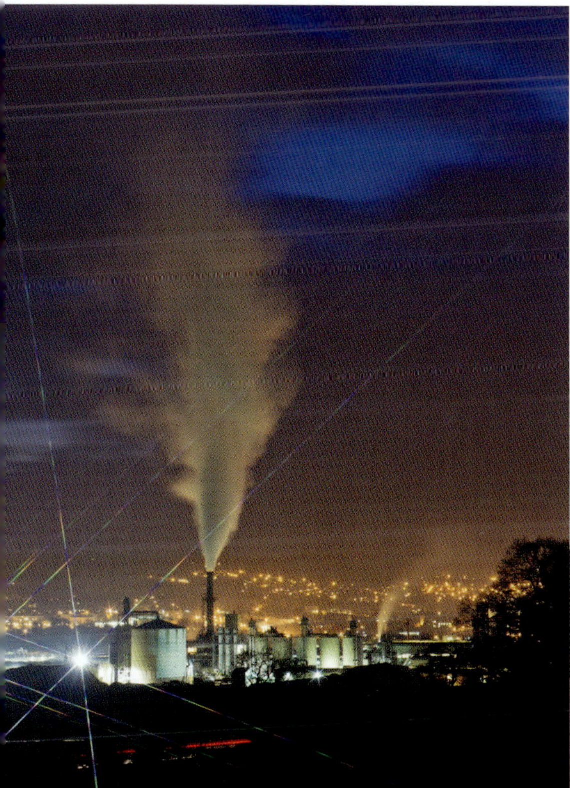

Tip

Using a smaller aperture will cause point light sources to appear star-shaped, although the effect is not as dramatic as using a starburst filter.

STARBURST
The effect of a six-point starburst filter.

Canon EOS 7D, 17–40mm lens (at 40mm), 25 sec. at f/6.3, ISO 200

Polarizing filters

Light reflected from a non-metallic surface is scattered in all directions, causing glare and a reduction in color saturation. This scattered light has been polarized. A polarizing filter cuts out polarized light perpendicular to the axis of the filter. The most commonly seen use for polarizers is to deepen the color of blue skies. However, this effect only works when the polarizer is used at 90° to the sun (referred to as "Brewster's Angle"). The effect diminishes rapidly away from this angle, which can cause an unnatural banding effect across the sky when ultra wide-angle lenses are used with a polarizing filter.

Polarizing filters aren't just for sunny days: they also cut out reflections from wet surfaces and help to increase color saturation. This is particularly useful with woodland scenes and wet foliage.

In this situation, polarizing filters work best when used at approximately 35° to the reflective surface, and not at all at 90°.

The effectiveness of a polarizing filter is altered by turning it around the lens axis. Screw-in polarizers usually have a rotating front element, while polarizers designed for filter holders are rotated within the holder itself.

Notes

Polarizers are sold as either circular or linear. Linear polarizers are only suitable for manual focus cameras as they adversely affect both the TTL metering and autofocus systems of AF cameras. For that reason, you should buy a circular polarizer.

When using semi-automatic modes your camera will compensate for any light loss caused by filters fitted over the lens. When shooting manually, use the grid below to calculate how much exposure should be adjusted.

Filter exposure compensation table

Filter type	*Filter factor*	*Exposure increase*
Starburst	1x	0
Skylight/UV	1x	0
Polarizing filter	1x–4x	0–2 stops
0.3 ND filter	2x	1 stop
0.6 ND filter	4x	2 stops
0.9 ND filter	8x	3 stops

Neutral density (ND) filters

Low light photography doesn't necessarily mean waiting until light levels drop. You can artificially reduce the amount of light reaching the film or sensor by using a neutral density (ND) filter on the front of the lens.

Many digital cameras have a relatively high base ISO: often it is ISO 100, but sometimes it can be as high as ISO 200. This can prove very restrictive if you want to use a large aperture with a slow shutter speed. ND filters are available in a variety of strengths: the stronger the filter, the more opaque it is. A 1-stop ND filter has the same effect on the required exposure as changing from ISO 100 to ISO 50. A 2-stop is equivalent to changing the ISO from 100 to 25 and so on.

ND filters are also very useful if your camera is able to shoot video. Video often appears more pleasing when a relatively slow shutter speed is used—too fast a shutter speed and moving objects appear to move in a staccato fashion rather than smoothly.

> ***Tips***
>
> *ND filters are often sold using an optical density figure. A 1-stop ND filter has an optical density of 0.3, a 2-stop filter is 0.6, and a 3-stop filter is 0.9.*
>
> *A polarizer cuts out up to 2 stops of light, so it can also be used in the same way as an ND filter.*

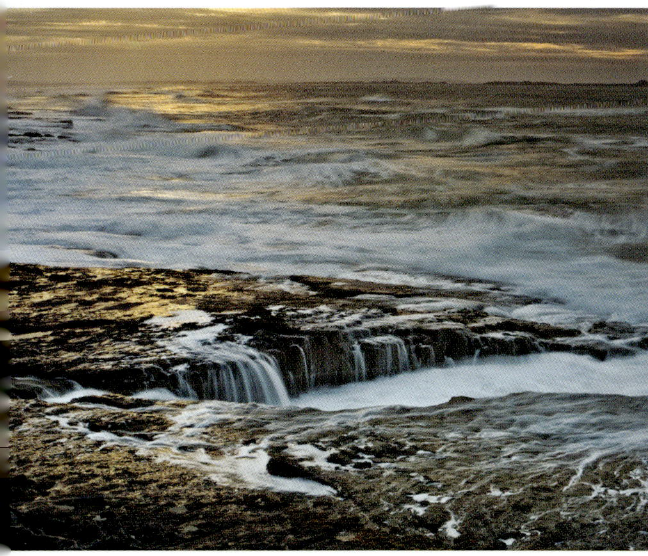

TIDAL
A 3-stop ND filter was used to slow the shutter speed from 1/15 sec. to 1/2 sec., allowing me to enhance the waves washing over the foreground rocks.

Canon EOS 5D, 50mm lens, 1/2 sec. at f/13, ISO 100

Extreme ND filters

A recent development is the general availability of very dense ND filters that reduce light by a greater factor than a few stops. These filters are so dense that to the naked eye they appear opaque, and shutter speeds can be increased from fractions of a second to several seconds or minutes, even in very bright light. Because shutter speeds lengthen so dramatically, extreme ND filters invariably require the camera to be mounted on a tripod.

As with standard ND filters, extreme ND filters are available in different strengths in either circular form, to fit directly onto a lens, or square for use in a filter holder. A good quality square filter should have a baffle around the circumference to stop light leakage around the edges during use.

Working smarter...

Apple iOS: *Longtime Exposure*

Android: *Exposure Calculator*

Both of these apps allow you to quickly calculate the difference in shutter speed needed for ND filters of varying strengths.

One problem common to all extreme ND filters is that they are never entirely neutral. They either display a warm, almost sepia, cast or a noticeable coolness. This varies from manufacturer to manufacturer and the information about individual filters can usually be found very quickly in online reviews and forums. If you are shooting with the intention of converting your images to black and white, the color cast won't be an issue. To counteract the color cast when shooting color you should either create a custom white balance for the filter and the current shooting situation, or be prepared to adjust the color later in post-processing.

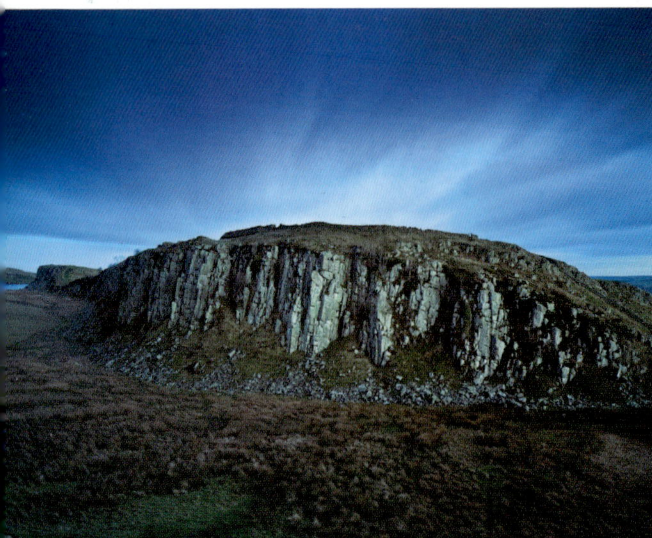

BLUE
I use a Hitech 10-stop filter, which has a cool color cast. However, this is easily corrected in post-production.

Canon EOS 7D, 10–22mm lens (at 16mm), 5 min. at f/4, ISO 400

Because extreme ND filters are so opaque you will need to compose, determine exposure and set the focus before fitting the filter. The exposure should be based on the settings taken without the filter attached and then altered depending on the strength of the filter. Use the grid below as guidance. As an example, if the shutter speed with no filter attached is 1/15 sec., you would need to change it to 2 seconds if a 5-stop ND filter is used, or 1 minute with a 10-stop ND filter. Using manual exposure will allow you to make the necessary changes more easily, as exposure compensation usually covers a 3–5 stop range.

The effect of using an extreme ND filter is very pronounced if there is any movement in the scene you are photographing. When used to shoot landscapes, moving clouds will lose definition and become more ethereal. Water, particularly tidal seawater washing back and forth, will cease to look like water, and take on a misty appearance. In many ways it is a look that suits black-and-white imagery better than color, as black and white offers an inherently less literal representation of the world.

Because shutter speeds are potentially so long when using an extreme ND filter it is recommended that fresh batteries are used in your camera whenever possible. If shooting digitally, Long Exposure Noise Reduction should be activated, while film users should apply exposure compensation to combat reciprocity law failure if necessary.

Extreme ND filter exposure compensation

Shutter speed	5-stop filter	8-stop filter	10-stop filter	*Shutter speed*	5-stop filter	8-stop filter	10-stop filter
1/8000 sec.	1/250 sec.	1/30 sec.	1/8 sec.	***1/8 sec.***	4 sec.	30 sec.	2 min.
1/4000 sec.	1/125 sec.	1/15 sec.	1/4 sec.	***1/4 sec.***	8 sec.	1 min.	4 min.
1/2000 sec.	1/60 sec.	1/8 sec.	1/2 sec.	***1/2 sec.***	15 sec.	2 min.	8 min.
1/1000 sec.	1/30 sec.	1/4 sec.	1 sec.	***1 sec.***	30 sec.	4 min.	16 min.
1/500 sec.	1/15 sec.	1/2 sec.	2 sec.	***2 sec.***	1 min.	8 min.	32 min.
1/250 sec.	1/8 sec.	1 sec.	4 sec.	***4 sec.***	2 min.	16 min.	64 min.
1/125 sec.	1/4 sec.	2 sec.	8 sec.	***8 sec.***	4 min.	32 min.	128 min.
1/60 sec.	1/2 sec.	4 sec.	15 sec.	***15 sec.***	8 min.	64 min.	256 min.
1/30 sec.	1 sec.	8 sec.	30 sec.	***30 sec.***	16 min.	128 min.	512 min.
1/15 sec.	2 sec.	15 sec.	1 min.	***1 min.***	32 min.	256 min.	1024 min.

Tip

When focusing, you could still use AF if you wish, but be sure to switch your lens to manual focus before fitting the filter (and without disturbing the focus as you do so). If the light levels are reasonably high, Live View may still work with a filter attached, and even allow you to focus. Experiment to determine if this is the case.

Tip

Extreme ND filters aren't just useful for landscape work. Anything that is moving relatively quickly will vanish from a photo if the shutter speed is minutes long. This is useful for architectural subjects that have people milling around them and where the ideal is a relatively people-free shot. Only someone who stops moving for a reasonable period of time will register in the final image. Whether you try to keep that person moving along is your esthetic choice!

WAVES

The use of a 1 minute exposure makes this coastal scene appear very tranquil. In reality, the waves were pounding against the rocks in the foreground.

Canon EOS 1Ds MkII, 70–200mm lens (at 70mm), 1 min. at f/16, ISO 50

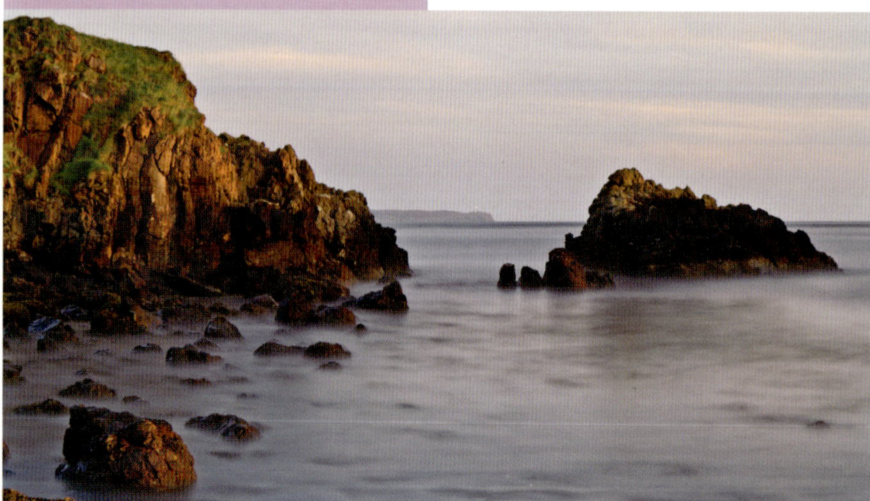

Graduated ND filters

ND filters are used across the entire scene. However, the graduated ND filter is more specialized. The graduated ND is divided into two. The bottom half of the filter is transparent; the top half is semi-opaque like an ND filter. The transition zone between the two halves can be soft, hard, or very hard, and graduated ND filters are available in different strengths (commonly 1-stop, 2-stops, and 3-stops).

Graduated ND filters are used to balance the exposure of a scene when one half is far brighter than the other half, and a "straight" exposure is impossible. The most common users of graduated ND filters are probably landscape photographers who often need to balance the different brightness levels of sky and foreground in their image. The greater the difference in brightness between the sky and the foreground, the stronger the graduated ND filter would need to be.

Graduated ND filters are available in screw-in form, but they work best in a filter holder. This way they can be moved up and down (or rotated) so that they can be precisely positioned where needed.

LANDSCAPE
This scene required the use of a 2-stop graduated ND filter (below right). Without the filter (below left) the sky and background are washed out.

Canon 7D, 17–40mm lens (at 22mm), 1/30 at f/8, ISO 400

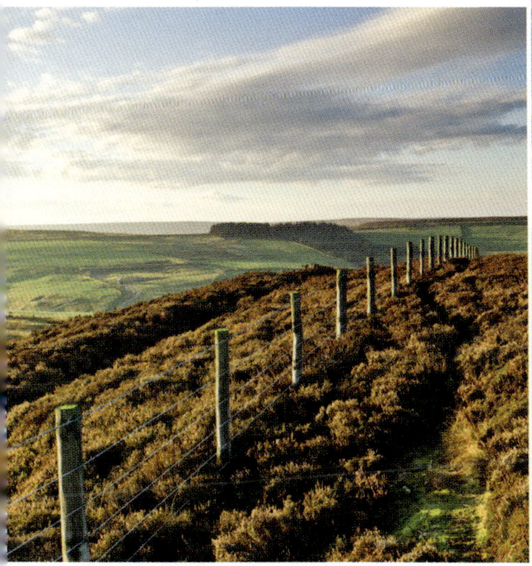

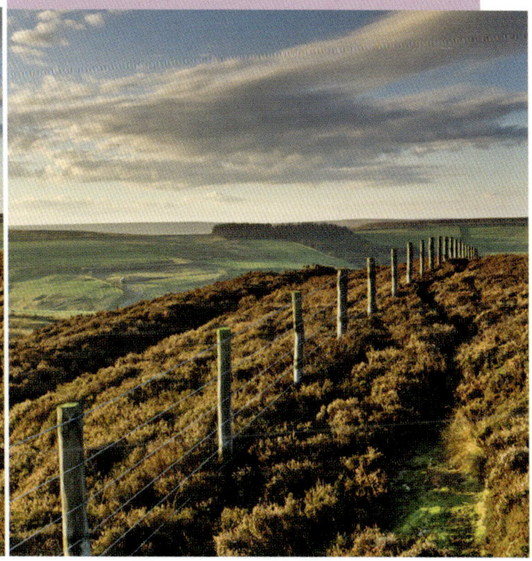

Metering with ND graduate filters

A very quick and crude method to assess whether a graduated ND is necessary is to squint at the scene in front of you. If the foreground and the sky appear equally bright then you probably don't need a filter. If, however, the foreground looks far darker than the sky, you will need one.

Metering method #1

1) Switch your camera to manual exposure and select center-weighted metering.

2) Meter from the foreground and set the correct aperture and shutter speed combination.

3) Point the camera to the sky and meter again. Note the difference in the exposure and select a graduated ND filter that reduces the difference to 1 stop.

4) Compose your shot and fit the filter, leaving the exposure set for the foreground.

Metering method #2

1) Switch your camera to manual exposure and select spot metering.

2) Take readings from a midtone area, such as grass or rock. Note the suggested exposure.

3) Take spot meter readings of the midtones in the sky. These are typically areas of blue sky or the undersides of darker clouds. Again, note the suggested exposure.

4) Calculate the difference in stops between your two readings and use a graduated ND filter that is equivalent to the difference.

REFLECTIONS

Don't use an overly strong ND graduate filter when shooting reflections. The subject should always be darker than its reflection.

Canon EOS 1Ds MkII, 70–200mm lens (at 70mm), 1/100 sec. at f/9, ISO 200

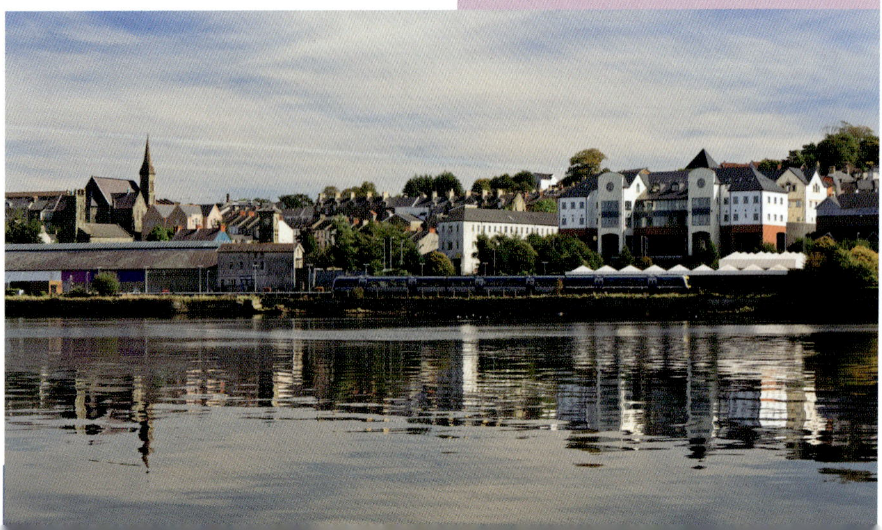

Other equipment

It's not just camera equipment that is useful when shooting in low light. There are gadgets and tools that will make your life easier both practically and photographically.

Batteries

The batteries used in modern digital cameras are extremely efficient for their size, but they will inevitably deplete. This is particularly true if you are constantly using the camera's Live View and image review functions, and when setting lengthy shutter speeds with Long Exposure Noise Reduction activated.

Film cameras are less battery dependant, but those with electronic shutters still require a healthy battery to function (film cameras with mechanical shutters often only need a battery for the lightmeter).

To prevent your photography session coming to a premature end, it's worth investing in a spare battery or two and keeping these charged up ready for use. Batteries are depleted more quickly when conditions are cold. Store your spare batteries inside your jacket to keep them warm until you need them.

Spirit level

In low light, it's often difficult to see whether your camera is level, but some tripods and tripod heads come with a built-in spirit level. Alternatively it's possible to buy a spirit level that clips into the hotshoe of your camera, or that can be balanced on the top plate of the camera if that is flat and parallel to the base of the camera.

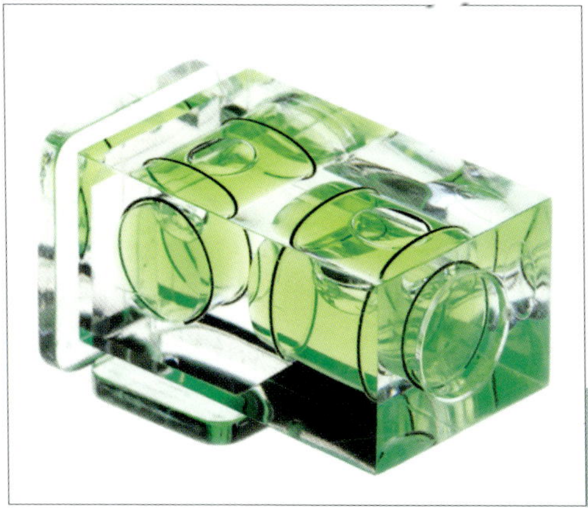

ON THE LEVEL
Hotshoe-mounted spirit level.

Working smarter...
Apple iOS: *iBubbleLevel*
Android: *Spirit Level Pro Free*
These apps use your smartphone's tilt detection to provide an electronic spirit level. However, you should only use them if you're happy to balance your phone on top of your camera!

Reflectors

A reflector is a surface—usually white—that is used to direct light into the shadow areas of your subject to reduce contrast. It's possible to buy reflectors in all sorts of shapes and sizes, though often a piece of card or paper is more than adequate, particularly when shooting macro subjects. Commercial reflectors are also available in metallic, either colored silver or gold. Metallic reflectors bounce more light back toward the subject and increase contrast compared to a pure white reflector. If you use a silver reflector outdoors this can have the effect of making the reflected light cooler, particularly when ambient light from the (blue) sky above is reflected. A gold reflector counteracts this and adds warmth to the light reflected back to your subject. Gold reflectors are often used in portraiture for this very reason; the warmer light adds a healthy glow to your subject.

> ***Notes***
>
> *Reflectors are most useful when you have one light source, such as the sun. Position the reflector on the opposite side of your subject to the light source and angle it so that the shadows lighten to the desired amount.*
>
> *Check that the reflector isn't intruding into the image before you press the shutter-release button on your camera!*

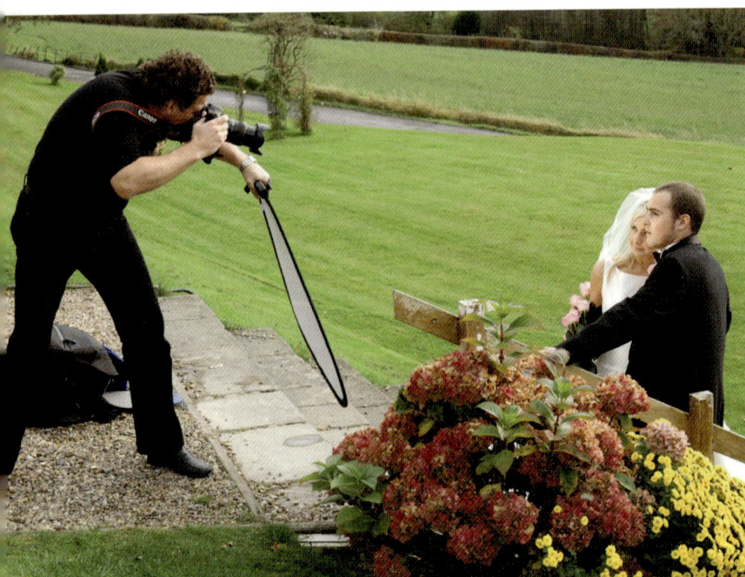

LASTOLITE
The name most associated with reflectors (and other lighting control systems) is Lastolite.
Image © Lastolite

Camera: Canon EOS 7D
Lens: 50mm lens
Exposure: 1/25 sec. at f/10
ISO: 100

SHADOWS

The low, raking light of morning creates long, often dense shadows. For this beach still life I shot without a reflector (top) and with a reflector just out of shot on the left (bottom). The reflector "bounced" sunlight into the shadow area, reducing contrast, as well as adding overall warmth to the image.

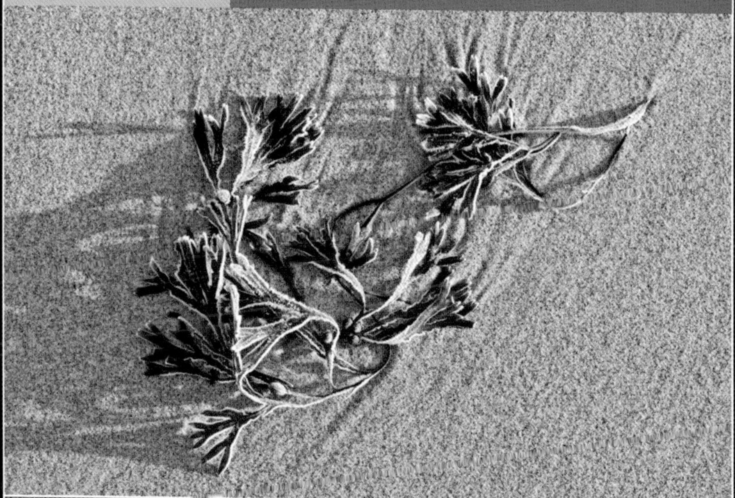

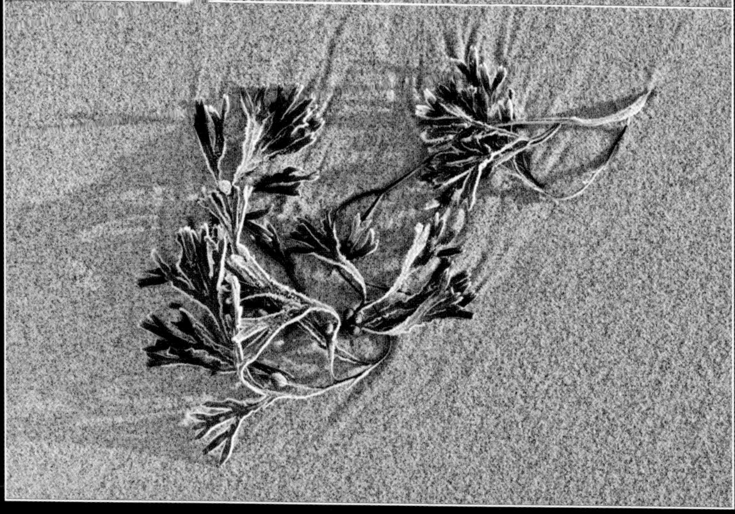

Flashlights

I have a variety of flashlights that all have a different purpose when I shoot in low light. The least powerful of my flashlights is an LED headlamp that frees up my hands to carry other equipment such as maps and to operate the camera once I'm ready to set up. LED flashlights are very power-efficient and last far longer on one set of batteries than conventional flashlights. However, they are not particularly bright and the light generated is very "cool" in color. If I want a flashlight to illuminate my photographic subject—known as "painting with light"—I use a large rechargeable flashlight with an incandescent bulb. Not only is the light more powerful, it also has a "warmth" that I find esthetically pleasing.

Notebook

Images from a digital camera have one big advantage over those shot on film: shooting information such as the date, exposure details, and lens focal length is embedded into the image file as metadata. This information can be viewed after shooting using image-editing software such as Adobe Photoshop, and reviewing the exposure details is a good way to learn and understand what you did well, and sometimes more importantly, what went wrong.

Not all shooting information is stored in metadata. Your camera certainly doesn't know when filters were added or what your location was (unless your camera is equipped with a GPS facility). For this reason it's still useful to keep a notebook of how you work for future reference—tying your notes to the relevant image file names.

Working smarter...
Apple iOS: *Notebook*
Android: *Color Note*
Both of these apps allow you to make extensive notes using your smartphone and then sync them with your computer.

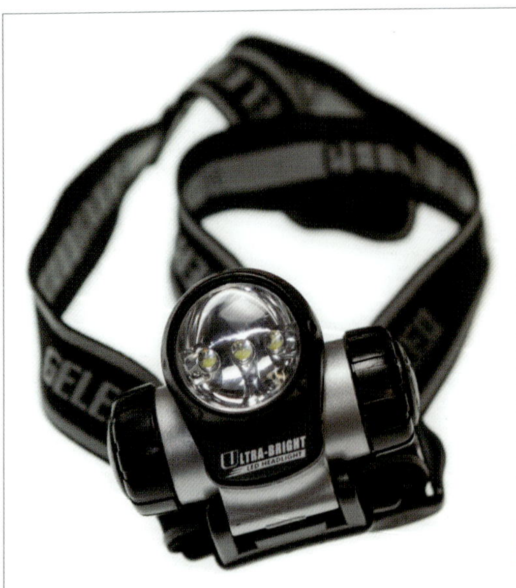

LED HEADLAMP
Useful when you need to keep your hands free and your way illuminated.

Smartphone

A smartphone is a hybrid of a cellphone and a pocket-sized computer. At the time of writing there is a number of smartphone standards competing for market share, with the two most popular being those based on Apple's iOS system and Google's Android standard. Also available are smartphones from BlackBerry and Nokia that use their own proprietary operating systems (the latter developed with Microsoft).

A good smartphone can run mini-programs known as apps (short for application), and there are hundreds of thousands of apps available, many of which are free or can be purchased for a very small fee.

From a safety point of view, it's useful to carry any kind of mobile phone when out and about—walking around in the dark has its hazards and it's better to be safe than sorry. Calling out the emergency services should always be a last resort though, rather than the easy option if you're just lost.

Notes

Devices such as Apple's iPod Touch and iPad also fall into the smartphone category, they just don't have the phone element.

When shooting star trails, exposures can be in excess of one hour, so having music to listen to, or games to play on your phone can help to pass the time!

Most smartphones have a built-in camera, but the small sensor size means they are far from ideal for low light photography.

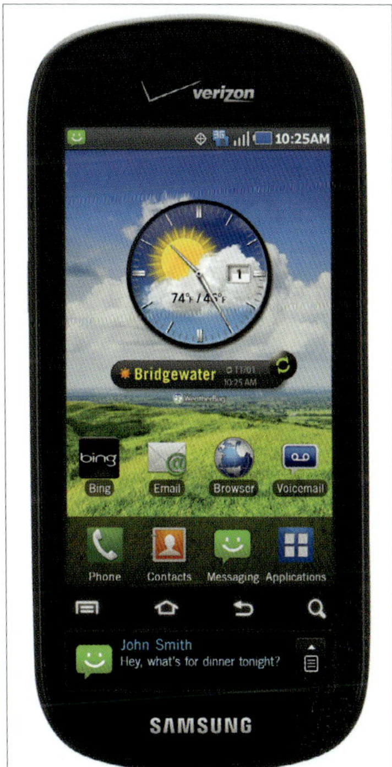

ANDROID
The Samsung i400, an Android-based smartphone.
Image © Samsung

Movement

Extreme ND filters are particularly useful in bright conditions when it would be otherwise impossible to achieve a slow shutter speed. I wanted to use a shutter speed of 4 seconds to blur the wind-blown leaves and simplify the background behind this statue. Because the statue was in bright sunshine this was only possible by using a 5-stop ND filter.

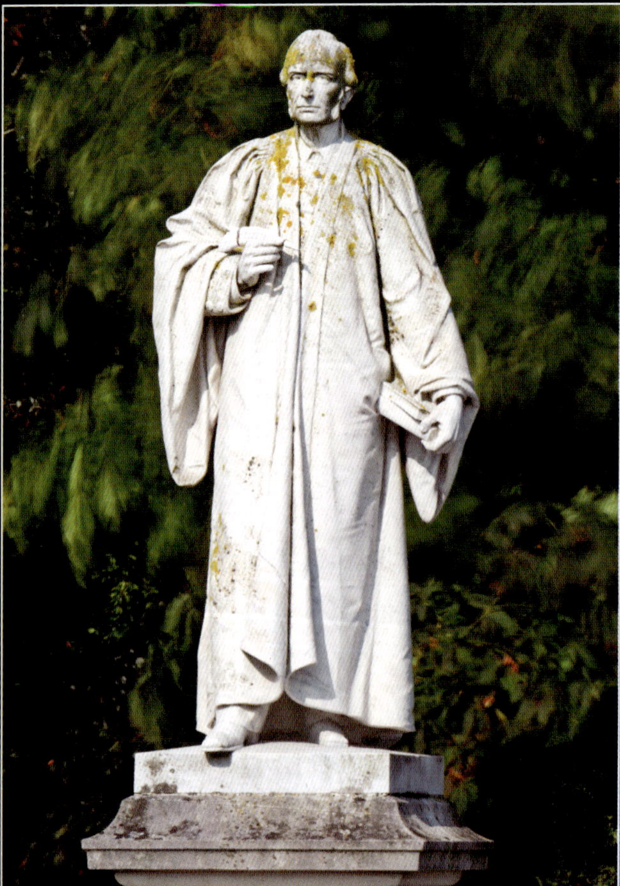

Camera: Canon EOS 7D
Lens: 70–200mm lens (at 180mm)
Exposure: 4 sec. at f/11
ISO: 100

Combination

Filters can be combined to achieve different things in the same image. For this shot I used a 2-stop graduated ND to balance the exposure of the brighter sky to the foreground. I also used a plain 3-stop ND filter to slow the shutter speed and make the water appear more ethereal.

Camera: Canon EOS 7D
Lens: 10–22mm lens (at 10mm)
Exposure: 3 sec. at f/14
ISO: 100

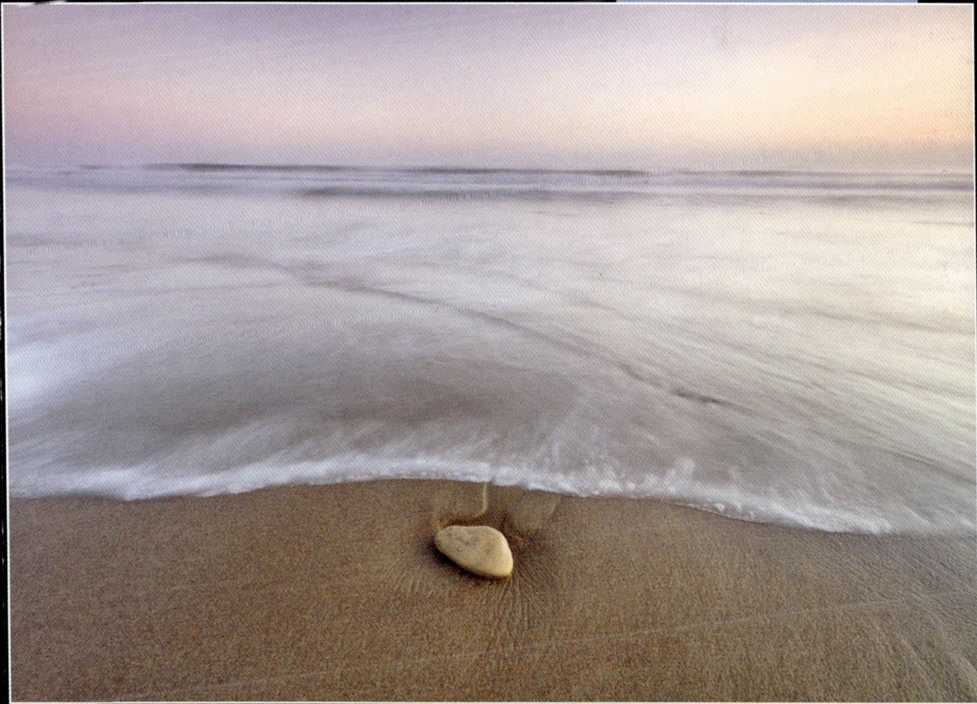

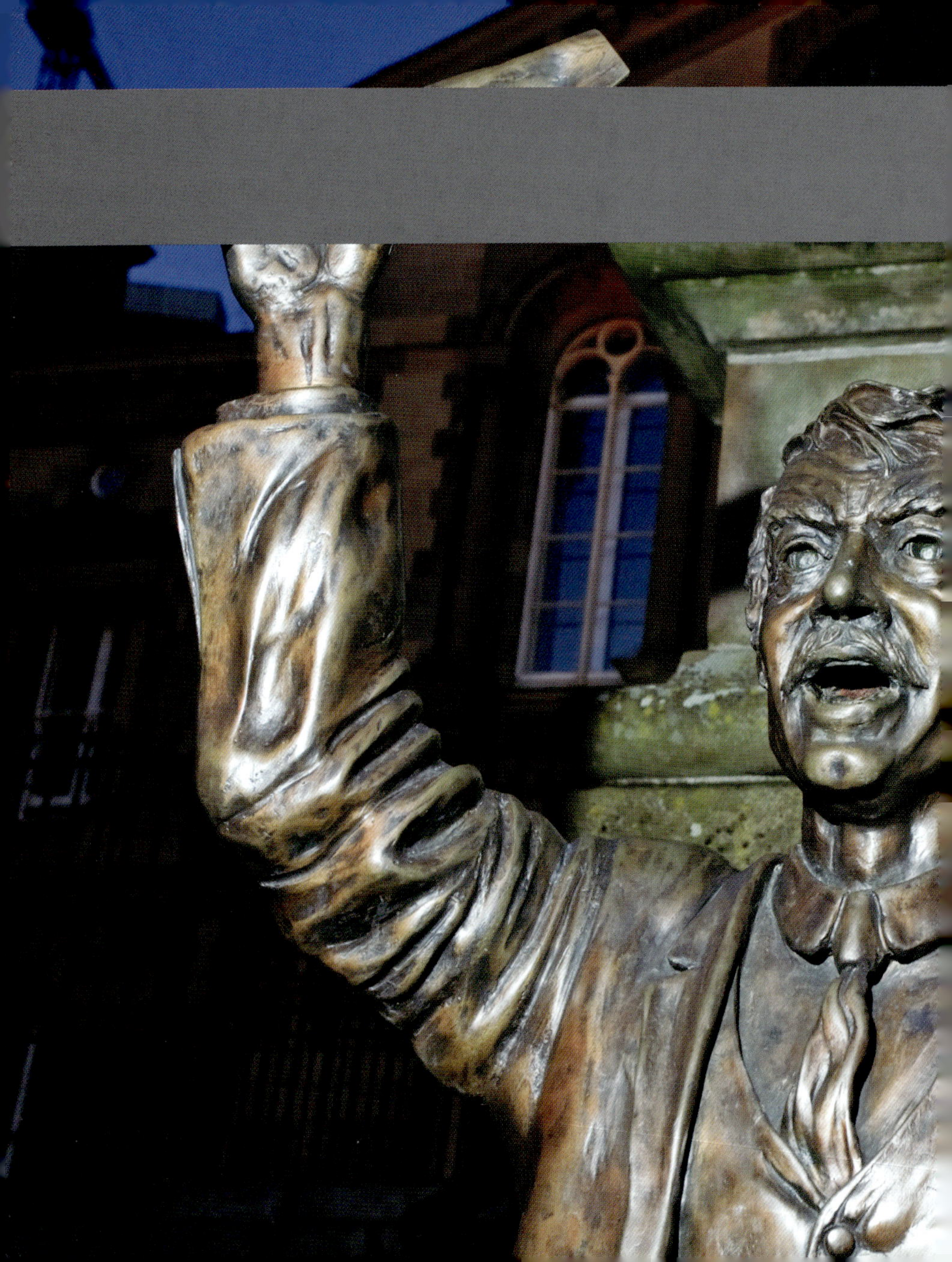

CHAPTER 4 FLASH

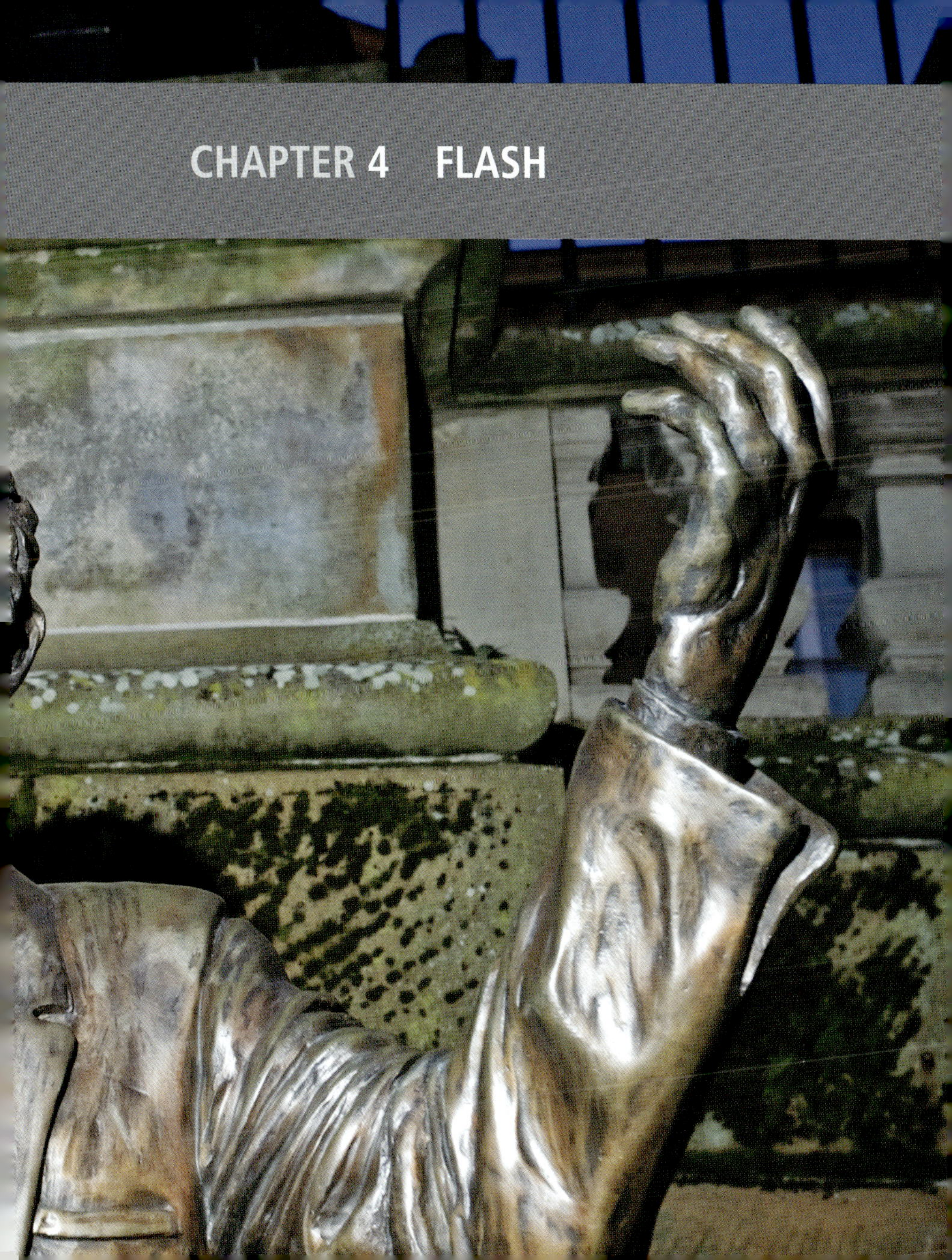

Flashes

There is a bewildering choice of flash units on the market today, with an equally confusing range of functions and modes.

What's in a name?

Manufacturers use a variety of different names for their flashes: Canon uses Speedlite to describe its products, Nikon uses Speedlight, and so on. To avoid confusion I'll use the generic "flash" or "flash unit" to cover all such devices.

Flash types

Before buying a flash it's worth thinking about how often you'll use it. It's all very well buying the biggest and best, but not if it's only used once a year. It's a better policy to buy a mid-range flash and then, if you find yourself using it frequently, consider buying a more powerful model. The smaller unit could then be used as a slave flash in multi-flash set-ups.

Built-in flash

A built-in flash is the most common type of flash that you will encounter. They are either permanently available on the front of the camera, or pop-up from the top-plate when they are needed.

Although it's useful to have a flash that is always available to provide a fill-in light, built-in flashes are usually relatively low powered.

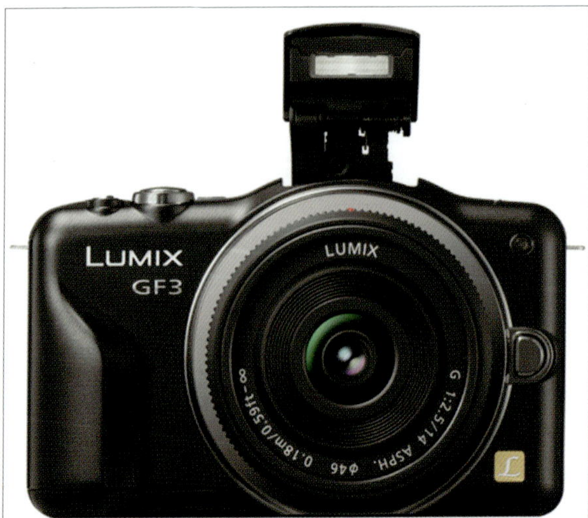

POP-UP FLASH
Panasonic DMC-GF3 with a built-in pop-up flash.
Image © Panasonic

Manual flash

This type of flash fits onto your camera via the hotshoe or PC connector. This flash does not communicate exposure information to your camera, so to obtain the correct exposure you need to change the power output of the flash and/or adjust the aperture or ISO setting on your camera.

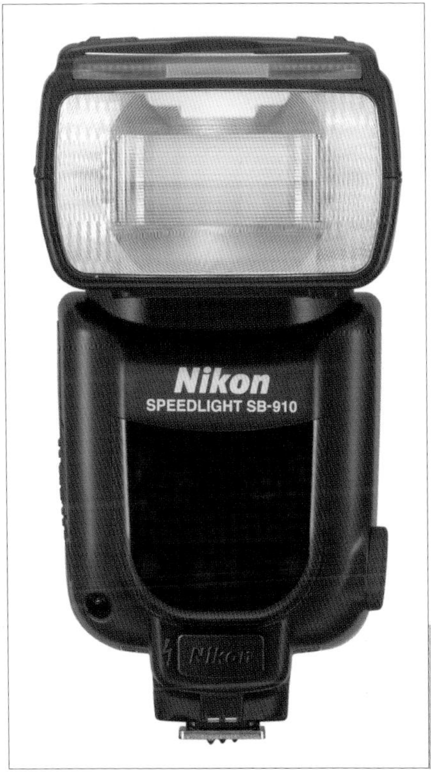

DEDICATED FLASH
Nikon Speedlight SB-910.
Image © Nikon

Automatic flash

An automatic flash is slightly more sophisticated, and offers a selection of "automatic aperture settings." By setting your lens and flash to the same aperture setting, the correct exposure is obtained within the possible flash-to-subject range for that particular aperture. A sensor on the flash will automatically cut the flash output to prevent overexposure.

Dedicated flash

These flash units communicate directly with a camera to produce the correct exposure. The various flash settings can usually be set on the menu system of the attached camera, as well as on the flash itself. A lot of dedicated flashes also work in conjunction with a camera's AF system, either to provide light to allow autofocusing, or to use the AF information to calculate the correct exposure. As this sort of technology is specific to a particular camera system, most camera manufacturers only produce dedicated flashes for their own cameras—Sigma is one exception to this rule.

Anatomy of a flash

The flash shown on this page is the Canon Speedlite 430EX II, which is a mid-range model that is compatible with Canon's EOS range of cameras. Its features are found on comparable flashes produced by other manufacturers.

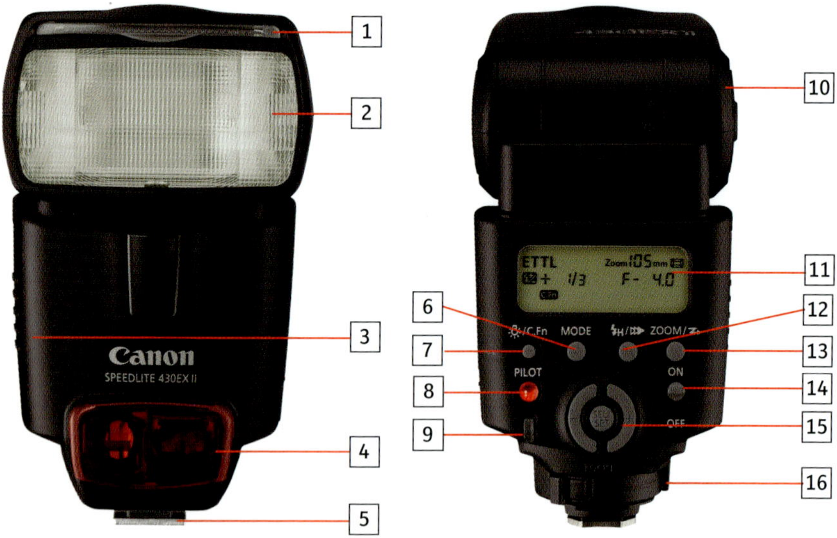

Image © Canon

1 *Wide-angle diffuser panel*

Increases the angle of coverage of the flash so that scenes are lit evenly when using a wide-angle lens.

2 *Flash head*

3 *Battery access panel*

4 *AF assist lamp*

If there is not enough ambient light for the camera's AF system to work normally, the AF assist lamp pulses light to compensate.

5 *Mounting foot*

6 *Flash mode button*

Selects the various metering modes the camera and flash combination uses to determine the correct exposure.

7 *LCD panel light/Custom function button*

8 *Flash charge light/Test fire button*

Lights when the flash is fully charged. The fresher the batteries, the more quickly the flash charges.

Canon EOS 7D, 10–22mm lens (at 17mm), 1/10 sec. at f/4, ISO 100

TTL FLASH

Using flash off-camera is simplified if both your camera and flash are compatible and support TTL exposure.

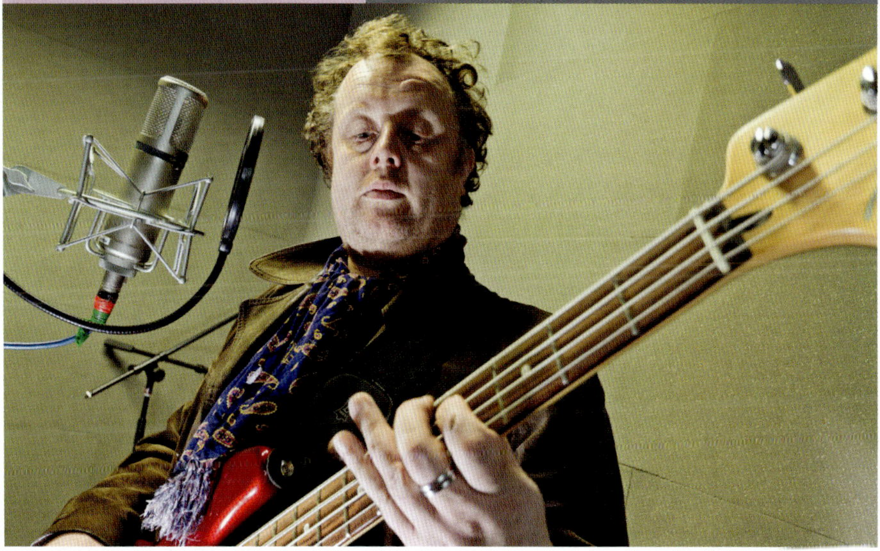

9 ***Flash exposure confirmation light***
Illuminates when the flash has fired and correctly exposed the subject.

10 ***Bounce angle index***
Shows the angle that the flash head is pointing when using bounce flash.

11 ***LCD information panel***

12 ***Hi-speed sync/Curtain sync button***
Sets Hi-speed and 1st or 2nd curtain synchronization.

13 ***Zoom setting***
Adjusts the coverage of the flash to suit the focal length of the lens used.

14 ***Power switch***

15 ***Option setting buttons***

16 ***Locking collar***

Using your flash

Working with flash can be daunting, but the following pages will explain some of the basic concepts that will help you get the best from your flash.

Guide numbers

All flash units have a maximum power output, which is represented by a numerical value known as the guide number (often shortened to GN). The GN allows you to calculate the flash's effective range in either feet or meters: the higher the GN, the greater the power of the flash. If you increase the ISO you effectively change the GN, so for this reason ISO 100 is the standard value that most (but not all) manufacturers use when quoting the GN of a flash.

If you know the GN of a flash you can also use it to either manually calculate the aperture value needed to correctly expose a subject at a given distance, or calculate the effective range of the flash at a chosen aperture. The formula to calculate this is:

GN/distance=aperture

GN/aperture=distance

As an example, the Canon 430EX II on the previous page has a GN of 141 feet (43 meters) at ISO 100, so if you set the aperture on the lens to f/5.6, the effective range of the flash would be 25.2 feet (7.68 meters). Doubling the ISO increases the effective flash distance by 1.4, so at ISO 200 (and with the aperture still to f/5.6), the effective flash distance would increase to 35.63ft (10.86m).

Working smarter...

Apple iOS: *Photocalc*

Android: *Photo Tools*

These apps take the sweat out of calculating the values needed for the correct flash exposure. However, if you memorize the equations for determining distance and aperture using the guide number, then an equally accurate result can be achieved using the standard calculator app on your smartphone!

Sync speed

The fastest shutter speed available when shooting flash is known as the sync speed. This varies between camera models, but is typically in the range of 1/125 sec. to 1/250 sec. Most modern camera systems will not let you set a shutter speed faster than the sync speed when using flash (although there is an exception to this—see p98).

It is important to note that the shutter speed you use does not affect the flash exposure. If you were to shoot with your flash at full power—with no automatic adjustments—you could control the range of the flash by varying the lens aperture. The smaller the aperture, the less range the flash will have, but varying the shutter speed will only affect the exposure for those areas in an image that are lit by ambient light, and not by the flash.

If you are using your flash as a fill-in light, a shutter speed close to the sync speed will be appropriate, but when ambient light levels are low, longer shutter speeds can be used in a technique known as slow sync flash.

Modern flash systems use a metering system that is known as TTL, or through-the-lens metering. This works by firing a series of smaller pre-flashes before the camera shutter opens, with the power of the main flash based on the metering of these pre-flashes. This happens so quickly that it's almost impossible to distinguish that more than one flash has occurred.

This system is very reliable for general use, although most flashes still have a manual mode for those who want full control.

SYNC SPEED
This image was shot at the maximum sync speed of my camera and its lowest ISO setting. This was done to underexpose the background and therefore emphasize the subject.

Canon EOS 1Ds MkII, 70–200mm lens (at 70mm), 1/250 sec. at f/10, ISO 50

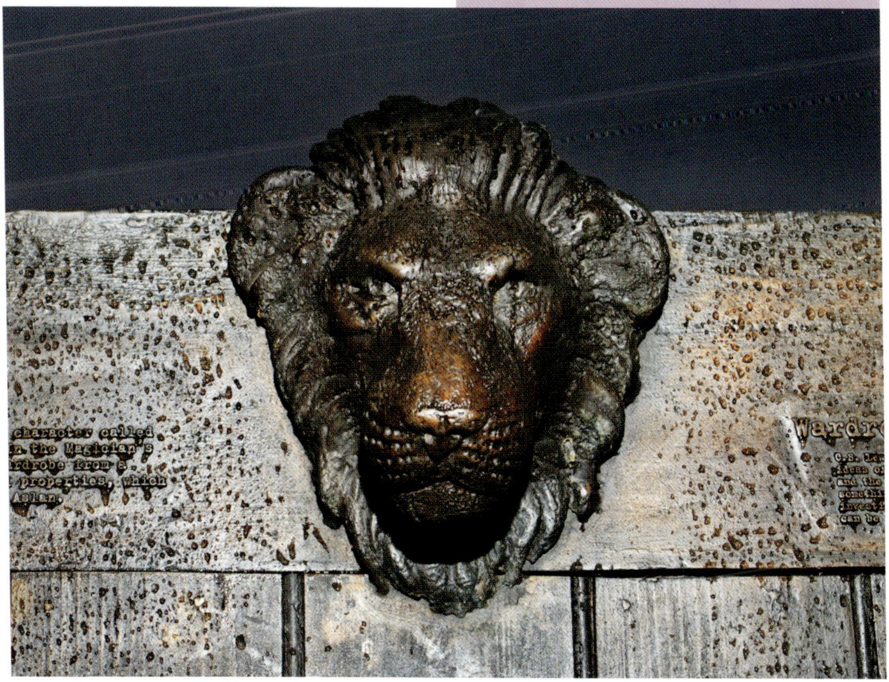

Hi-speed sync flash

The normal sync speed of a flash can occasionally be limiting, and there are times when you may need (or want) to use a shutter speed that exceeds the flash sync speed. This is particularly true on bright days, when flash is useful as a fill-in light. Fortunately, a lot of digital SLR systems will allow you to use hi-speed sync flash, providing you have a suitable, dedicated flash unit.

When a fast shutter speed is used (one that is higher than the sync speed), the distance between the 1st and the 2nd shutter curtain following on behind is smaller than the height of the sensor. Therefore the flash would illuminate only the section of the sensor that is revealed by the shutter when it fires—the area hidden behind the shutter would be literally left in the dark.

Hi-speed sync flash gets around this problem by pulsing the flash to simulate a continuous light source. The one drawback is that the power of each flash is reduced to ensure that the flash is able to recycle quickly between flashes. This means that the effective distance of the flash is reduced when hi-speed sync mode is used, and the higher the shutter speed, the lower the distance becomes. However, hi-speed sync is a useful tool when it's needed—even low light photographers venture out into bright daylight occasionally!

HI-SPEED FLASH
As I was using hi-speed flash for this image, the flash had to be close to the subject. In fact, it was just out of shot to the left of the camera.

Canon EOS 7D, 24–70mm lens (at 24mm), 1/320 sec. at f/8, ISO 100

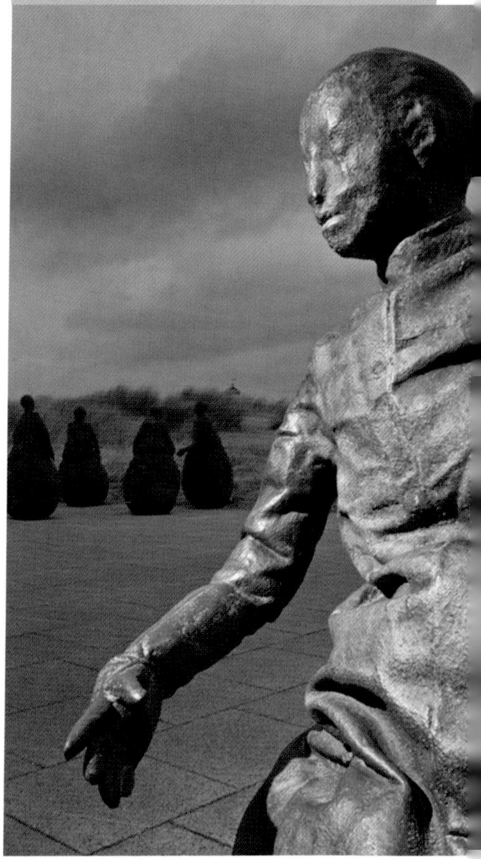

Red-eye correction

Red-eye can be gruesome, transforming friends and family members into strange-looking supernatural creatures. It is caused by the use of direct flash, when the light from the flash bounces off the back of the subject's eye, picking up the color of the blood vessels as it does so. The problem is made worse by the fact that flash is most often used in low light conditions, when your subject's pupils will naturally be at their widest.

Red-eye correction pulses a series of pre-flashes that cause pupils to contract, reducing the risk of the flash being reflected back out from the eye. The use of techniques such as bounce flash will also cure red-eye.

Fill-in flash

Flash is a useful technique to control contrast if your subject is backlit. However, it's easy to make your subject look like a card cutout if the flash output is too strong. To control this, you can either adjust the aperture used—making it smaller and reducing the effective distance of the flash—or alter the power of the flash. Most flashes should allow you to do this using either a camera menu or a control on the flash unit itself. The amount of adjustment you need to make will vary depending on the ambient light, but typically ½- to 1½-stops is a good starting point. TTL-controlled flashes generally cope with fill-in flash very effectively, and often require very little adjustment.

Canon 7D, 24–70mm lens (at 50mm), 1/250 sec. at f/4, ISO 100

FILL-IN FLASH
This mannequin was on a window ledge and was backlit by strong sun. I used off-camera TTL flash to lighten the shadow side of its body and reduce contrast.

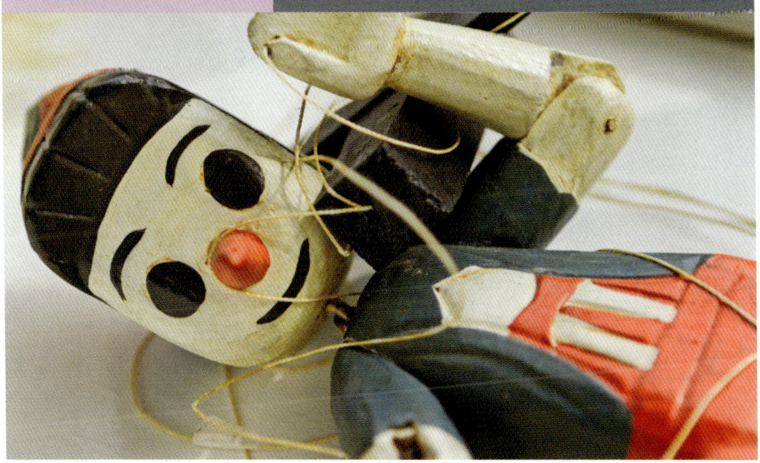

Bounce flash

One of the biggest problems with the light from a built-in or on-camera flash is that it delivers hard, frontal lighting that isn't particularly sympathetic to your subject. If your flash has an adjustable head, a technique known as "bounce flash" can be used to soften the light. By angling the flash head up or to the side, the light can be reflected from another surface back toward your subject. This has the effect of spreading the light, making it far softer. Flash softboxes and diffusers work in a similar way.

The easiest surface to bounce the light off from a flash is a ceiling, but this will obviously only work if you're shooting inside! If you are outside and your camera is mounted on a tripod, or you have an assistant, then a large sheet of card held above the flash is equally effective. What is important is that the surface that the flash is bounced off must be neutral in color, as the light will pick up any color and tint your subject accordingly.

The more powerful your flash, the more effective this technique is. This is because the surface you bounce the light from will absorb some of the flash and you are also increasing the distance the light has to travel before it reaches your subject: the higher the ceiling, the more light is needed to be effective.

Flash diffusers

A diffuser works in a similar way to bounce flash by spreading the light from a flash to soften it. This helps to reduce hard shadows and creates a far more pleasing, natural effect, especially for

BOUNCE FLASH
With the flash pointing forward, the result is not great (below left), but by pointing the flash upward and bouncing the light off a sheet of white card it is far more acceptable (below right).

Canon EOS 7D, 50mm lens, 5 sec. at f/9, ISO 100

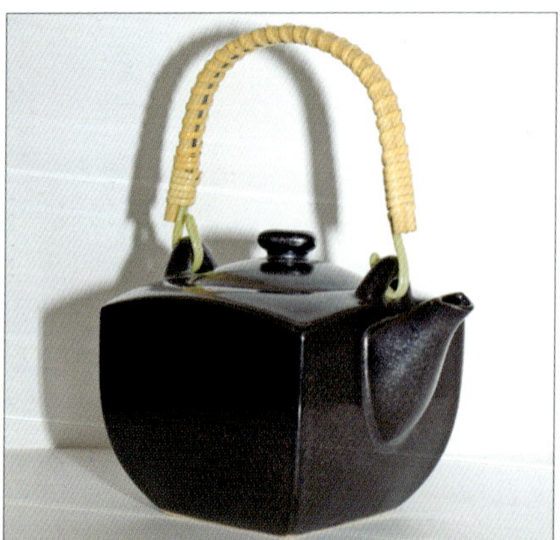

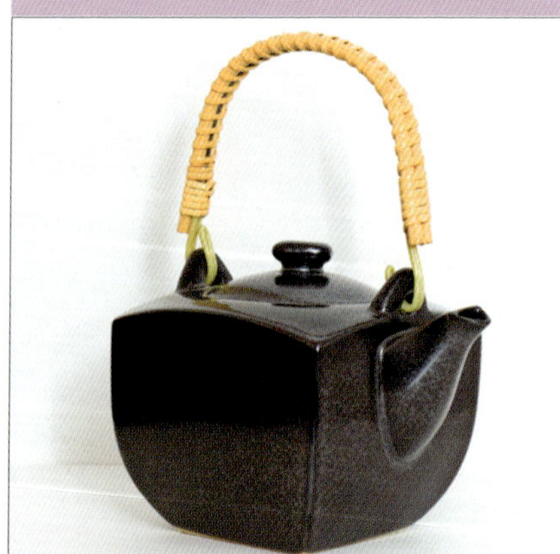

portraits. Diffusers are available in a variety of different sizes, from very simple and small push-on devices to more elaborate and larger types that are taped to the flash head. The greater the frontal area of the diffuser, the softer the light will be. However, as with bouncing the light from your flash, a diffuser will absorb some of the light, so your flash will need to be proportionately more powerful in order to illuminate your subject.

Third-part manufacturers of flash diffusers include Sto-Fen and Lumiquest. A less effective (but undoubtedly cheaper), method of diffusing a flash is to tape thin, neutrally colored tissue paper over the flash head.

Off-camera flash

A flash doesn't necessarily need to be attached directly to the hotshoe of your camera. Moving your flash away from the camera is a good way of controlling how your subject is lit. For example, moving a flash to the left or right of the camera will change the flash from a frontal light source to a side light for greater interest.

The simplest way of getting your flash off-camera is to use an extension cord. These are available in different lengths and connect either to the hotshoe of your camera or to a PC connection socket.

An alternative option is wireless flash. There are two methods of shooting wirelessly, the first of which uses the camera's built-in flash to trigger a compatible off-camera flash unit. The drawback with this system is that there has to be line of sight between the two flashes for this to work correctly—if not, the off-camera flash simply will not fire.

The second method uses a radio transmitter to connect the camera to the flash. This method allows a greater working distance between camera and flash, but it does require the purchase of a much more expensive radio transmitter: third-party companies that make these include PocketWizard and Cactus.

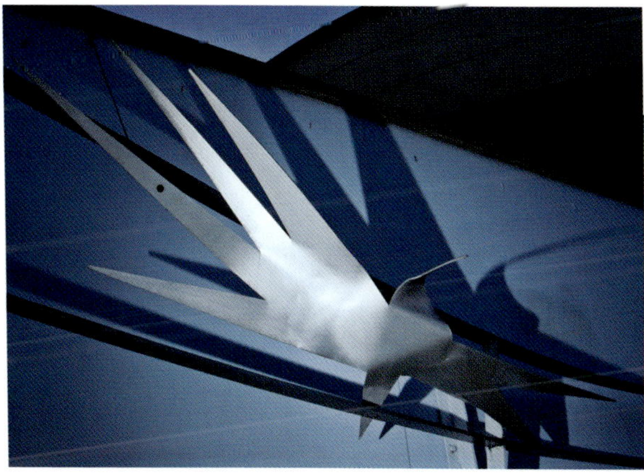

OFF-CAMERA
For this shot I used a 3-foot (1m) long extension cord to move my flash to the left of the camera. This made the shadows behind the subject far more interesting.

Canon EOS 1Ds MkII, 17–40mm lens (at 22mm), 1/60 sec. at f/11, ISO 100

Flash light

The light from an electronic flash has a nominal color temperature of 5500K, which, like midday sunlight, is very neutral in color. This makes flash perfect as a fill-in light source during the day, but the light can appear overly cool when you are shooting at dusk. Skin tones can also benefit from being photographed under a slightly warm light. You could alter the white balance setting of course, but this can prove tricky when shooting in mixed lighting such as street lighting.

Fortunately the light from a flash can be modified very easily and cheaply using colored gels that tape over the flash head. It's possible to make your own using discarded candy wrappers, or to use professional gels made by accessory manufacturers such as Rosco or Lee Filters. The DIY approach is arguably more fun (you get to eat the candy first), but the manufactured route is more consistent.

Gels are readily available that will convert the color temperature of your flash so that it matches the output from other light sources such as tungsten lighting (requiring an 85 gel to change the color temperature of the flash from 5500K to 3200K). For a more theatrical look it can also be fun to use brightly colored gels such as red or green.

Notes

All gels will absorb some light from the flash, and the more intense the gel's color, the greater the light loss.

Bouncing flash from a brightly colored surface will have a similar effect on the color of flash to using a gel.

GELS
Colored gels can be taped to the flash simply and quickly to change the color of the light.

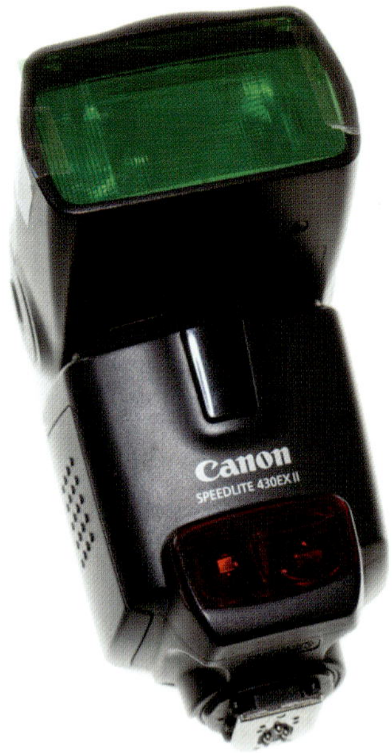

FLYING *(Opposite)*
This mannequin was photographed in a darkened room. A red-filtered flash was fired from one side, and a green-filtered flash from the other.

Canon EOS 7D, 17–40mm lens (at 30mm), 30 sec. at f/11, ISO 100

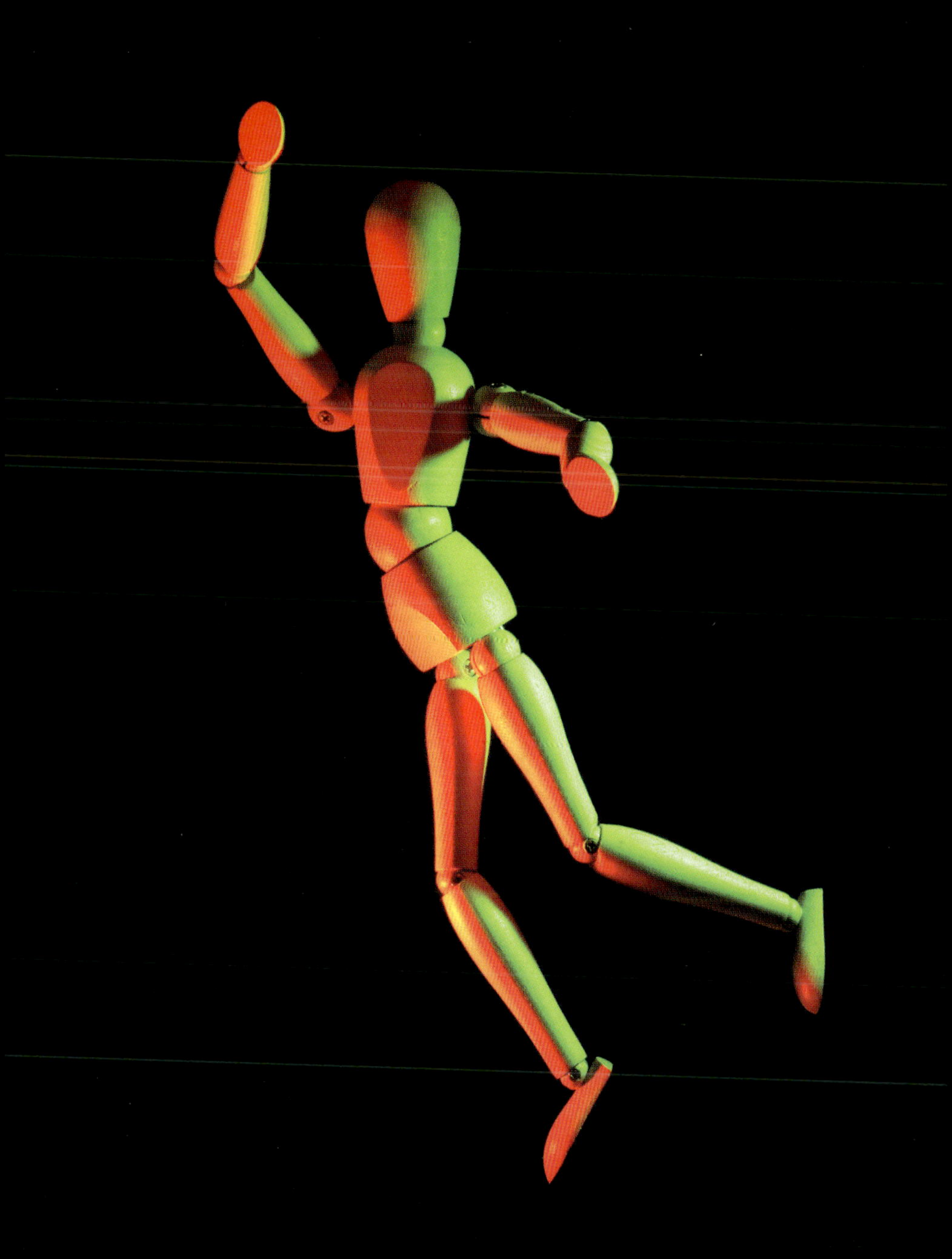

Illumination

Flash was used as a fill-in light for this image, softening some of the shadows cast across the sculpture by the streetlighting.

Camera: Canon EOS 1Ds MkII
Lens: 17–40mm lens (at 21mm)
Exposure: 1/100 sec. at f/10
ISO: 200

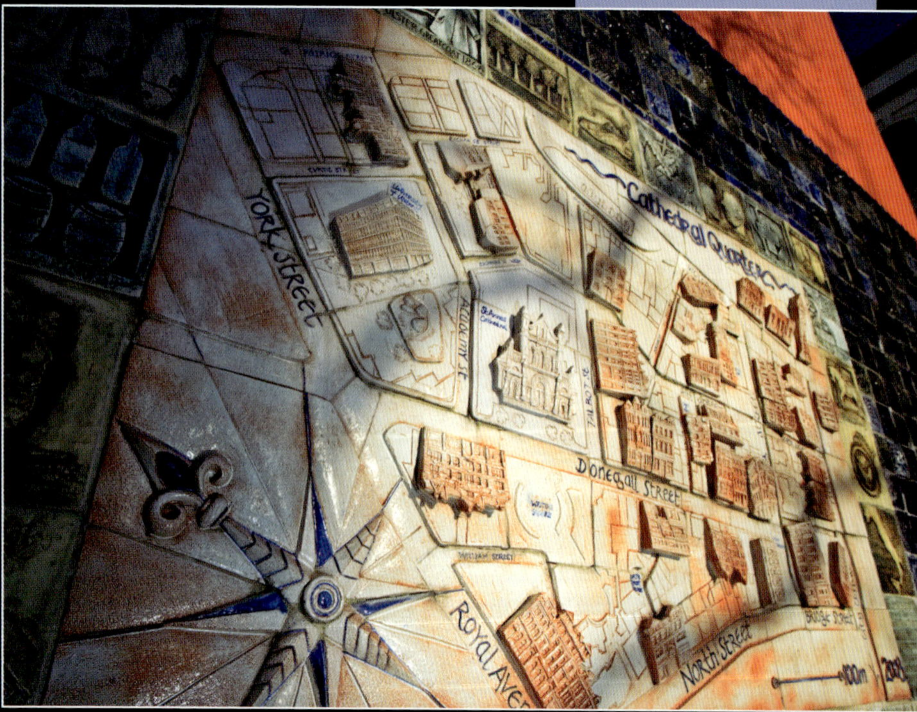

This image was shot using slow sync flash. During the exposure the zoom ring on the lens was turned to create a "zoom burst" effect. The sharpness in the image is entirely due to the flash freezing any movement at the point of firing.

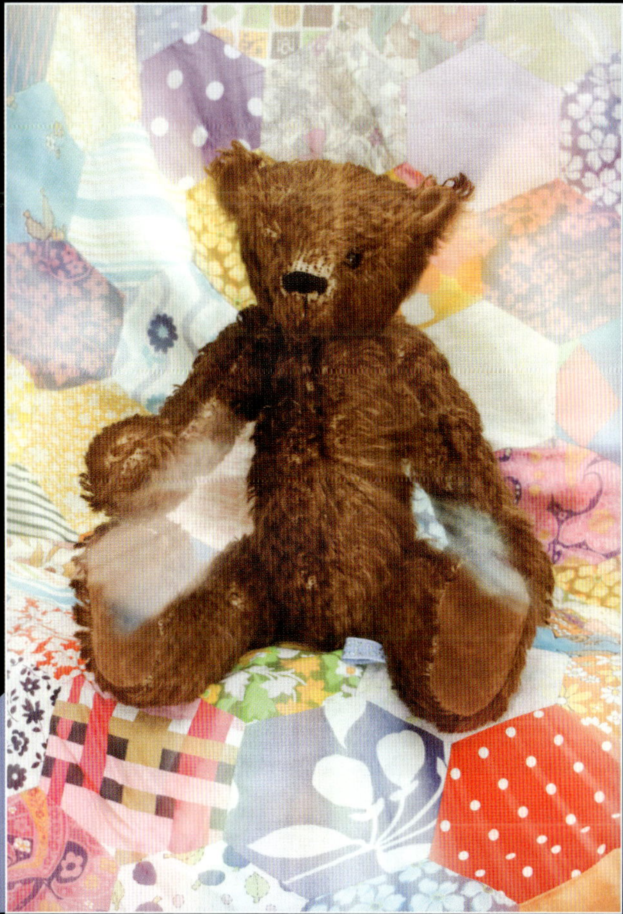

Camera: Canon EOS 7D
Lens: 70–200mm lens (focal length adjusted during exposure)
Exposure: 1 sec. at f/20
ISO: 100

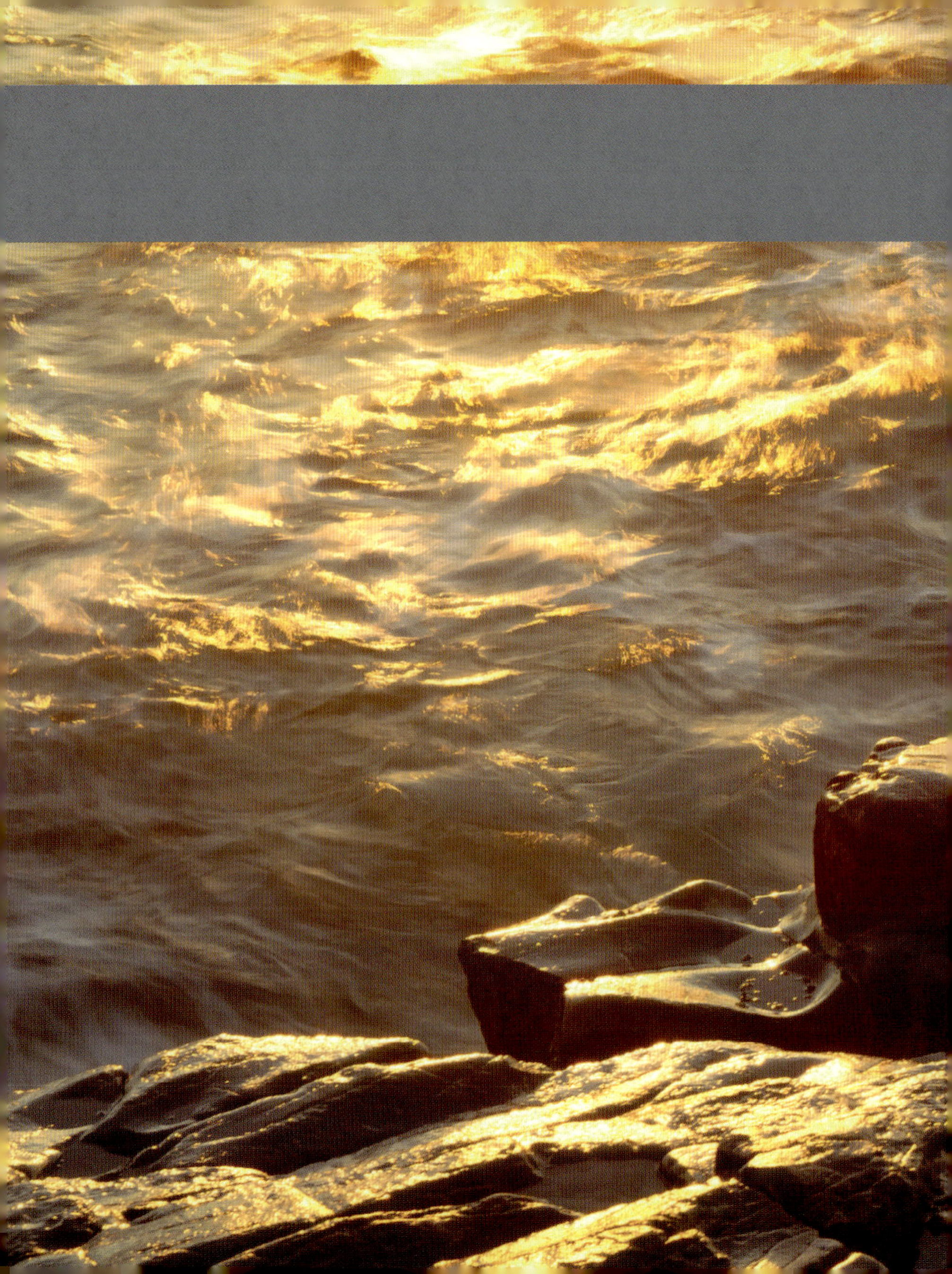

CHAPTER 5 LANDSCAPES

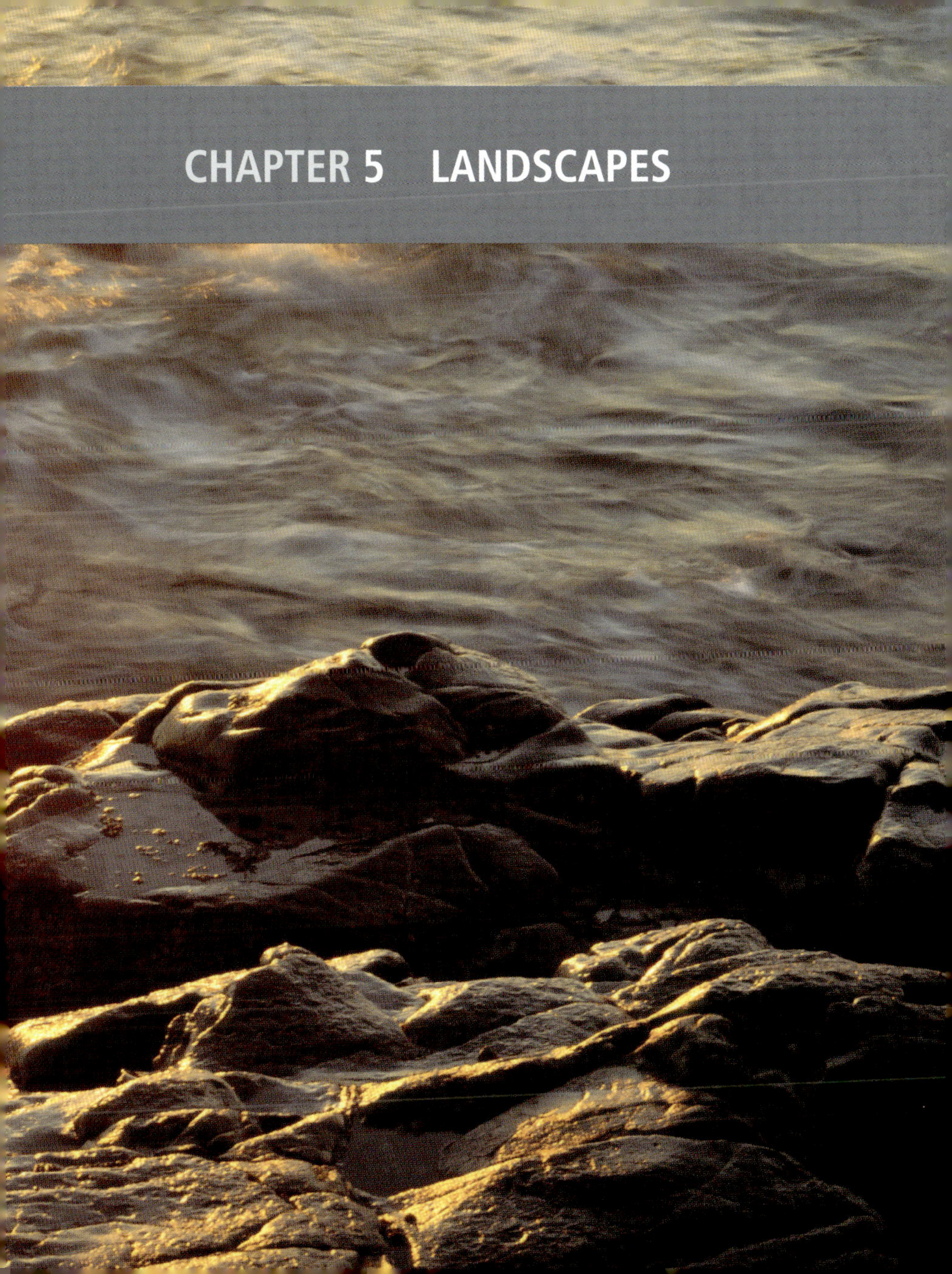

Landscapes

Landscape photography isn't just about blue skies and good weather: low light landscape photography often involves being out in all weathers and at either end of the day.

Caring for yourself

There's no photograph that's worth sustaining injury for. Low light photography introduces a few more potential hazards than photographing during the hours of daylight, but these can be minimized with careful planning.

RAIN
Bad weather can often hit unexpectedly when out in the hills. This is why preparing for this eventuality is so important when it comes to remaining safe.

Canon 1Ds MkII, 100mm lens, 1/100 sec. at f/11, ISO 100

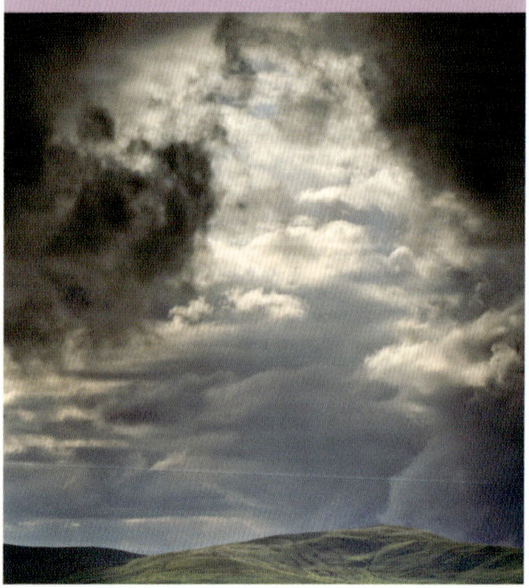

Once you've decided on your location, let someone else know where you're going. If possible, also let that person know an approximate time of return. In mid-summer it's possible to be out until very late in the evening, far later than most non-photographers would expect.

Take a headlamp: low light photography invariably means being out when it's dark, and wearing a headlamp will free up your hands to hold a map or to keep your balance when walking over rocks. Modern LED headlamps are extremely power-efficient, but it doesn't hurt to keep spare batteries in your equipment bag.

A cell phone is useful for all sorts of reasons, but make sure it is fully charged—particularly if you plan to use photography-related apps. Only use your phone to call the emergency services in an emergency; being lost doesn't count. If your phone has a built-in GPS (Global Positioning System), make sure you know how to use it so that you can pinpoint your location on a map, but don't rely solely on your GPS to navigate—always carry an up-to-date map and compass as a backup.

WATERFALL *(Opposite)*
Although this composition looks precarious, I didn't take any risks when setting up the shot.

Canon EOS 5D, 24mm lens, 1/10 sec. at f/13, ISO 100

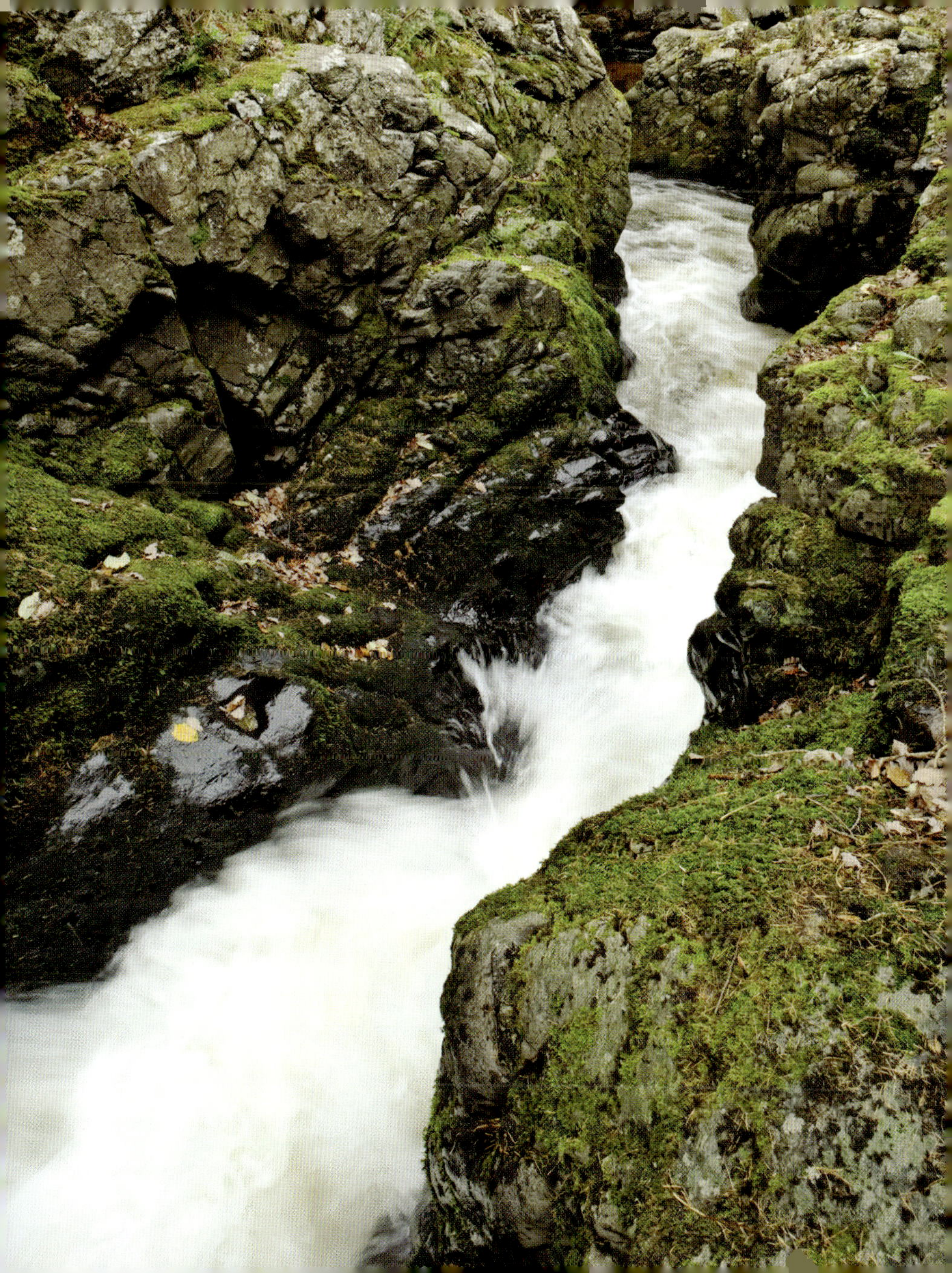

In the wild

Out in the countryside you will be away from artificial lighting (unless you take your own). This means learning to work with the different lighting conditions that nature can throw at you.

Preparation

Landscape photography often succeeds (or fails) based on the amount of preparation that you do beforehand. This involves looking at maps to work out a route to a particular location, as well as determining whether the sun will be in a favorable position for your chosen subject.

The biggest problem is often timing: it's comparatively easy to be at a particular spot for sunset, as you have all day to get there, but sunrise is a different matter. The simplest approach is to wild camp (if permissible) at the location so that you're on the spot immediately. However, this isn't always practical. If you intend to drive to a location on the morning itself, it pays to have everything ready the night before so that it's just a case of waking up and setting off. Allow yourself plenty of time, and aim to be at the location at least 45 minutes before sunrise so you can get set up without panicking. It helps if you scout out a location beforehand and have a composition already planned. You'll also need to factor in the time it takes to walk from your car to your chosen spot—there's nothing worse than realizing you've misjudged the distance from your car to your shooting position and that you'll not make it in time.

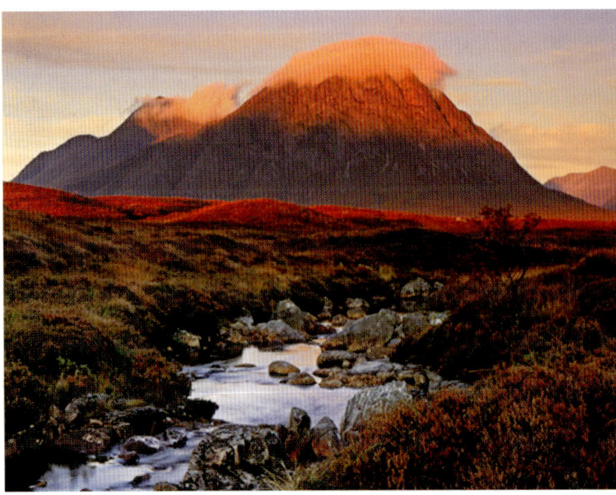

LEISURELY
Although this looks like a desperately wild place, it was only a five minute walk from the car—and only a 10 minute drive to the lodging house. So it was comparatively easy to be on location at the right time.

Pentax 67, 105mm lens, exposure details unrecorded, ISO 50 (Fuji Velvia)

Camera: Pentax 67
Lens: 150mm lens
Exposure: Unrecorded
ISO: 50 (Fuji Velvia)

This image required me to spend a night in the refuge hut just visible at the end of the path. Sometimes this is the only way to be at a location in time for sunrise.

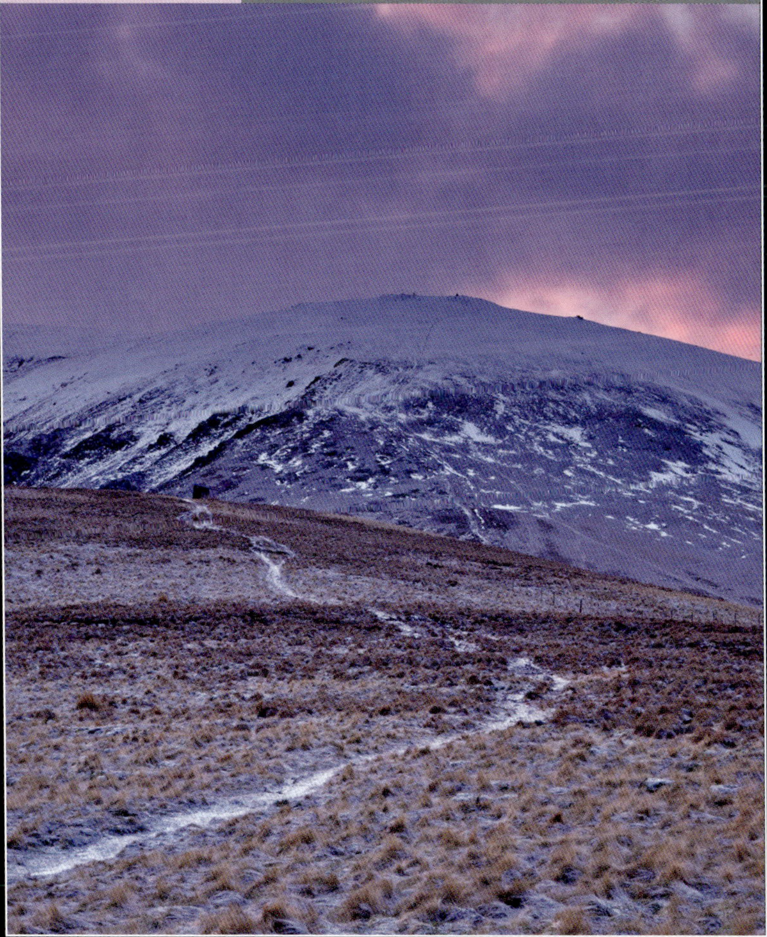

Woodland

In sunny weather, woodland can be a confusing mess of bright highlights and deep shadow. In using it as a subject, it's often better to wait until the sun is low in the sky or when it's overcast or even raining. Foliage on trees often benefits from the use of a polarizing filter, which helps to reduce any glare and saturates the colors of the leaves.

LEAVES
When the sun is shining I prefer to look for details, such as these backlit leaves.

Canon EOS 1Ds MkII, 200mm lens, 1/3 sec. at f/9, ISO 100

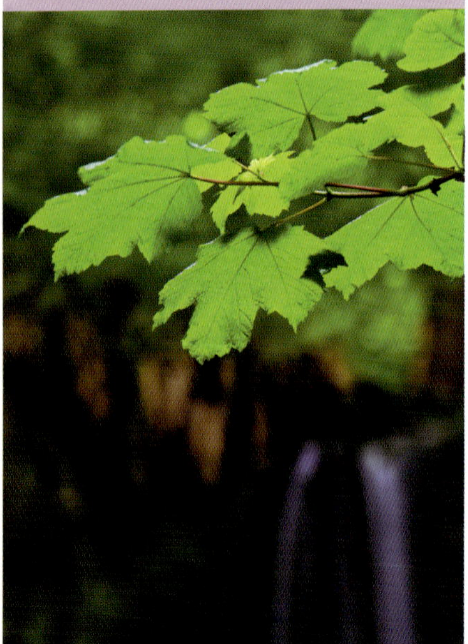

The most colorful season is fall, when the leaves of deciduous trees begin to turn yellow and red. There are several factors that affect the color of fall leaves, but the conditions earlier in the year are important. A good indication of the strength of fall color is when a warm and wet spring is followed by good summer weather. When fall arrives, the most colorful displays are likeliest to occur when there is a run of warm days with sunshine, followed by cooler nights.

Fall also heralds the arrival of fungi, which often grows in damp, dark conditions. Again, shooting on an overcast day will help to control contrast, but be aware that fungi create their own shade as well, so there's often a big difference in contrast between the top of the cap and the underside. Using a reflector will help to push light underneath. You may also find that if your tripod has a removable center column, you can take it out and reinsert it upside down to get your camera closer to the ground (albeit upside down). Live View is useful when composing in this situation.

> ***Tip***
> *On overcast days use the Cloudy or Shade white balance preset to warm up woodland color.*

Camera: Canon EOS 7D
Lens: 70–200mm lens (at 70mm)
Exposure: 1 sec. at f/11
ISO: 100

To get down to the level of these toadstools I mounted my camera upside down on the tripod.

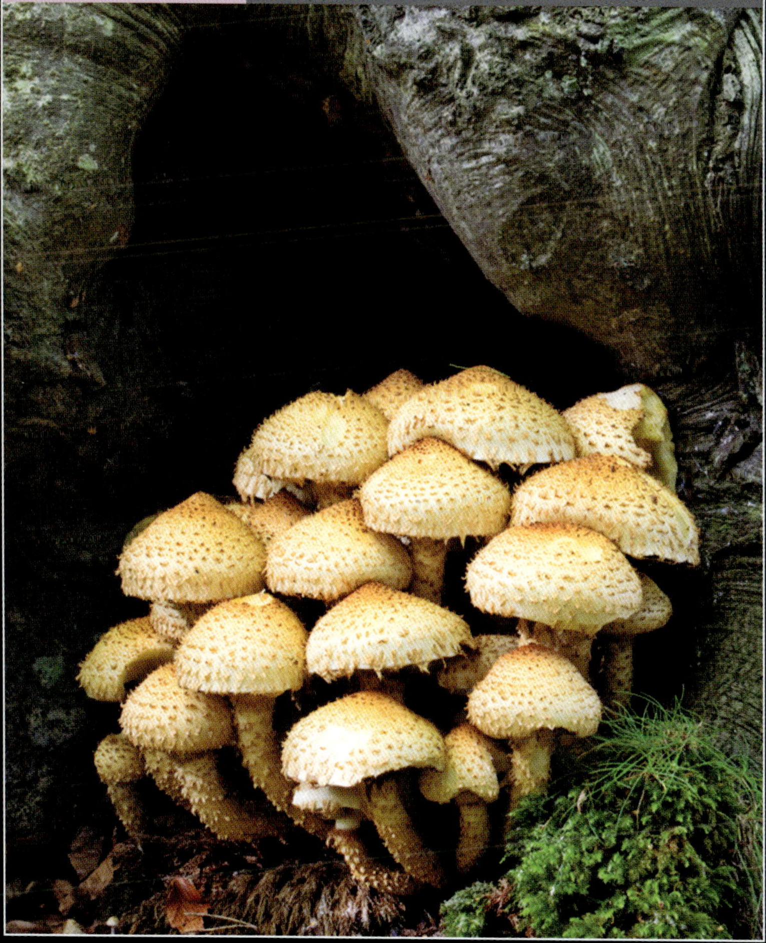

Water

The correct shutter speed to use when shooting watery subjects such as rivers or the sea is a contentious subject for photographers, but there is no right or wrong answer. Some prefer to see the individual drops of water, which involves a fast shutter speed, while others prefer water that looks as smooth as glass. In low light, unless you're prepared to use a large aperture or high ISO, you'll often have little choice but to use a slow shutter speed, and a shutter speed of even 1/2 sec. will be enough to add some blur to water. The key is to experiment and see which look you prefer. For the ultimate blurring effect, use an extreme ND filter to extend shutter speeds to whole minutes. This approach works best with tidal water, especially when you include something solid in the image as a contrast to the moving water.

Water is also reflective and will pick up the prevailing color of ambient light. This is most notable at either end of the day. Mornings are a good time to shoot lakes, as the air tends to be more still first thing in the morning, so lakes can often act like perfect mirrors. A still lake surface is also good for creating symmetrical compositions, but consider breaking the symmetry, and adding a note of tension, by looking for something such as a rock or branch poking out of the water's surface.

Tip

It's easier to see how seawater flows after it has washed up onto the beach. Fire the shutter just before it begins to flow back.

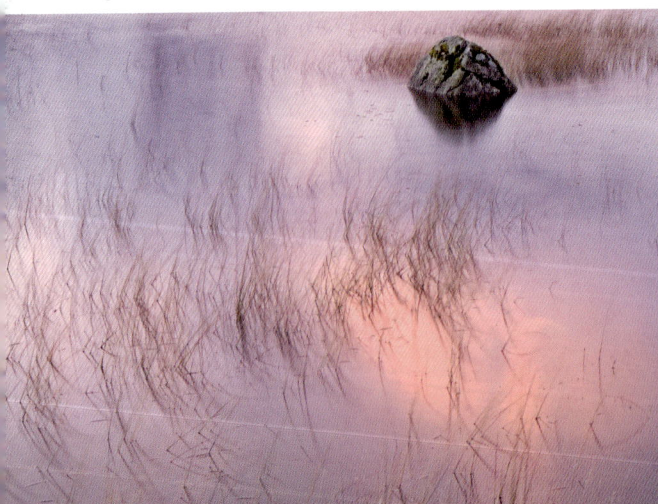

REFLECTIONS
There was no direct light on this lake, just the colors of the sky above.

Canon EOS 5D, 50mm lens, 5 sec. at f/16, ISO 100

Camera: Canon EOS 7D
Lens: 70–200mm lens (at 110mm)
Exposure: Various
ISO: 100

RIVER RUNNING
This sequence shows how the shutter speed can affect the look of moderately fast running water. Which do you prefer? Top left: 1/200 sec. Top right: 1/60 sec. Bottom left: 1/6 sec. Bottom right: 6 sec.

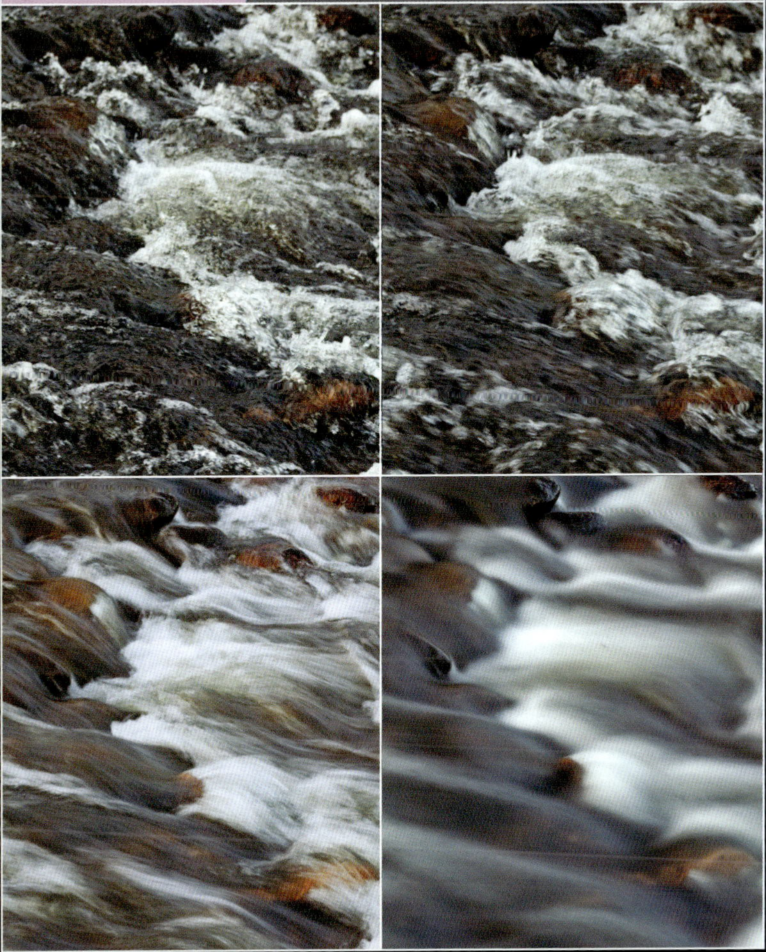

Seasons

Each season has its charm, but my personal favorite is fall. The golds, yellows, and reds of foliage are the main reason for the appeal of this season, and these colors are particularly striking in the soft light of an overcast day, such as this one in the Scottish Highlands.

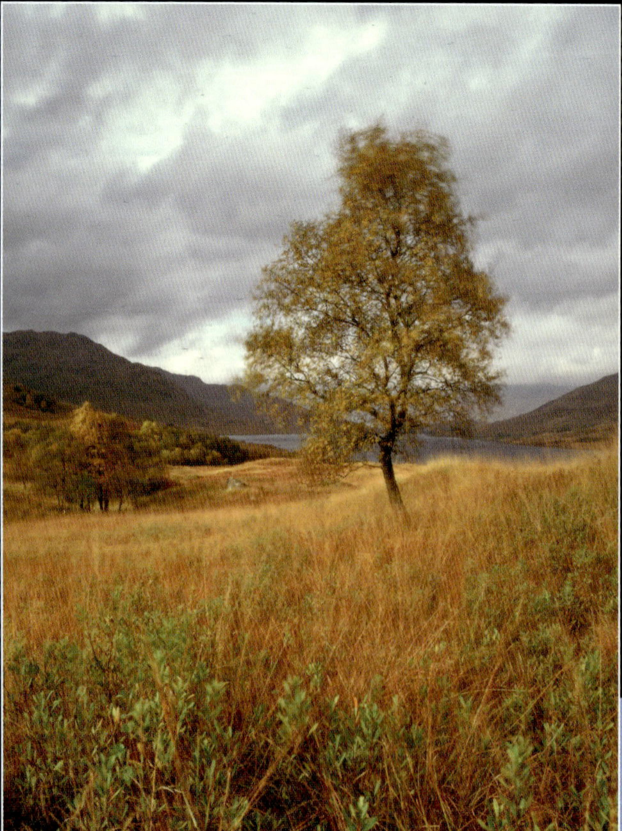

Camera: Pentax 67II
Lens: 105mm lens
Exposure: 1/2 sec. at f/16
ISO: 50 (Fuji Velvia)

The end of the day

Sunset is almost the easy option for a landscape photographer: there is no waking up early to face potential disappointment, and a good sunset is often the climax to a good day's photography.

Camera: Canon EOS 7D
Lens: 10–22mm lens (at 22mm)
Exposure: 1/100 sec. at f/10
ISO: 100

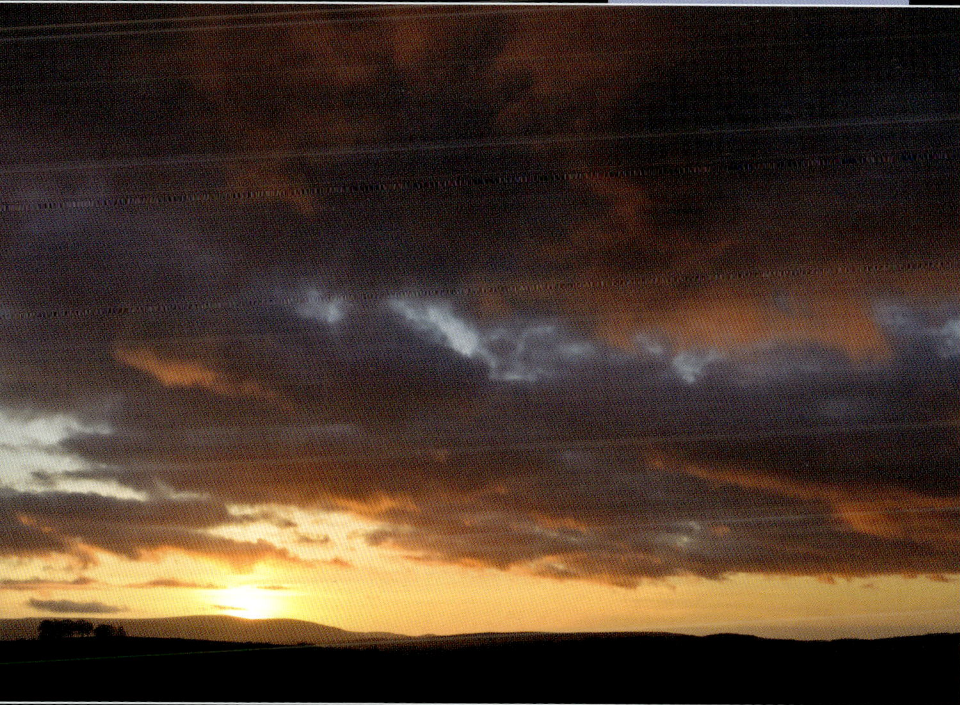

The weather

When the weather is bad, light levels can drop dramatically. However, there are still plenty of photo opportunities to be found when the sun isn't shining.

Changeability

Some parts of the world are blessed (or sometimes cursed) with weather that changes little over the seasons. The further north or south you are though, the more the weather can change, not just over the course of a year, but sometimes in the space of a few minutes.

The cause of weather is air pressure. When there is low air pressure air begins to rise. As it does it begins to expand and cool. As cold air can't retain moisture, clouds begin to form, and if the air continues to cool, rain begins to fall. The opposite is true during periods of high pressure. Air begins to fall, becomes more dense, and warms up. Warm air is efficient at retaining moisture so rain is less likely and there is a greater chance of fine weather and clear skies.

Ironically, fair weather is often the least interesting time to be out creating landscape photographs. There is little drama to a clear blue sky and, as previously mentioned, sunrises and sunsets are often disappointing. The only times that crisp, clear skies are welcome (for this photographer) is when shooting astronomical subjects at night and on frosty days in winter. Long periods of high pressure can also cause smog and dust to build up and this reduces visibility. Summer is the season most prone to the build up of this kind of haze.

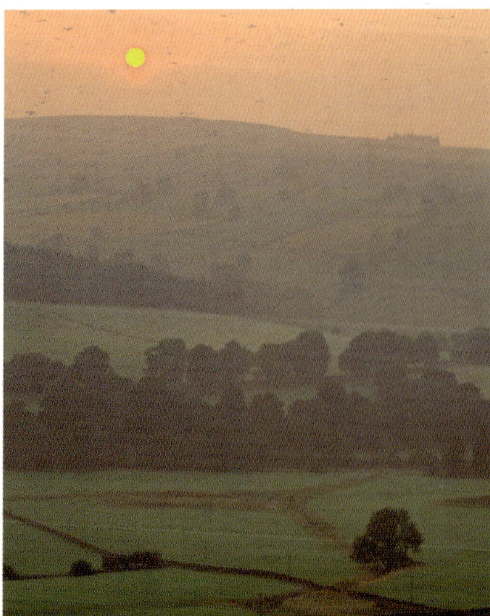

HAZY
This image was shot after a few days of high pressure. The hazy conditions gave the sunrise a suitably misty feel, but the reduction in visibility meant the rest of the day was a photographic washout.

Pentax 67, 180mm lens, exposure details unrecorded, ISO 50 (Fuji Velvia)

Predicting the weather

The ability to predict what the weather will do over the course of a few hours is a useful skill to learn. Although professional weather forecasting is generally accurate, it can't always be right about localized weather conditions. Plus, when you're in the middle of nowhere it's not always possible to receive up-to-the-minute weather reports. If you know what the weather will be doing, you will have more confidence to set your alarm for a sunrise excursion (or to abandon a trip as a total loss).

> ***Working smarter...***
> Apple iOS: *Accuweather*
> Android: *iMap weather*
> If you can get a signal, both of these apps will keep you up to date with the local weather forecast.

Condition	Result
Red sky at night...	Suggests that the following day will be clear.
Red sky in the morning...	Means that rain is possible later in the day.
Mackerel skies	Rain is likely within 24 hours.
Halo around the sun	Seen in summer this means rain is possible.
Heavy dew in the morning	Indicates a period of fair weather.
Flowers smell stronger	Scent is strongest in moist air, indicating potential rain.
Strong winds	Means air pressure is changing, bringing wet weather.
High flying birds	Fair weather probable.
Cloud cover builds up slowly	Indicates a warm front bringing prolonged rain with it.

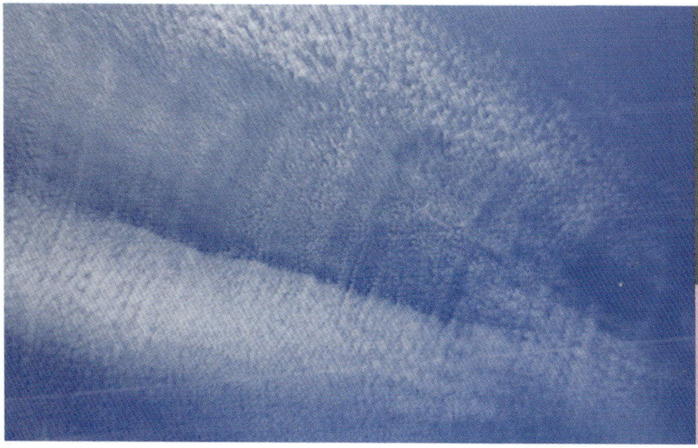

MACKEREL
Altocumulus (or mackerel) clouds make pleasing images, but also warn of rainy weather to come.

Canon EOS 1Ds MkII, 17–40mm lens (at 24mm), 1/160 sec. at f/11, ISO 100

Rain

Rain brings practical challenges to photography as it is of course wet and this can be potentially damaging to equipment. Some high-end cameras are weather sealed (although not to the point of being completely waterproof), but regardless of your camera, with care it's still possible to shoot in rain without damaging your equipment.

Umbrellas are very useful, and small, fold-up umbrellas generally fit into the pockets of equipment bags. Held above a tripod-mounted camera they can help to keep the rain at bay, but if you need to wait for a period of time, a plastic bag fitted loosely over the camera is also an effective way of keeping it dry. For the ultimate in protection, some companies such as Optech and Storm Jacket sell fully waterproof covers to fit most cameras.

The most rewarding time to photograph rain is when storm clouds roll in. There's often a wonderful contrast between the sunlit areas of the landscape and those under the shadow of rain. This is also the time when "Jacob's Ladders" are often seen.

These are the dramatic shafts of sunlight that burst through breaks in cloud, but they are often fleeting and so leave little time to set up your camera on a tripod. However, because you are photographing reasonably bright light, it's more than possible to handhold your camera and shoot. If you don't include much foreground you also won't need a large aperture—f/5.6 or f/8 is

SUNBURST
I anticipated that the sun would break through the gap in the clouds, which gave me time to set up my camera and tripod.

Canon EOS 1Ds MkII, 17–40mm lens (at 40mm), 1/2 sec. at f/16, ISO 100

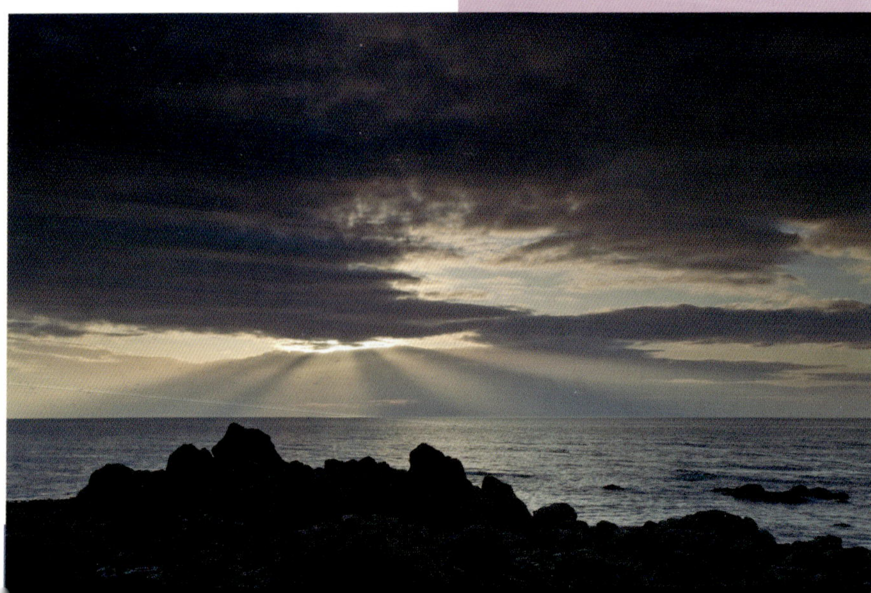

usually enough—and this will help to keep the shutter speed relatively high.

To freeze raindrops falling, you will need to use a shutter speed of at least 1/250 sec. This is often difficult when it's raining, as the light levels are low, but using flash is an effective way to freeze raindrops—and add sparkle to a scene. However, your flash will need protecting from the rain more than your camera, so it's a good idea to cover it in a transparent plastic bag.

Rainbows

Rainbows are caused by sunlight refracting through droplets of rain, and are another rain-related phenomenon that is often fleeting. They form a circle with the sun perpendicular to the center of the circle, but because the ground is in the way, part of the circle is cut off. If the sun is on the horizon, almost half the potential circle will be visible: the higher the sun rises in the sky, the smaller the visible arc and the lower the rainbow. Rainbows cannot form when the sun is higher than 42° from the horizon, as the circle of the rainbow is effectively below ground level.

Experiment with different focal lengths when shooting rainbows. Wide-angle lenses will help you capture the full span of the rainbow, while telephotos are useful when it comes to filling the frame with the bands of color. Rainbows form natural lead-in lines, so try to find a position where they will point toward an interesting feature in the landscape.

RAINBOW
The combination of showers and sunshine is a good time to see rainbows. It's often possible to see showers approaching and so be prepared.

Canon EOS 1Ds MkII, 70–200mm lens (at 135mm), 1/3 sec. at f/16, ISO 100

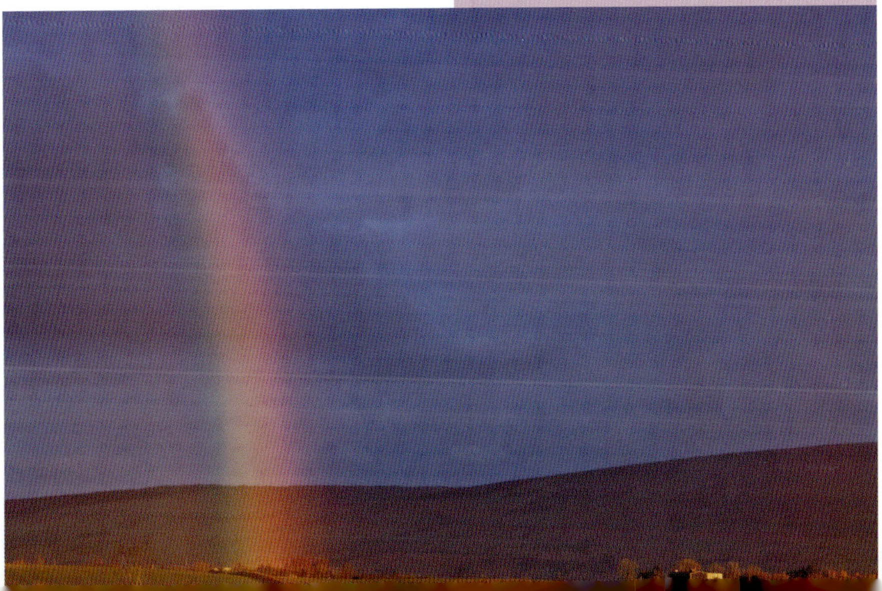

Drama

The landscape is often at its most dramatic when the weather is changeable. On photography trips this means preparing for all eventualities to keep both you and your equipment safe.

Camera: Canon EOS 5D
Lens: 17–40mm lens (at 22mm)
Exposure: 1/15 sec. at f/14
ISO: 100

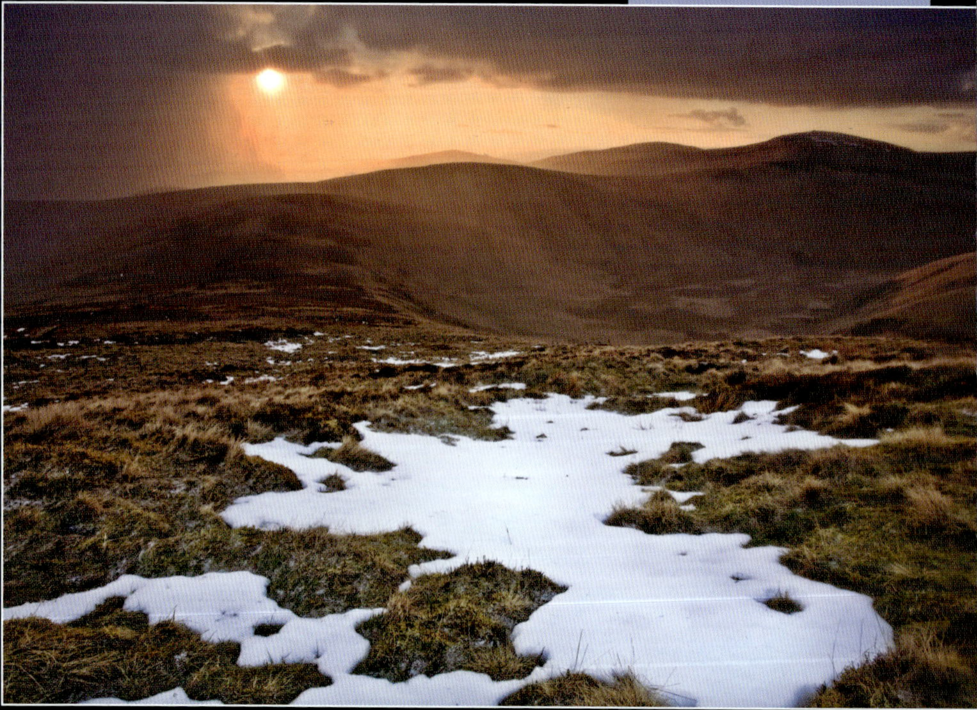

Low light and the need to use a long shutter speed can help to simplify an image. Wind was whipping across this open moor, disturbing the surface of this pool, but a shutter speed of 6 seconds softened the ripples away. Ironically, the image looks calm and tranquil even though in making it I had to lean against my tripod to keep it steady!

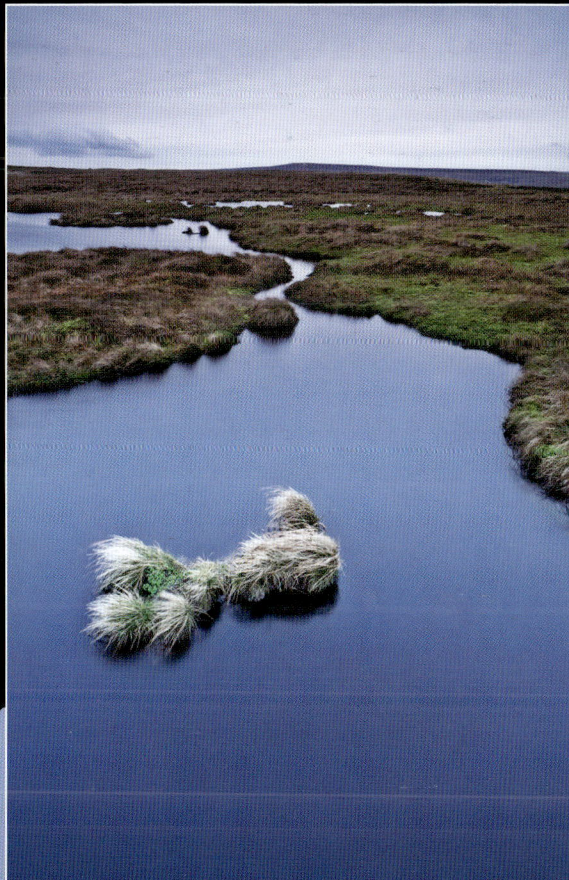

Camera: Canon EOS 1Ds MkII
Lens: 24mm lens
Exposure: 6 sec. at f/18
ISO: 50

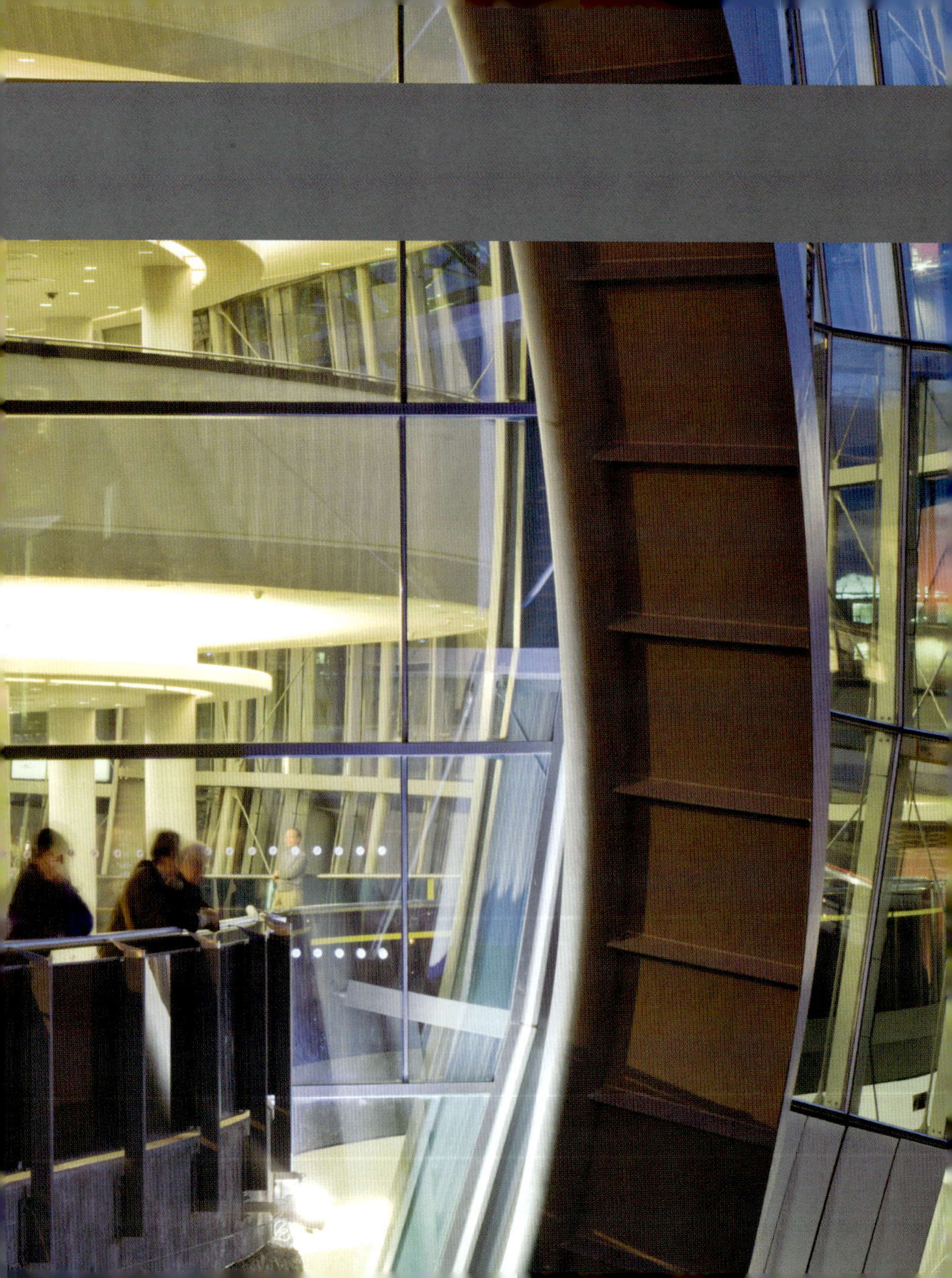

CHAPTER 6 THE URBAN ENVIRONMENT

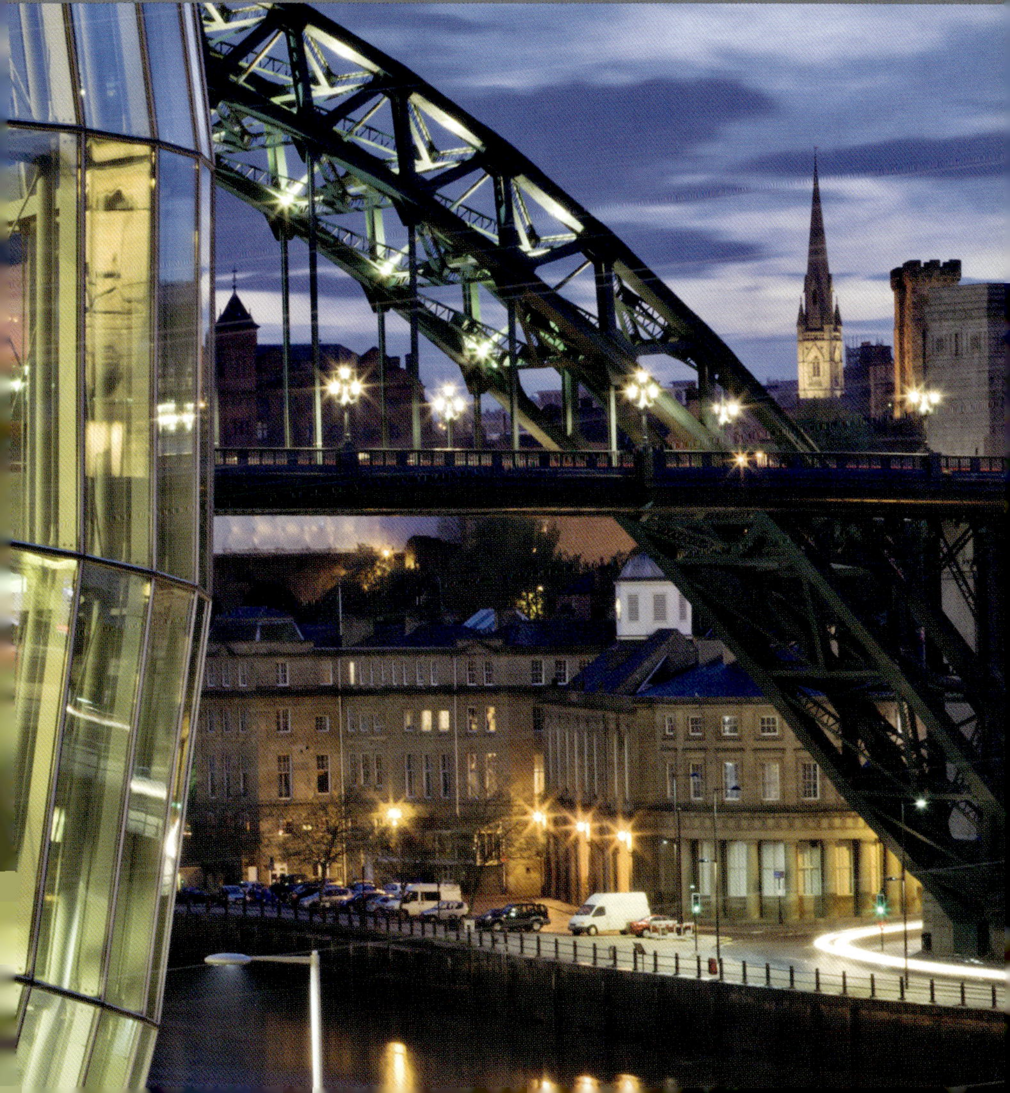

The urban environment

Cities and towns are exciting places to photograph in the evening. When the lights are turned on even the humblest urban space can be transformed.

Timing

With rural landscape photography, a location will either be most suitable in the morning or evening, but cities and towns are often more interesting with the onset of night. For a start, there will be more people around than there will be first thing in the morning, particularly in winter when night falls earlier, and shops will be open and window displays illuminated. Buildings are also more likely to be floodlit; this varies, of course, but floodlighting is often switched off at midnight for reasons of economy. The urban environment just seems more alive later at night than it does in the morning.

Ironically, the wrong time to be photographing a city is when night has fallen completely and the sky is black. The tops of buildings are rarely lit and once the sky is black you'll lose the shape of the roofline. The optimum time to shoot is when there is still color in the sky, which happens earlier in winter than it does in summer, but is roughly 25–40 minutes after sunset. If you have a number of different subjects to shoot during this period, start with those that face west as the sky will darken sooner looking east. Once you've finished photographing all of the west-facing subjects you can move on to those that face east.

If you're in an unfamiliar city it pays to walk around during the day to learn how to get about. This will also allow you to pre-visualize the shots you want to take so you can set up in the evening with the minimum of fuss: you want to optimize the time you have.

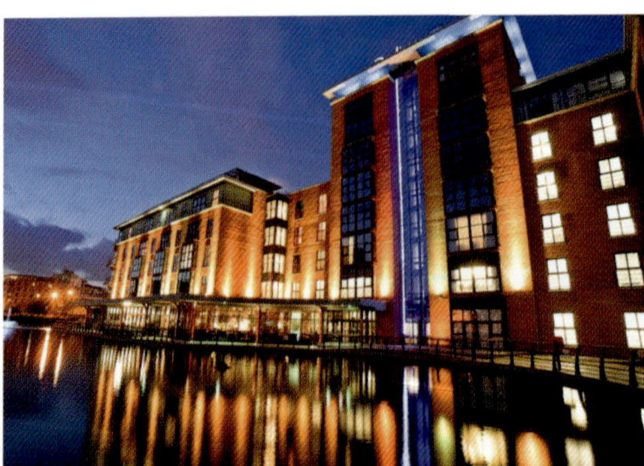

PREPARED
These two very different buildings are within 10 minutes of each other. By scouting the location during the day I was able to walk from one to the other on the same evening.

Canon EOS 1Ds MkII, 17–40mm lens (at 17mm), 20 sec. at f/11, ISO 100

(Opposite) **Canon EOS 1Ds MkII, 70–200mm lens (at 160mm), 6 sec. at f/10, ISO 100**

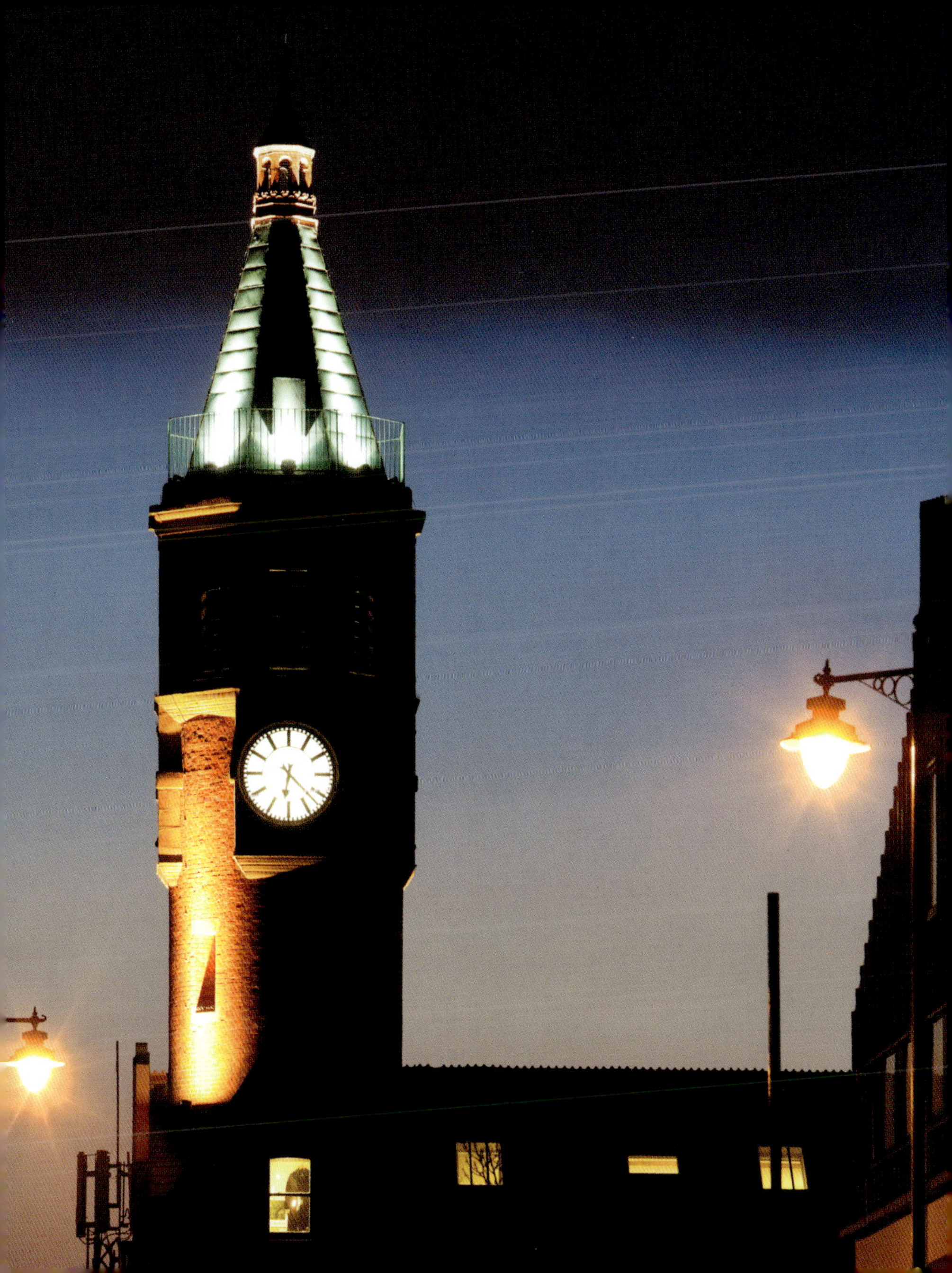

Lenses

A good selection of lenses will help you get the most out of your low light city photography.

Focal length

City streets are often just not wide enough for the photographer, so a wide-angle lens is often needed to make sure that the whole of an urban space is captured. Even so, it's often necessary to tilt a lens upward to fit everything in, which can cause a visual phenomenon known as "converging verticals," where a building appears to be falling backward. So, wide-angle lenses—though often necessary—should be used carefully. Use a hotshoe-mounted spirit level to make sure that your camera is straight, both forward and backward, as well as from side to side.

Another approach is to embrace the limitations of wide-angle lenses and deliberately use your camera at odd angles. As a visual style it can be very effective, although there's a definite "sweet point" to be found: too little looks like a mistake, and too much can produce feelings of vertigo in anyone who looks at the resulting image.

The most useful type of lens to have when shooting architecture is a tilt-and-shift. A tilt-and-shift lens allows you to keep the back of your camera parallel to a building, but move the lens up or down to bring the top or bottom of the building into the shot without introducing distortion. Unfortunately these lenses tend to be very expensive, so where space allows I prefer to use longer focal length lenses instead. These lenses have a flatter perspective than wide-angle focal lengths and produce a more natural looking image.

LONG
By stepping back I was able to use a reasonably long lens for this image. This enabled me to keep the buildings looking parallel to each other.

Canon EOS 5D, 100mm lens, 1 sec. at f/16, ISO 100

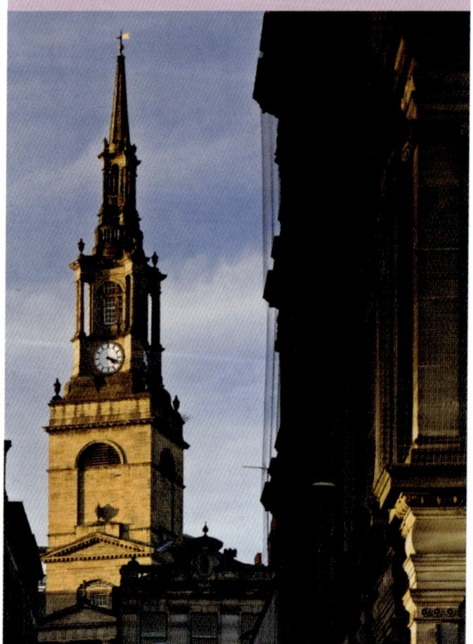

Camera: Canon 1Ds MkII
Lens: 17–40mm lens (at 20mm)
Exposure: 5 sec. at f/11, ISO: 100

I took a different approach to this image. By looking up with a wide-angle lens the perspective is far more dramatic.

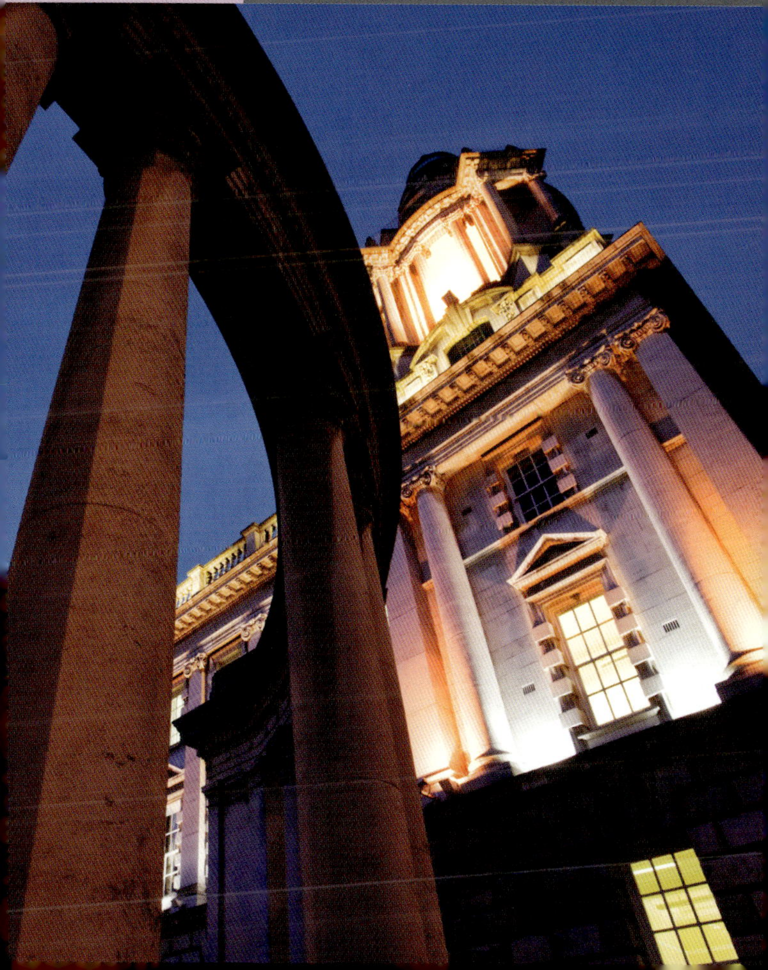

What to photograph

There is an infinite number of stories to tell in the urban environment, but your personal interests are what will guide you when it comes to the story you choose to tell.

The bigger picture

There is no single approach to urban photography; you must decide what "story" you want to tell. This is often easier when you're in a familiar location as you will know what aspects of a place will be appealing and areas you'll want to avoid.

My personal preference is for cities with a river: I'm fascinated by rivers and the reflections you see in them at night. Rivers are also good because they allow you to get an unimpeded view across to the buildings on the other side. The one big problem with the urban environment is that it can be cluttered, making it difficult to set up a satisfactory composition.

Another approach I often take to overcome this is to try and find a viewpoint over a city from either a bridge, hill, or tall building. City parks are also a good place to find interesting views, and there is a natural contrast between the rigidly straight buildings that surround parks and the more organic shapes of trees and bushes.

RIVER REFLECTIONS
Rivers are a great spot to see a city or town from. To make the most of this viewpoint I shot a series of images from left to right to create a panoramic stitch in post-production.

Canon EOS 1Ds MkII, 100mm lens, 10 sec. at f/11, ISO 100

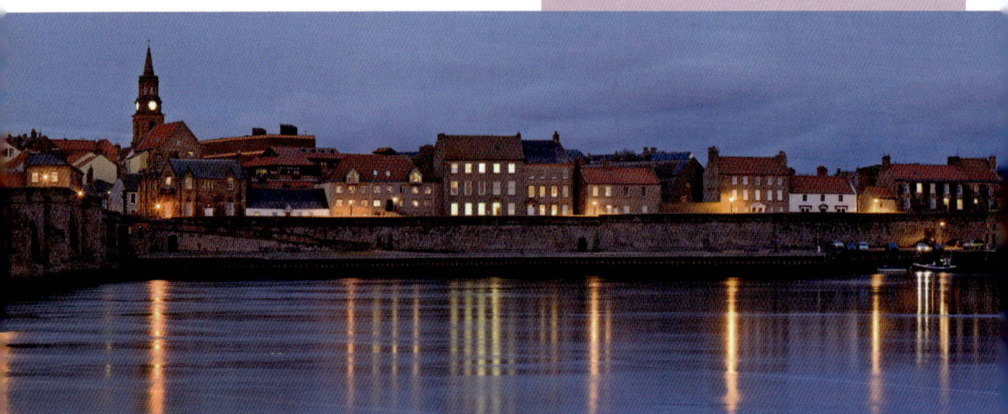

Details

The urban environment isn't just about architecture on a grand scale—interesting smaller details can be found wherever you look. One of my favorite times for shooting in a city is after rain, when the pavements are wet and highly reflective. Any light that falls on them—and this includes ambient blue light from the sky—will glow on the wet surface. If a recognizable object is being reflected, focus on the reflection if you want that to be sharp, rather than the wet surface itself. If you want both to be sharp you will need to use a small aperture to increase the depth of field.

Another subject to look out for in the urban environment is illuminated neon signs. These make great subjects, whether you include them as part of the wider urban scene or you crop in tightly so they fill the entire frame. Use a longer focal length for the latter, and remember that as they are a relatively flat surface the depth of field you'll require will be minimal, so you won't need a particularly small aperture if you shoot from straight on.

Statues and art pieces are common in the urban environment, but these are rarely lit intentionally. If the statue is relatively small, and you can get close enough to it, use flash as illumination. If you can take your flash off-camera, move it to the side of your subject to make the texture of the piece more prominent. If the statue is large enough, or you can get low enough so that it's framed against the sky, shoot it as a silhouette. It will help if you can find a position so that the shape isn't too complex and the subject is easily recognizable.

COLOR

The golden light on these wet cobbles is from a streetlamp, while the blue is ambient light from the sky above. It was this color contrast that I found most appealing about this scene.

Canon EOS 1Ds MkII, 50mm lens, 15 sec. at f/16, ISO 100

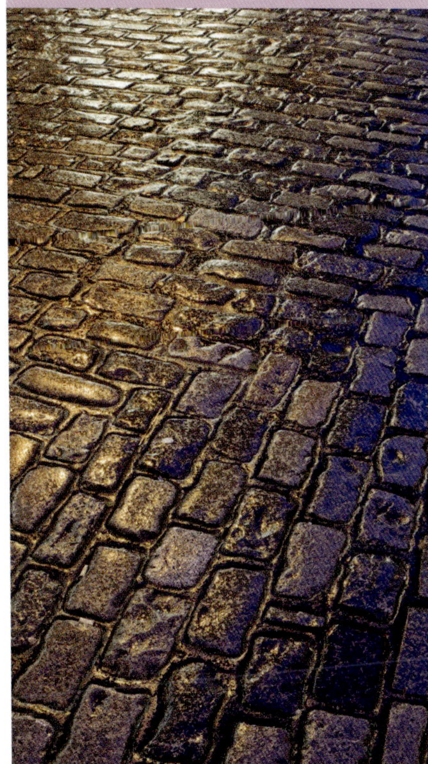

Traffic trails

Moving traffic at night, combined with long exposures, adds zip to urban scenes. Because the cars are moving, only the trails of their lights are recorded.

Shooting light trails is easiest when the busiest time on the roads coincides with dusk. Depending on your latitude this will usually be in the spring and fall months, when dusk is around 5.00pm.

There are several approaches to shooting traffic trails. The first is to find an elevated spot, such as a footbridge, so that you look down on the traffic. This will help to convey a powerful sense of perspective with the trails following the

SERENDIPITY
The appealing aspect of shooting traffic trails is the unexpected, but interesting, results. A bus passed during this exposure, and the lights from the upper deck neatly framed the buildings in the background.

Canon EOS 1Ds MkII, 17–40mm lens (at 40mm), 6 sec. at f/16, ISO 100

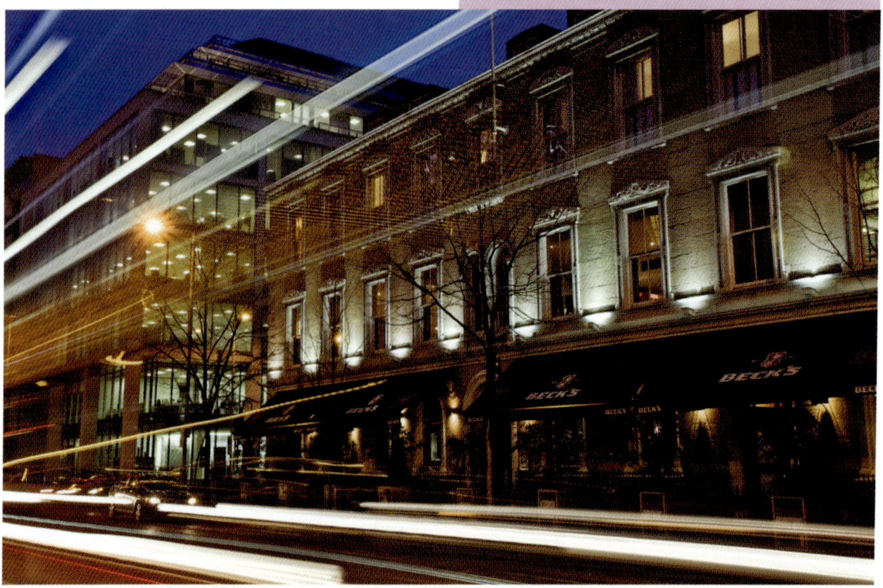

line of the road. The more lanes on the road, the greater the number of trails, and the more complex the potential composition will be as cars change from lane to lane.

The second approach is to shoot from street level (without actually standing in the road itself). This will allow you to include buildings in the composition, but try to avoid locations near traffic lights or bus stops where the traffic is likely to come to a regular standstill.

Shooting traffic trails

What you'll need: Tripod, fully charged batteries, remote release, black card (optional).

1) Arrive at your chosen location before dusk and set your camera up on its tripod.

2) Choose your composition. A wide-angle lens will exaggerate the width of the road; a telephoto lens will give a "'flatter" look.

3) Switch your camera to manual focus and focus a ∞ (infinity).

4) Plug in your remote release and turn your camera to Bulb. Set the aperture to f/16. Wait until the light levels have dropped to the point where your shutter speed is roughly in the range of 30 seconds–1 minute.

5) Fire the shutter when the traffic is flowing reasonably quickly. If long gaps appear between vehicles hold the black card in front of the lens.

> ***Note***
>
> *If there are illuminated buildings in your shot, base your exposure on these by using your camera's spot meter.*

6) Release the shutter and review the results. Traffic trail images can be hit and miss, so it's worth continuing shooting until the street is completely dark.

> **COMPOSITION**
>
> The line of the road will give you an idea of how the traffic trails will flow, so use that as a guide when composing your shot.

Canon EOS 7D, 70–200 lens (at 200mm), 30 sec. at f/16, ISO 100

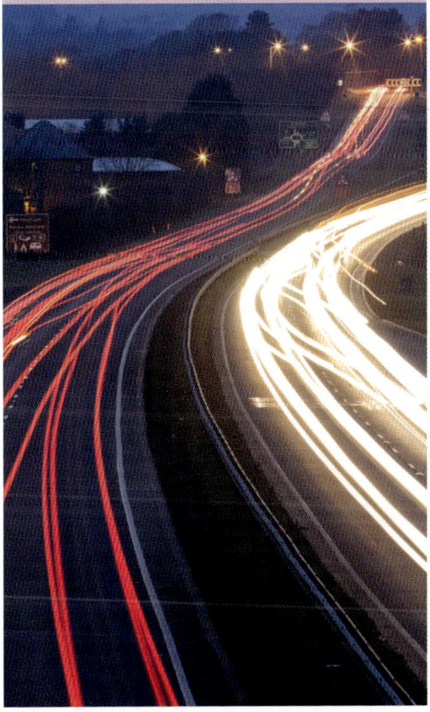

Warm and cool

Frosty winter mornings are a great time to be out and about with your camera. The low winter sunlight is warm in tone and brings out the color of materials such as sandstone. For this image I was in shade, and it was the contrast of the cool blue shadow and the warm light on the building that appealed.

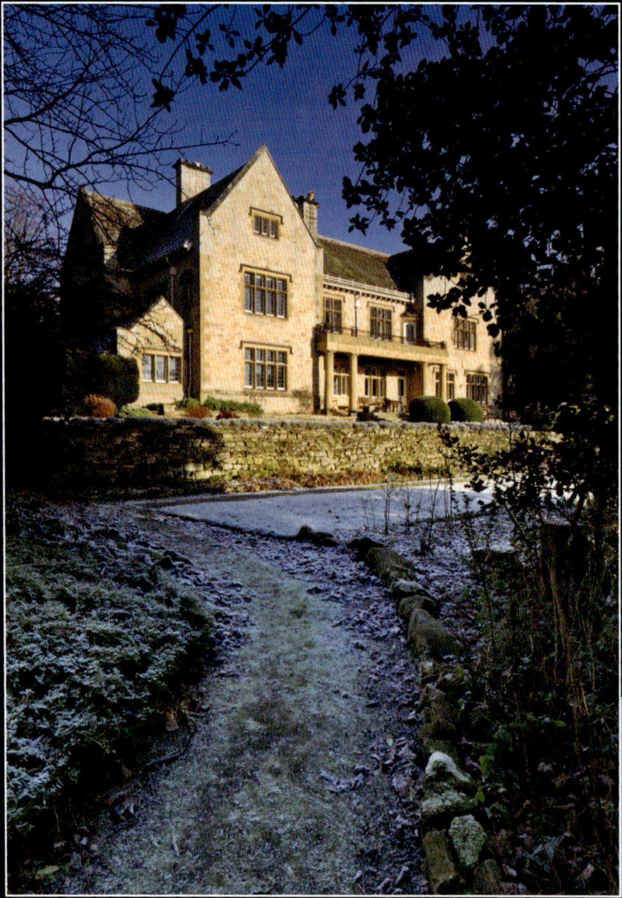

Camera: Canon EOS 1Ds MkII
Lens: 100mm lens
Exposure: 6 sec. at f/11
ISO: 100

Ambience

Not every building is floodlit, but nature sometimes provides a helping hand. The warm pink glow on this decommissioned lighthouse was from vividly colored pre-dawn clouds behind the camera. Sometimes you don't need to be pointing your camera at the most dramatic part of a sky for a good picture.

Camera: Canon EOS 7D
Lens: 10–22mm lens (at 14mm)
Exposure: 1/2 sec. at f/14
ISO: 100

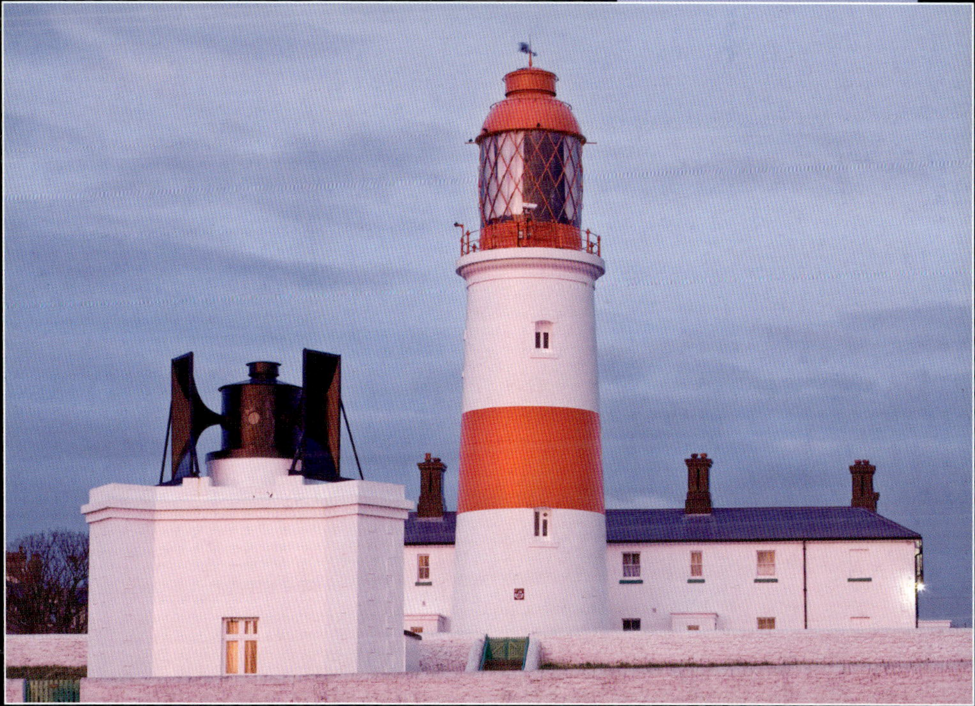

Christmas and other festivals

Mid-winter festivals, such as Christmas, are celebrations that involve lights, and when the sky is at its darkest, interiors and urban spaces are often at their most colorful.

'Tis the season

City streets at Christmas are usually jolly places, combining a blaze of light with happy people milling around shopping or soaking up the atmosphere. Dusk, half an hour after sunset, is the best time to be out shooting, although some days will be busier than others. Saturdays are generally a good day for photography if you want to capture people out enjoying themselves. Other days will be quieter, but this is no bad thing if your intention is to capture the lights only.

Take a selection of lenses with you. Wide-angle lenses are ideal for street scenes, while longer focal lengths will allow you to crop more tightly on individual lighting displays. Because the light levels will be low, a tripod is a necessity, but take care when setting up so that you don't block busy through-routes. Christmas is also the time when filters such as starburst filters come into their own—their effect is perhaps too obvious at other times of the year, but Christmas seems to suit the slightly unreal look these filters create.

Shop window displays also make interesting subjects. Bigger department stores often have animated displays showing festive scenes, but the lighting tends to be relatively subdued so to avoid blurring set the maximum aperture and a high ISO. The windows will pick up reflections from lights around you, so try to keep your lens as close to the glass as you can. If you have a willing assistant get them to hold a coat over you and your camera to block out the light. Don't forget the people watching the displays as well—their reaction to the display will often be unguarded and even an adult's face can break out into expressions of childlike wonder.

DETAILS
A long lens was used for this shot. As I also used a large aperture the lights behind have been left pleasingly out of focus.

Canon EOS 1Ds MkII, 200mm lens, 1/8 sec. at f/2.8, ISO 100

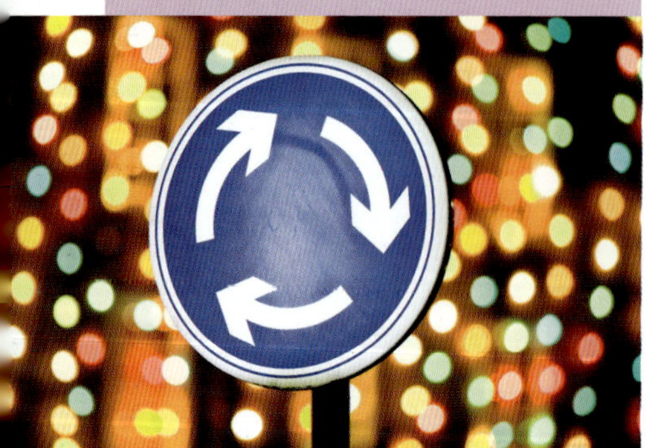

Camera: Canon EOS 5D
Lens: 24mm lens
Exposure: 3 sec. at f/16
ISO: 100

Keep yourself wrapped up warm when you are out shooting in midwinter. There is often a lot of standing around, so it's easy to become chilled.

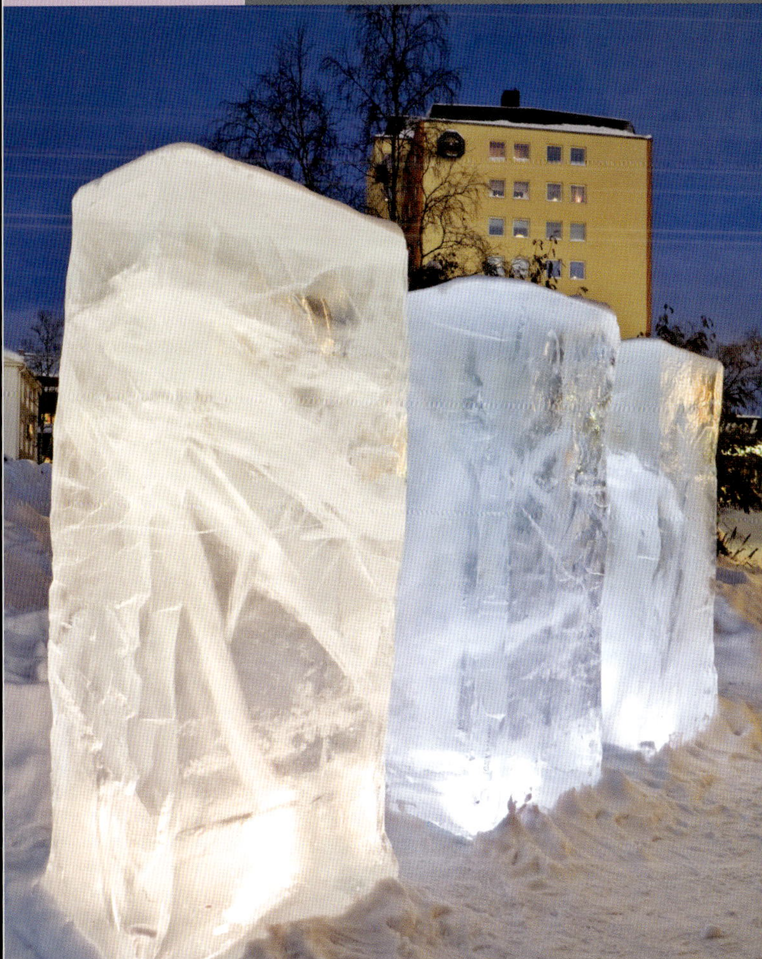

People

An urban area is as much about the people who live there, as it is about the buildings they live in.

The approach

A documentary photographer is the fearless type who goes out into the world and shoots images regardless of the feelings of the subjects. A few bruised egos are a small price to pay in the quest to reveal an underlying truth about the world.

There probably isn't any photographer who's that blinkered to people's feelings, but it's certainly more comfortable to shoot candidly when out on the city streets. It doesn't have to be that way though. People are often amenable to being photographed, and with practise it gets easier to spot those who are not. The most important qualities you'll need are being friendly and honest with people—and not being too upset when they refuse to take part. If this happens, be polite and move on. Don't wait until they're not watching and then shoot them candidly. If your subject agrees to be photographed, be prepared to show them the results on your camera's LCD.

In low light, a prime lens with a fast aperture is going to see a lot of use—shoot at maximum aperture to maintain the fastest shutter speed you can. You'll have very little depth of field, so if you're shooting close-up portraits, be sure to focus on your subject's eyes. It's uncomfortable to look at a portrait image when the subject's eyes are noticeably unsharp.

KEEPING IT SIMPLE
I prefer to keep my portrait shots very simple; usually just head and shoulders.

Canon EOS 5D, 50mm lens, 1/200 sec. at f/4, ISO 400

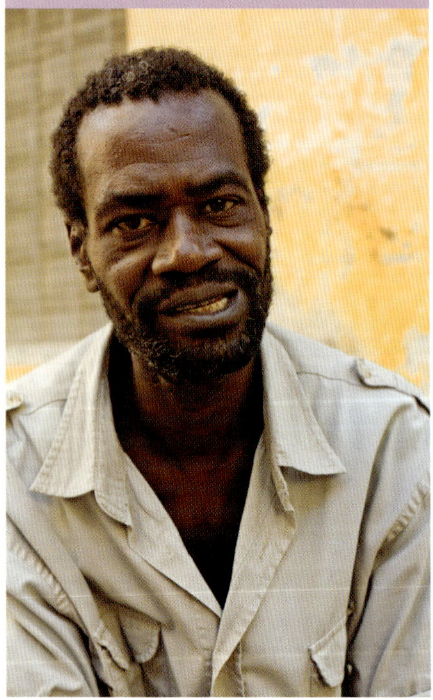

Interiors

The inside of a building often has more character than the outside. The interior is shaped over time by the people who live and work there.

Equipment

The one big problem often encountered with interiors is size. The cavernous space of a cathedral is easy to work in; a cramped domestic interior is less so. The obvious solution is to use a wide-angle lens, but wide focal lengths need to be used with caution to avoid converging verticals. Wide-angle lenses also introduce another problem in the form of distortion—what should be perfectly straight lines end up with a distinct curve.

Distortion can either be "barrel" or "pincushion," but barrel distortion is the one that will be encountered with wide-angle focal lengths. Barrel distortion causes straight lines to bow out from the center toward the edge of the image, while pincushion distortion causes straight lines to bow inward toward the center.

An increasing number of cameras have options that will endeavor to fix lens distortion in-camera at the time of capture when you're shooting JPEGs. If you're shooting Raw files, lens distortion correction will need to be done at the post-production stage—software such as Lightroom 3 (and above) offers this facility.

One type of lens that you wouldn't correct is a fisheye lens. These lenses usually have 180° angle of view, so are very wide angle indeed, but while the distortion is extreme, this is part of their charm. Fisheye lenses are not lenses you'd want to use for every image you shoot, but they do provide a unique look that's impossible to replicate otherwise.

VERTICAL
This was the interior of an ice hotel. With the camera mounted on a tripod I tried to keep it as level as I could to avoid converging verticals. Keeping the camera vertical emphasized the shape of the interior too.

Canon EOS 5D, 24mm lens, 10 sec. at f/16, ISO 100

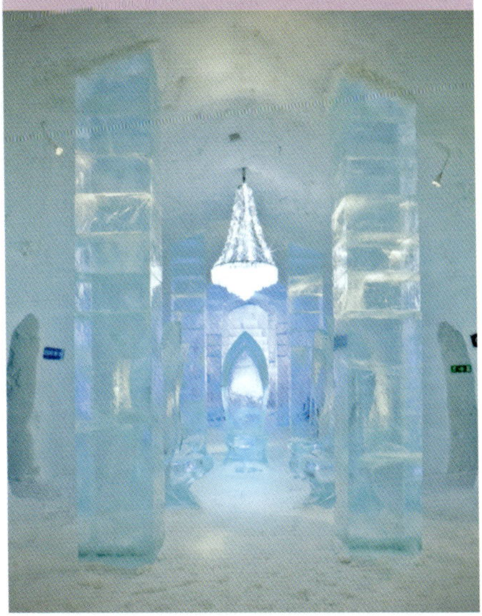

Lighting

How an interior is lit will often depend on the age of a building. Modern buildings often use fluorescent striplighting, while older buildings are more likely to use tungsten lighting. The other source of lighting is of course daylight, although older buildings tend to have smaller windows than newer buildings.

Each of these different types of lighting has a different color temperature. If a room is lit by one source only, this is not a problem—it's simply a case of using the correct white balance preset or creating a custom white balance. However, when you have mixed lighting the results can be ghastly, and while a custom white balance will help to a certain degree, it will not solve the problem entirely. I prefer to avoid mixing lighting whenever possible, which often means switching off the artificial lighting and relying on the ambient light from outside, or using artificial lighting and waiting until dusk so that the ambient light outside is low and becomes less of a problem.

If contrast is a problem in an interior (artificial lighting doesn't always completely illuminate an interior space) be prepared to use flash to "paint" with light, as outlined in the following chapter. Flash is very different in color temperature to most forms of artificial lighting, but you can use color correction gels to modify the color temperature of your flash.

MIXED
The solution to shooting with mixed lighting (daylight and artificial) in this hotel room was to close the curtains—sometimes the simplest answers are the best.

Canon EOS 5D, 17–40mm lens (at 30mm), 18 sec. at f/14, ISO 100

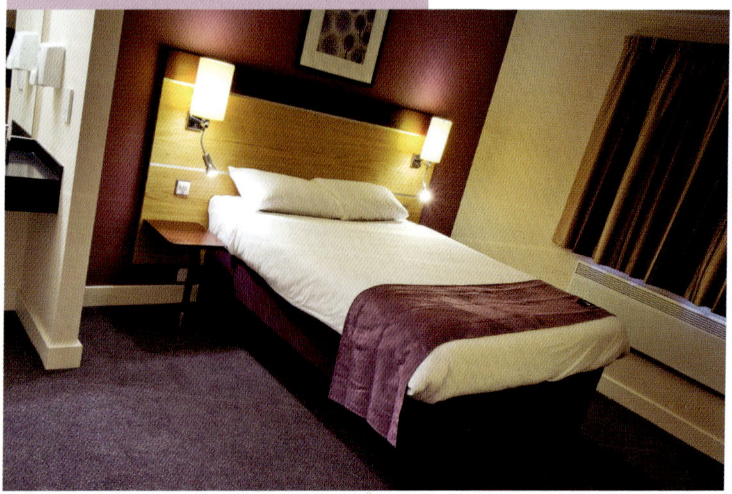

Camera: Canon G10
Lens: 6.1–30.5mm (at 7mm)
Exposure: 3 sec. at f/4.5
ISO: 80

This image was shot with a compact camera—all I had to hand at the time. To avoid camera shake I rested the camera on a balcony ledge.

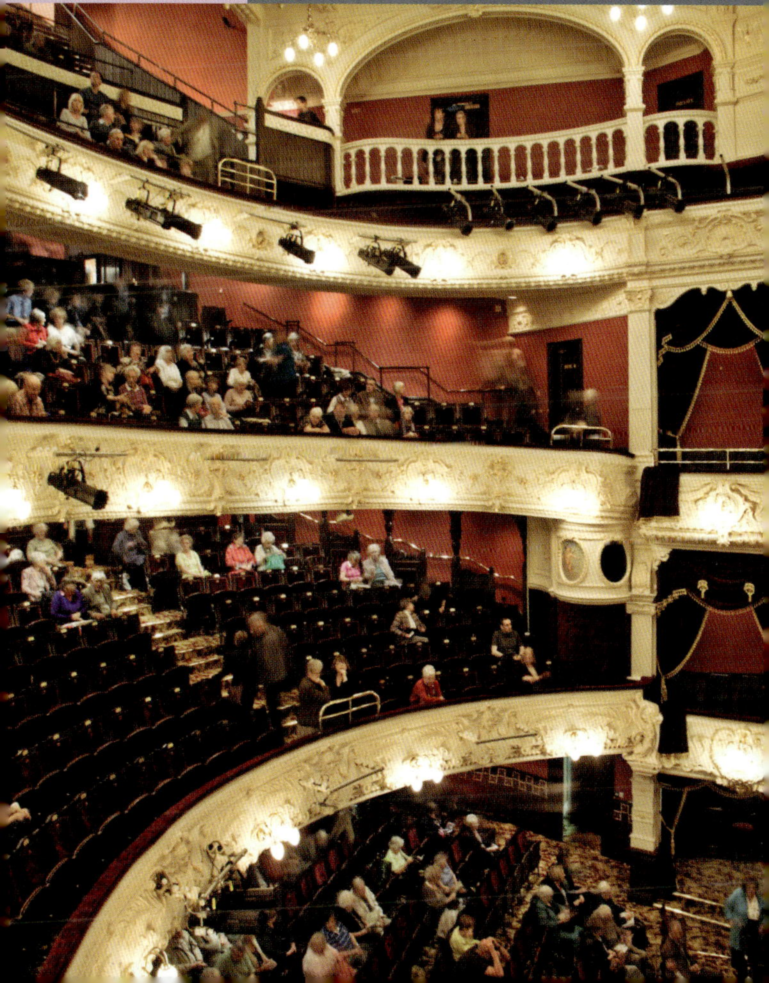

Public spaces

Photographing in a public space is often tricky, as you are sharing that space with other members of the public and ultimately you shouldn't inconvenience anyone.

Museums and art galleries

One of the first problems you will encounter is establishing whether photography is permitted in your chosen venue. A lot of museums and art galleries don't allow photography either for security reasons or the fear that the use of flash may damage the exhibits—it's worth contacting the venue before a visit to see what is and isn't allowed. If photography isn't allowed don't try and sneak pictures when you think no one is looking, as being evicted is embarrassing and will not endear the venue to the idea of photography in the future.

If the museum or art gallery does allow photography, you need to be prepared to handhold your camera only. A tripod may prove a nuisance to other visitors to the venue, so lenses with a large aperture or image stabilization will be most useful.

Wide-angle lenses will allow you to cover the broad sweep of the venue's interior, which is useful to create context for your chosen subjects, while a fast prime lens, such as a 50mm "standard" lens, is ideal for homing in on details.

Once you're at the venue, what do you shoot? The most obvious approach is to produce record shots, similar to those you'd find in a brochure promoting the venue. This is fine, but isn't very imaginative.

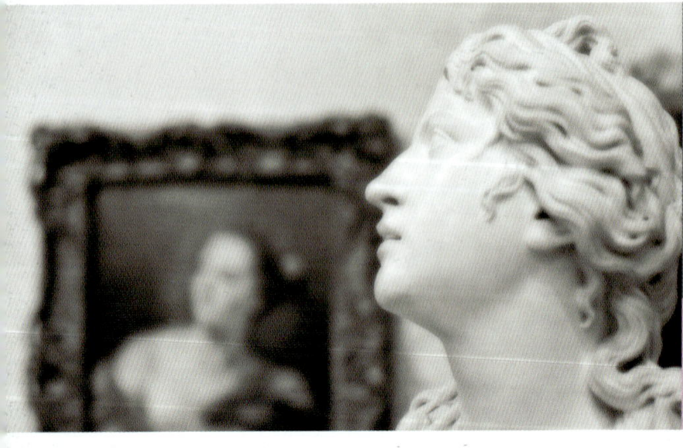

LOOKING UP
Despite the need to use a large aperture, there is just enough depth of field to see that the two subjects are both looking at something outside the frame. They weren't really, but that's the way I saw it at the time.

Canon EOS 5D, 50mm lens, 1/40 sec. at f/2.8, ISO 500

Camera: Canon EOS 5D
Lens: 50mm lens
Exposure: 1/100 sec. at f/2.8
ISO: 500

For a more timeless look I'll often process images from museums with less color saturation.

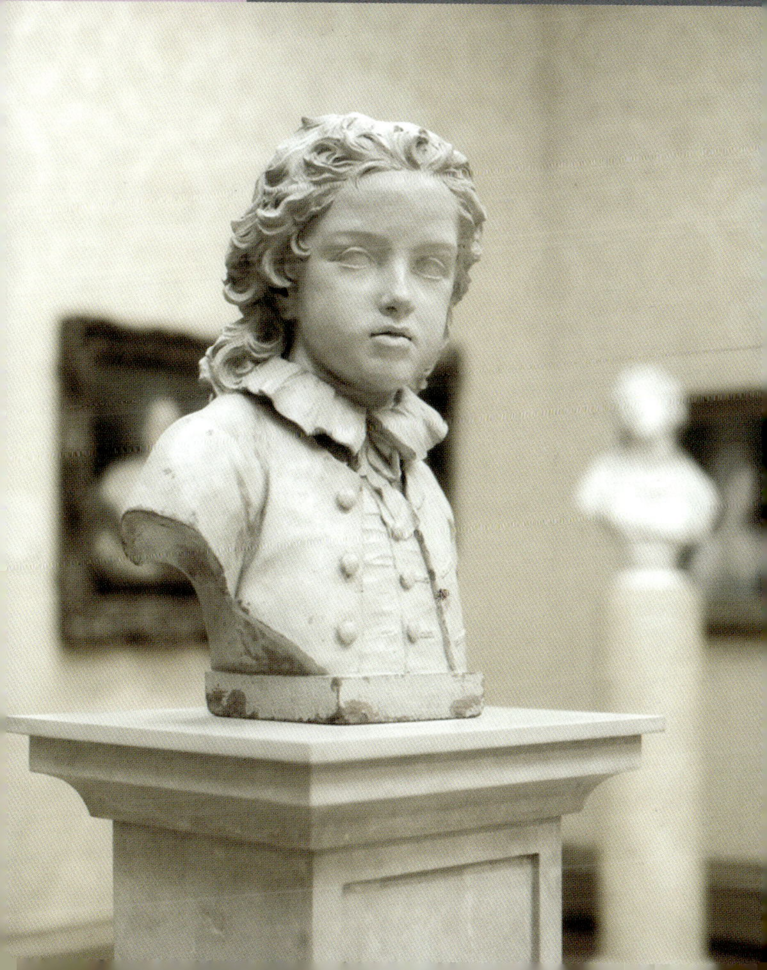

My personal way of working is to look for unusual juxtapositions between the exhibits and visitors. This approach can either be humorous or thought provoking, but hopefully never dull.

Reflections

Exhibits in museums or art galleries are often behind glass, and glass creates reflections and reduces contrast. Place your lens against, or as near to, the glass as possible, but don't press against the glass too hard. This is partly because you don't want to damage the glass, but also to avoid straining the AF motor in the lens. Glass is often covered in dust or fingerprints so you may want to clean it with a soft cloth beforehand.

The most obvious solution to cutting out reflections is to use a polarizing filter. However, polarizers are most effective when they are used at an angle to a non-metallic surface such as glass: they will not cut out reflections when you're looking straight at the glass, which will result in a self-portrait. Museums and galleries are often dimly lit so a polarizer will require a high ISO or restrict the range of usable aperture and shutter speed combinations.

> ***Tip***
>
> *Don't forget to look at the architecture of the building you are photographing in, as many older galleries are works of art in themselves. It often pays to look up, as ceiling decoration can be highly decorative.*

SELECTION

This display was protected by glass, but by holding the camera against the glass, I was able to avoid reflections and, as a bonus, this also helped me keep the camera steady during the long shutter speed that was required.

Canon EOS 7D, 10–22mm lens (at 10mm), 1/2 sec. at f/5.6, ISO 200

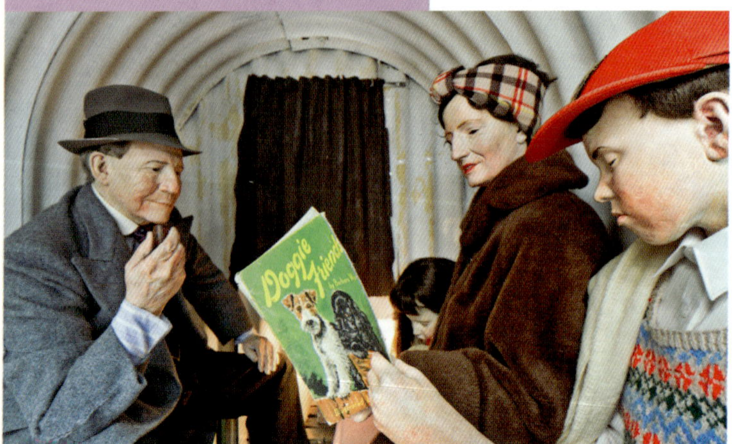

Camera: Canon EOS 7D
Lens: 70–200mm lens (at 70mm)
Exposure: 15 sec. at f/8
ISO: 100

I like to look for quirky details that bring a smile to the face.

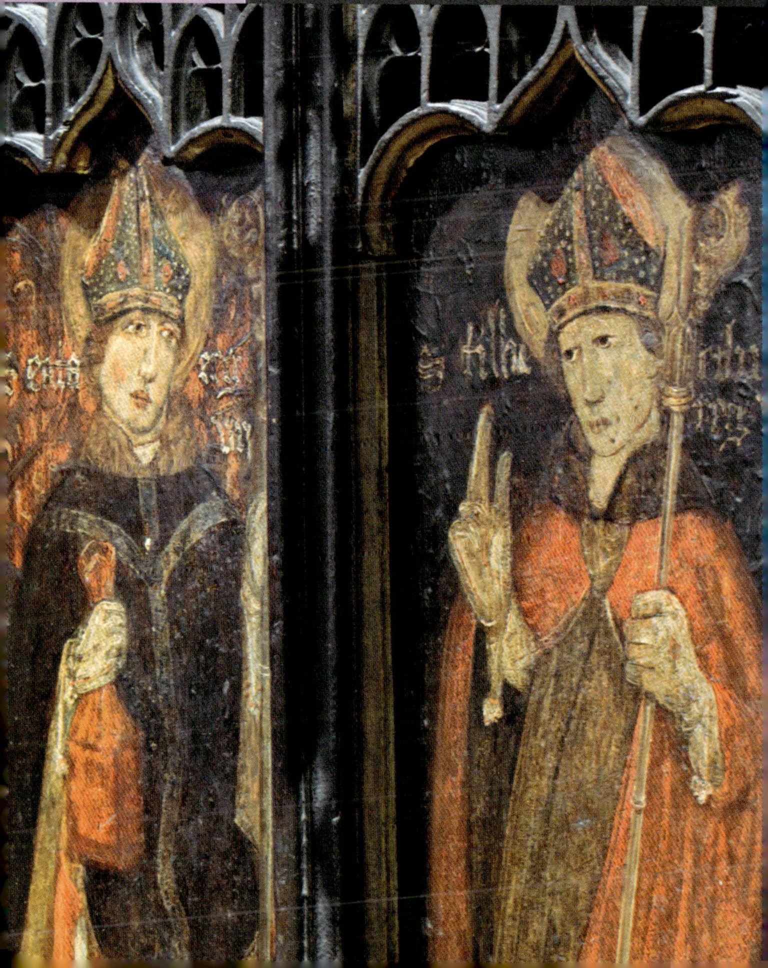

Stained glass windows

One of the most esthetically pleasing aspects of churches—and other older municipal buildings—is their stained glass windows. Capturing the color is best achieved on overcast days when the light outside is softer. Longer lenses are useful to home in on small, distant details. Generally, if maximum aperture is used, it's also possible to handhold the camera.

Correctly exposing a stained glass window along with a building's interior can be more problematic, as the contrast between the relatively bright window and darker interior is usually greater than a camera's dynamic range. If you're allowed to use a tripod, shooting a sequence of bracketed shots and then using HDR or exposure blending in post-production is a perfectly valid solution. Another solution is to use an off-camera flash to "paint with light," although this will require a tripod and also permission from the owners of the building.

Another very photographic aspect of stained glass windows is the way that they transmit light. This light will change throughout the day as the sun moves across the sky, throwing color onto the various elements in the building. Metallic surfaces will pick up and reflect the colors most readily, but stonework and wood can be just as beautiful bathed in colored light.

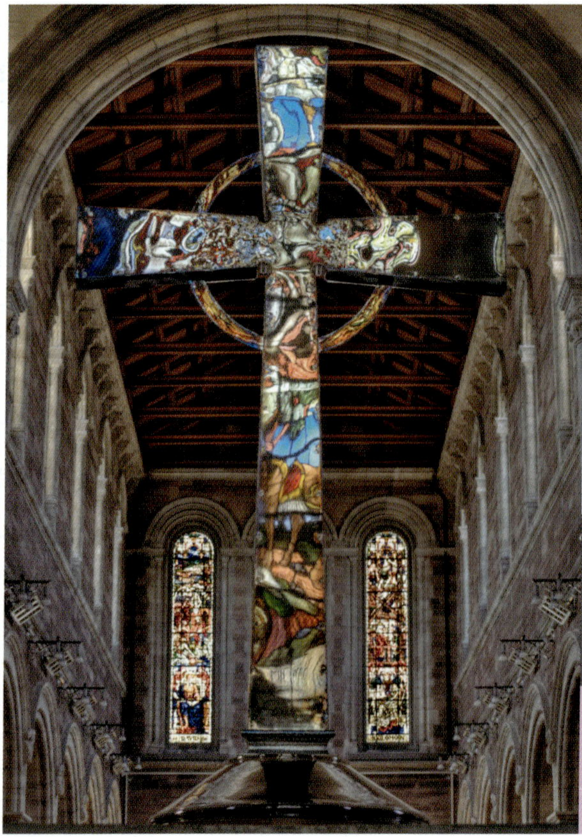

REFLECTIONS
The colors on this metal cross come purely from a stained glass window behind the camera.

Canon EOS 1Ds MkII, 70–200mm lens (at 70mm), three blended exposures at f/18, ISO 100

Camera: Canon EOS 7D
Lens: 50mm lens
Exposure: 1/80 sec. at f/2
ISO: 800

I enjoy creating images of stained glass windows that don't tell the whole story, leaving the viewer of the image to work out what is happening.

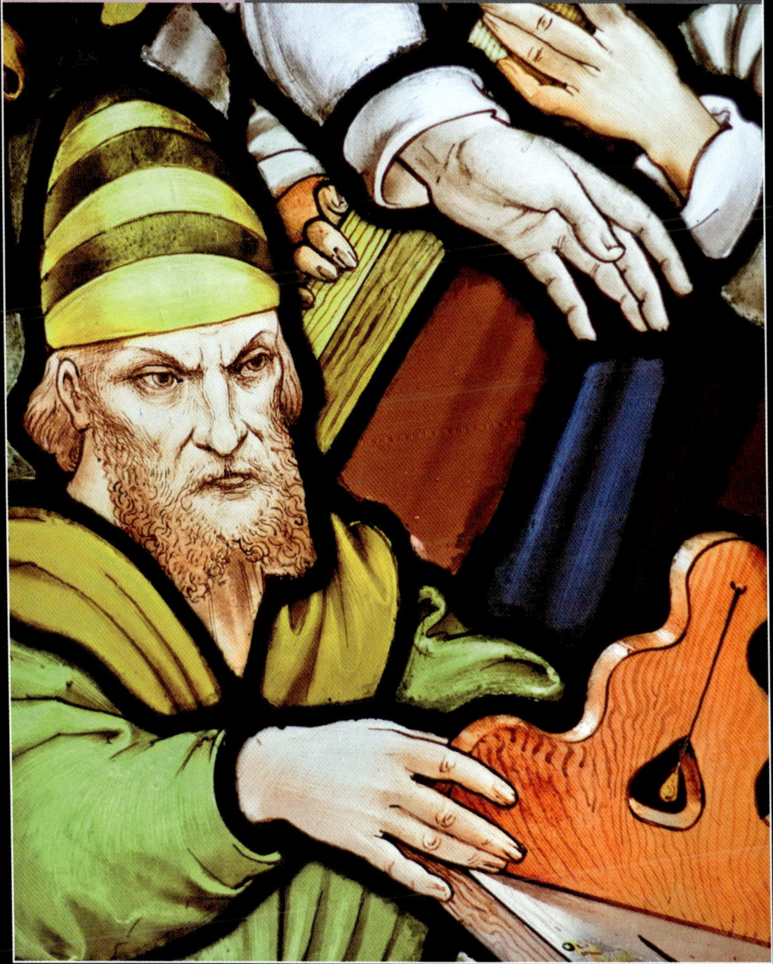

Music and sporting events

As with museums and art galleries, there are often restrictions on using cameras at music and sporting events. The first task is therefore to make sure that you can actually use you camera. The larger the venue, the less likely it is that photography will be allowed. For this reason it's often easier to shoot at smaller events, when amateurs or semi-professionals are performing. Another benefit of a smaller event is that it's easier to get close to the performers, reducing the need to use longer lenses.

At pop-music events lighting is often part of the show, and the intensity, direction, and color of the light can vary rapidly. This makes for an exciting evening for the audience, but will make your life as a photographer more difficult. The first practical problem to overcome is determining the correct exposure. The most accurate way is to use the spot meter facility on your camera and meter from one of the performers. Fire a test shot and check the histogram. If the performer was under a spotlight the background will be dark and the shadow details will probably be clipped, but this is relatively unimportant; the key is assessing the histogram to see if the performer is well exposed. Adjust the exposure if necessary and use your new exposure as the base from which to work for the rest of the event.

Tip

Flash isn't usually very useful for music and sporting events, as it has such a limited range. Even if it is viable, its use can destroy the atmosphere of the vibrant stage lighting.

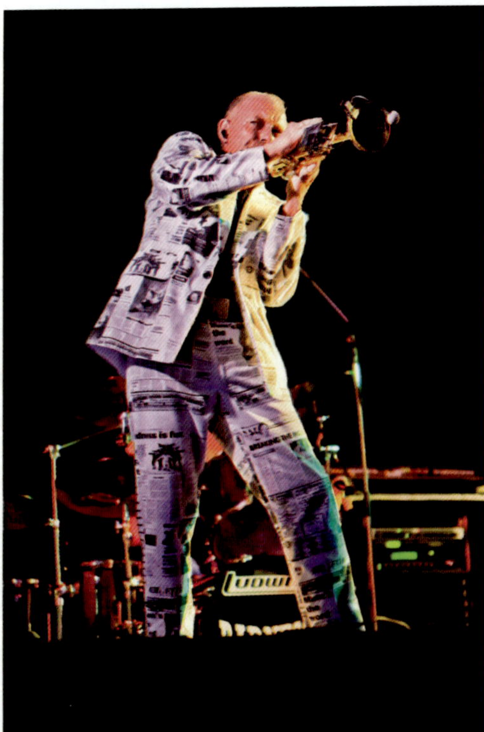

SPOTLIT

This musician was under a spotlight. The dark background would have fooled the camera's evaluative metering pattern into overexposing, but spot metering from the musician gave me a more accurate exposure.

Canon EOS 5D, 100mm lens, 1/100 sec. at f/2.8, ISO 1600

Although spotlights or floodlights can appear bright, you may still find that maximum aperture and/or a slow shutter speed is required for a correct exposure. If the performers or athletes are moving about, a slow shutter speed will result in motion blur, meaning there is often little choice but to increase the ISO setting. To shoot the image on the opposite page I set the ISO to 1600, partially to avoid camera shake, but mainly to make sure that the boisterous performer was captured as sharply as possible.

Noise can be a problem at higher ISO settings, but fortunately this will often work in your favor: a gritty image suits some performers and can actually add to the atmosphere of the piece. Converting to black and white in post-production is another effective approach to this kind of photography, with high levels of contrast and grain in an image arguably suiting black-and-white imagery more than color.

The color temperature of the lights will also vary from venue to venue: metal halide lamps used in floodlighting are relatively cool and using a daylight white balance will often give perfectly acceptable results. Lighting at music events can be a variety of colors, but a good start point is to use your camera's tungsten white balance setting initially, and refine this in post-production.

> ***Tip***
> *A prime lens with a large maximum aperture is very useful for music and sports photography.*

BLACK & WHITE
Shooting in Raw makes it easier to control white balance and apply processing effects, such as converting your images to black and white.

Canon EOS 5D, 200mm lens, 1/250 sec. at f/2.8, ISO 3200

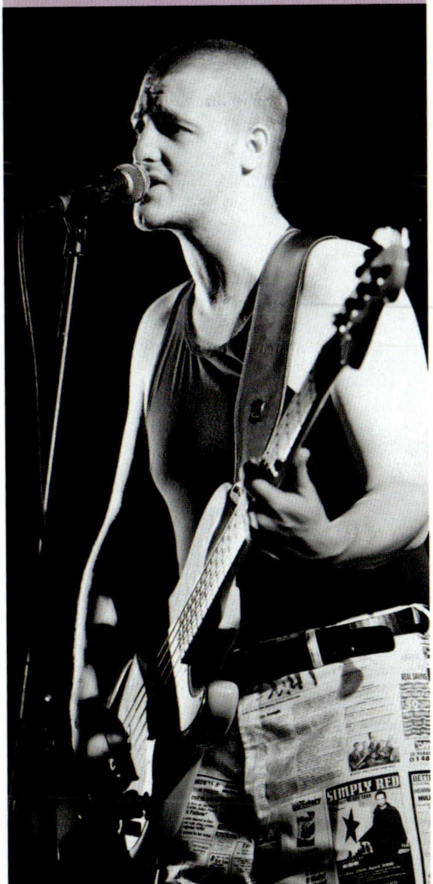

Look for interesting, and often overlooked details when you are photographing in museums and art galleries. This sculpture was only about 12 inches (30cm) high, so I had to move in close to fill the frame and exclude a distracting background. Because I was so close and using a large aperture, I focused precisely on the face of the figure in front as I knew depth of field would be minimal.

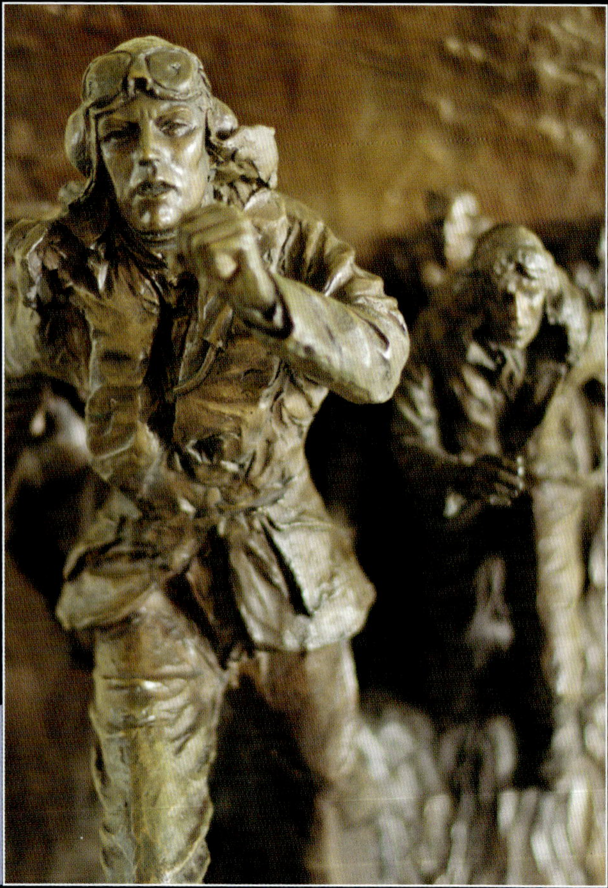

Camera: Canon EOS 7D
Lens: 50mm lens
Exposure: 1/60 sec. at f/1.4
ISO: 200

Light

I prefer to shoot interiors when the light outside is soft, so that any windows in the shot aren't overexposed. However, when time is limited this isn't always possible. For this shot I bracketed the exposure so that highlight detail was retained in one shot and shadow detail in another, with the correct exposure in the middle. The images were then merged using Lightroom and the Enfuse exposure blending plug-in.

Camera: Canon EOS 7D
Lens: 10–22mm lens (at 22mm)
Exposure: Three exposures (1/10 sec., 1/5 sec., and 1/2 sec.) at f/11
ISO: 400

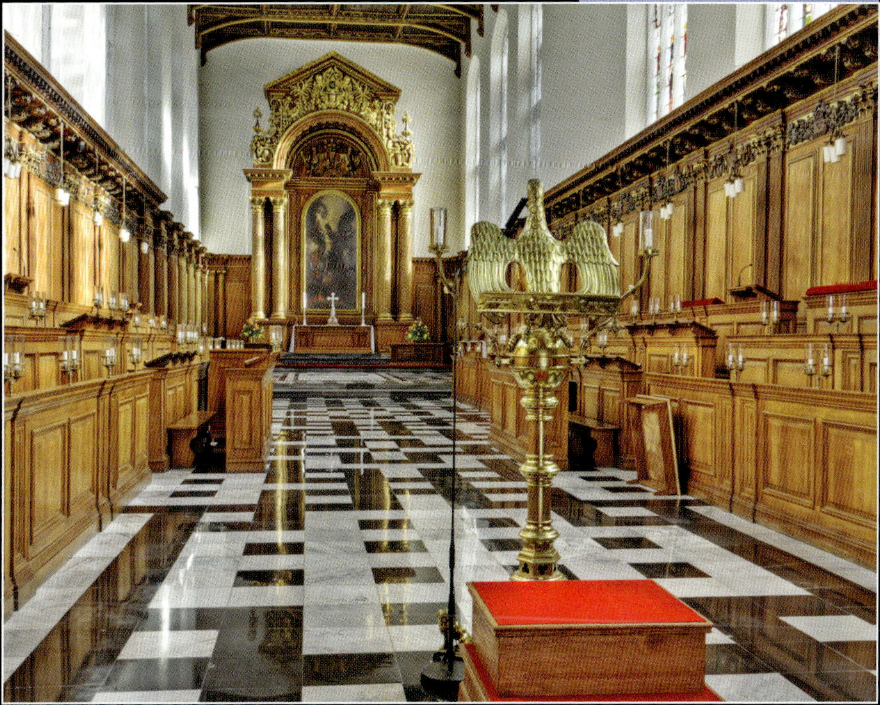

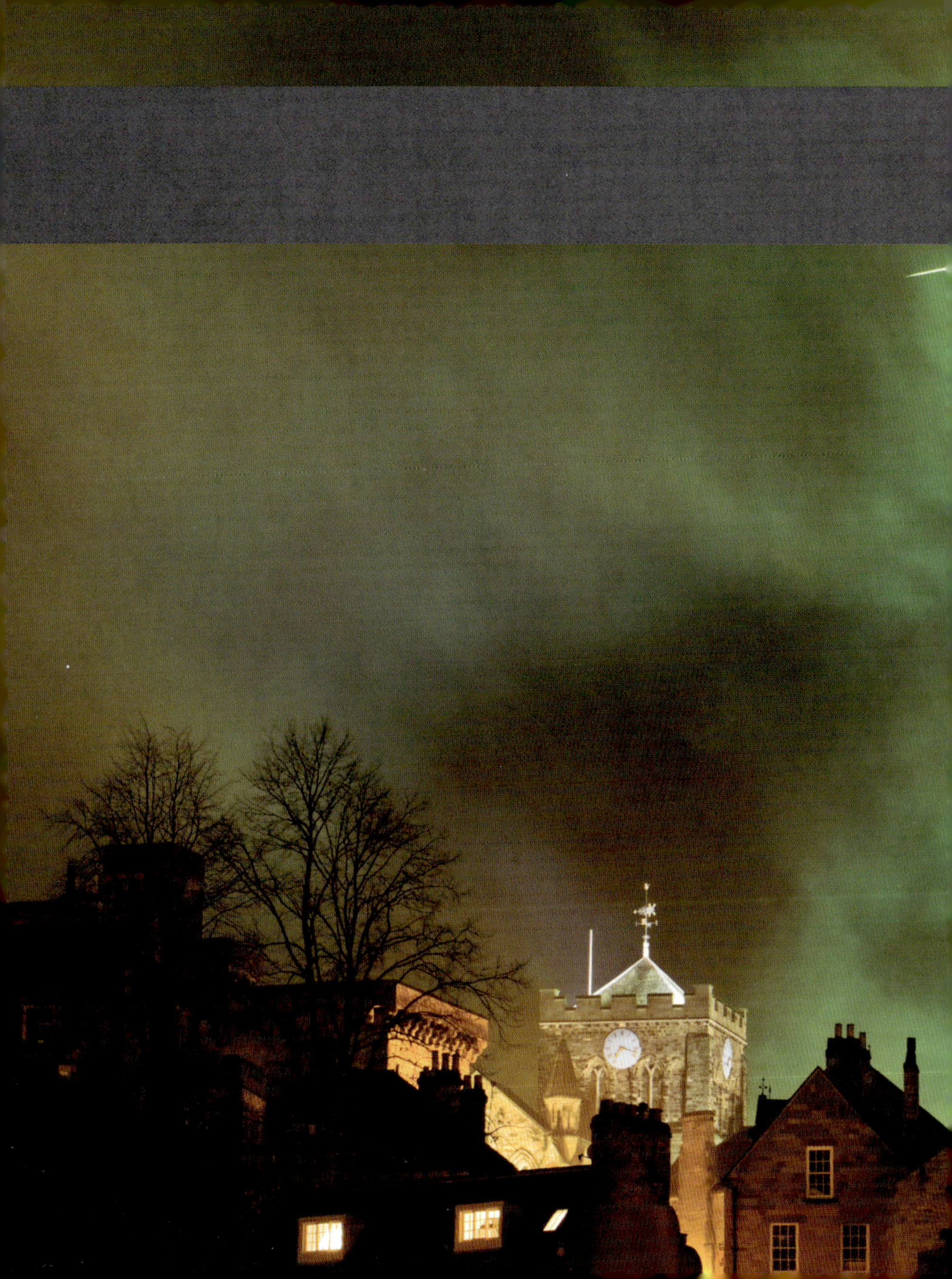

CHAPTER 7 SPECIAL SUBJECTS

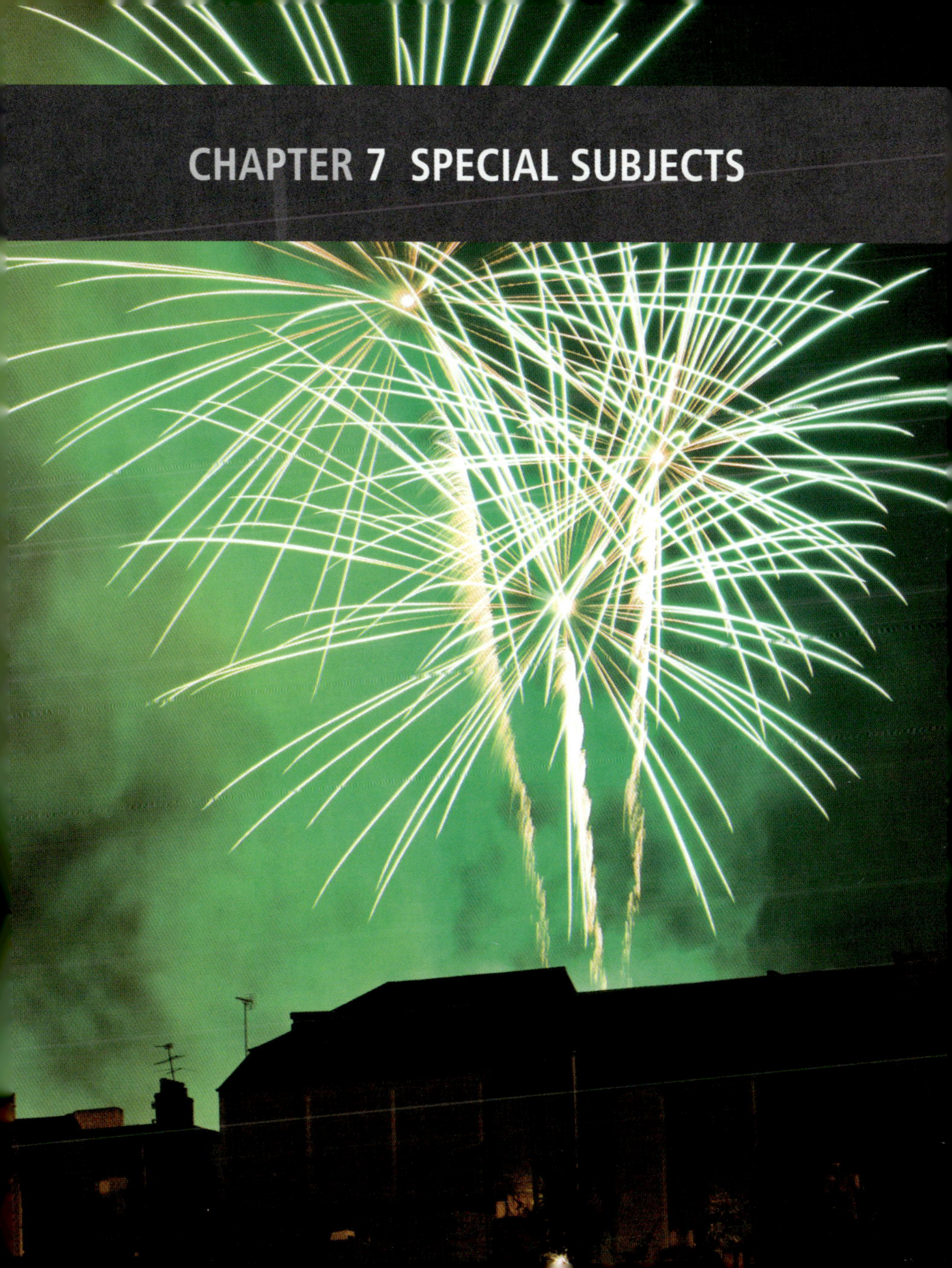

Introduction

There always seems to be an odd sock in the drawer that matches no other: this chapter covers the "odd socks" of low light subjects.

Experimentation

The one big benefit of digital photography is that it is free once the equipment's been paid for. This makes it easier to justify experimentation. Low light photography, by its very nature, can be hit and miss at times, but there is almost no limit as to what can be achieved with low light photography. All it takes is imagination and a willingness to try new things. In fact, there is probably more scope for individual creativity than there is with more conventional photography.

This chapter is a guide to some of the techniques that I've used to make images in low light. However, it's not a definitive guide as there are still techniques that I've yet to try myself. That's the most exciting aspect of low light photography – there's always something new to try.

WET WEATHER OPTIONS
It is a good idea to have a "reserve list" of ideas for photographs that can be taken indoors when the weather is less clement.

Canon EOS 1Ds MkII, 100mm lens, 1/3 sec. at f/4, ISO 100

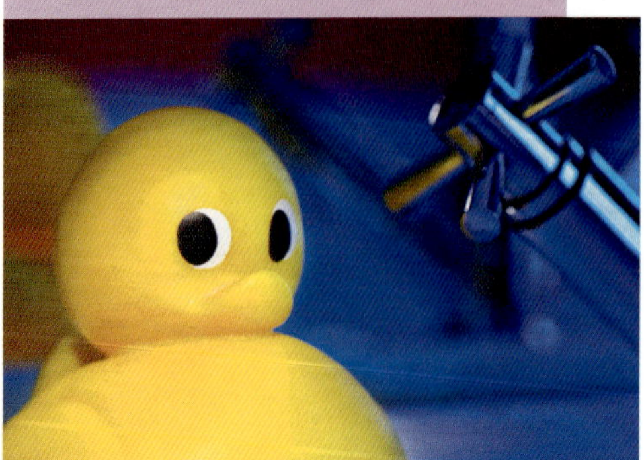

The story of a duck

Inspiration for low light photography can come from anywhere. Bad weather can disrupt photography plans, and in these situations I often prowl around the house looking for little projects to set up and experiment with. It's amazing what can be done with ordinary household objects to create striking images.

The handsome duck on this page was shot in a semi-darkened room, illuminated by torchlight. White balance was set to tungsten, turning what daylight there was a very cool blue.

FIREWORKS *(Opposite)*
Fireworks are a naturally photogenic subject, and I never miss an opportunity to shoot them.

Canon EOS 1Ds MkII, 50mm lens, 8 sec. at f/11, ISO 800

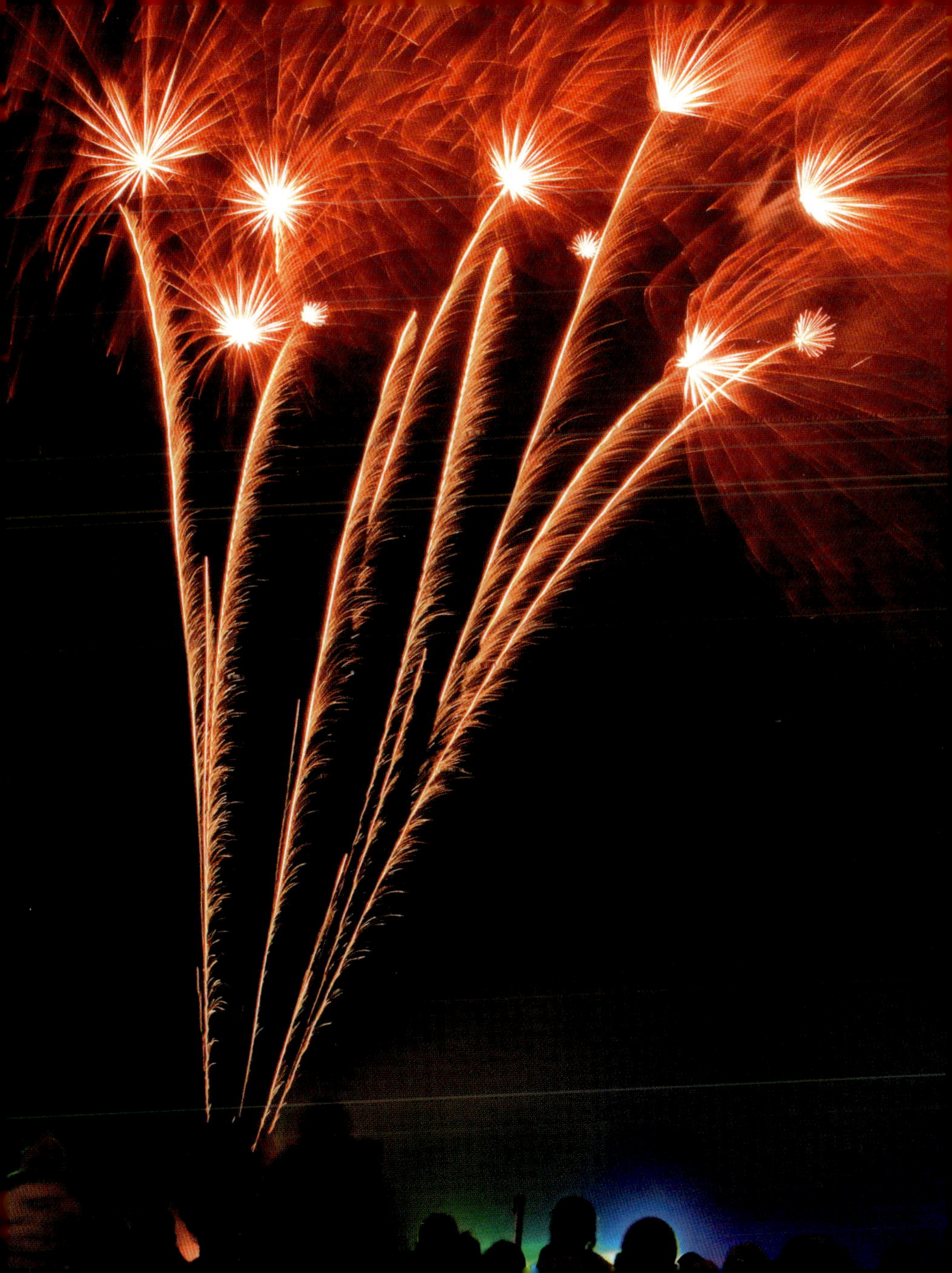

The night sky

The hours of darkness are when low light photography is at its most extreme. However, even on moonless nights, there is still enough light to create images.

Stars

There are approximately 6000 stars visible to the unaided eye, but it's impossible to see all of them in one go, as only a limited portion of the sky is viewable at any particular point in time. There are also stars that are seen only in the northern or southern hemispheres, and the number of stars visible also depends on ambient lighting conditions: light pollution drastically reduces the number of stars that can be seen in urban areas. Far more stars can be seen in the countryside, away from sources of light.

However, the number of stars that can be recorded by a camera is potentially far greater than 6000. This is because using a long shutter speed will allow light from fainter stars to build up to a point where an image is formed. Unfortunately this creates another problem—the earth rotates and, as it does so, the stars appear to move across the sky. This means that when a long shutter speed is used, stars won't be recorded as points of light, but as a trail.

Astronomers avoid this by using telescopes that are fitted with tracking mounts that move to match the rotation of the earth, keeping the stars in the same position within the telescope's field of view so that they can be recorded as sharp points of light.

Working smarter...

Apple iOS: *Planets 3.1*

Android: *Google Sky Map*

These apps allow you to explore the night sky, including moon phases.

STREAKS

The longer the focal length you use, the shorter the time it takes stars to appear as trails in your image.

Canon EOS 7D, 70–200mm lens (at 200mm, image cropped), 30 sec. at f/4, ISO 400

Shooting stars

What you need: Tripod, fully charged batteries, remote release.

1) Choose a night with settled weather and clear skies. A moonless night away from urban lighting will make the sky appear blacker in the final image.

2) Arrive at your chosen location before total darkness so you can see what you're doing when setting up.

3) Choose your composition. If you're using a wide-angle lens, pick something recognizable in the landscape that would make a good silhouette—this will help to give your image a sense of scale.

4) Switch your camera to manual focus and focus at ∞ (infinity).

5) The ISO of your camera will need to be set high to capture as much light as possible in as short a time as possible. But don't set the ISO so high that stars are lost in any resulting noise. Experiment with your camera to find the optimum ISO value.

6) Switch the camera to Manual and set the widest aperture. The shutter speed will depend on the aperture, the ISO, and the focal length of the lens. Try a series of shots in the range 1/4–4 sec. to see what works best for your camera and lens combination.

7) Make an exposure using the remote release to fire the trigger.

> **Note**
>
> *No matter how long a lens, or how powerful a telescope you use, stars will only ever be seen (or recorded) as points of light. If a star in an image is recorded as a disk, this is most likely the result of a focusing error—or it is one of the planets in the solar system.*

SHARP

By increasing the ISO I was able to reduce the length of the shutter speed to record the stars as sharp points of light.

Canon EOS 7D, 70–200mm lens (at 200mm, image cropped), 3.2 sec. at f/4, ISO 6400

Star trails

Stars rotate around an imaginary point in the sky known as the celestial pole. In the northern hemisphere, the Pole Star (or Polaris) is close to, but not exactly at, the northern celestial pole. Sigma Octantis is the equivalent in the Southern hemisphere, but as it is not a particularly bright star, it is often difficult to locate.

Creating star trails involves exposing an image for a lengthy period of time so that as the stars move across the sky they are recorded as arcs of light—the longer the shutter speed, the longer the arc. If you were able to expose the image for a full twenty-four hours, the arcs would eventually form a perfect circle as the stars returned to their start point.

Film is ideally suited to the creation of star trails, simply because film cameras tend to be less battery dependant and film itself is not affected by lengthy exposures (other than by reciprocity law failure). Digital cameras, on the other hand, are heavily reliant on their batteries, and noise can become a problem with exposures of 60 seconds or more. Blending (or stacking) a series of shorter exposures is one solution to these problems, as outlined on p162.

> ***Tip***
>
> *If your camera has a viewfinder curtain close it to prevent light leakage back into the camera.*
>
> *The direction that you point your camera in will determine how the star trails arc across your image. Facing your local celestial pole will produce circular arcs that spin around that point. Facing east or west will create a more subtle effect.*

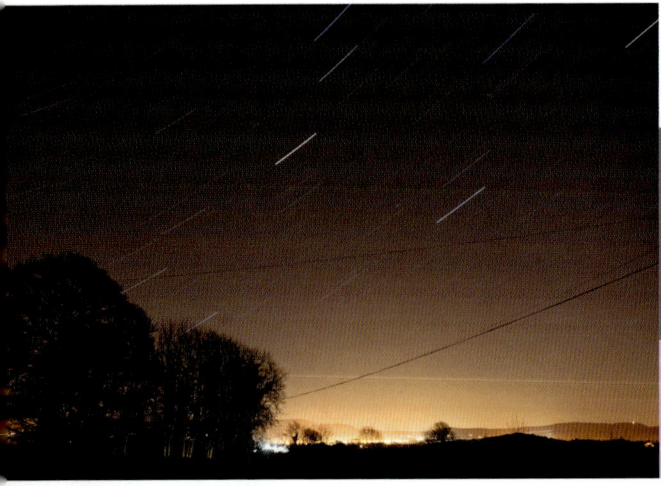

LIGHT POLLUTION
The closer you are to urban areas, the more color and light will be added to the sky by street lighting.

Canon EOS 1Ds MkII, 17–40mm lens (at 24mm), 17 min. at f/4, ISO 200

Shooting star trails

What you need: Tripod, fully charged batteries, remote release, stopwatch.

1) Follow **Shooting stars** steps 1–4, as outlined on page 159.

2) Choose your lens. I usually use a wide-angle lens as they create more dramatically circular star trail arcs in the final image.

3) Set the camera to Bulb mode and, depending on the base ISO of your camera (or the film speed), set the aperture to f/2.8 (ISO 100) or f/4 (ISO 200). If you use a higher ISO you will record fainter stars during the exposure, but also increase the amount of noise or grain in the picture.

4) Lock the shutter open using the remote release and start your stopwatch. The longer you lock the shutter open the longer the star trails will be. Remember that one hour equals 1/24 of a circle (or 15 degrees of rotation), so 12 hours would result in a semi-circular set of star trails.

5) Release the shutter after the desired length of time.

Note

If you're shooting digitally, your camera might apply Long Exposure Noise Reduction after the first exposure (if this option is set). This will take the same length of time as the original exposure. Some cameras will not allow you to shoot during this process, so if you wish to carry on shooting immediately after creating your star trail image, switch Long Exposure Noise Reduction off before you begin.

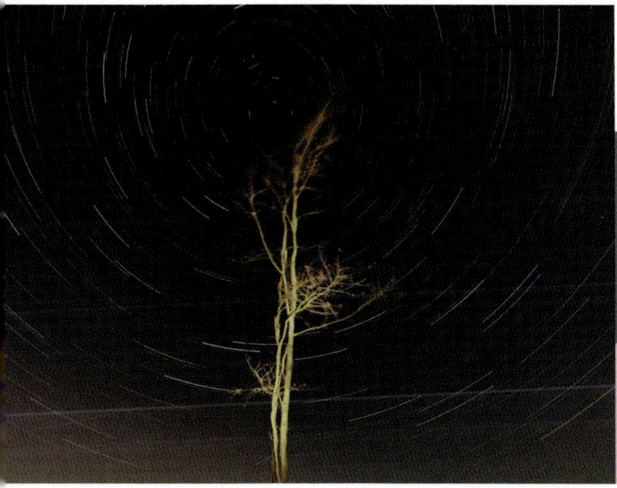

POLE STAR
For this image I pointed the camera north, toward the Pole Star. The tree in the foreground was lit using the "painting with light" technique.

Canon EOS 7D, 10–22mm lens (at 12mm), 110 stacked images, 30 sec. at f/4, ISO 200

Stacking images

Shooting a number of images of the night sky and then blending them in post-production can also create star trails. This technique is ideally suited to overcoming the limitations of digital cameras when it comes to long exposures. It is possible to stack images using Adobe Photoshop's layer functions, but a better solution is to use software designed specifically for the purpose, such as StarStaX.

What you'll need: Tripod, fully charged batteries, remote release with intervalometer function.

1) Follow **Shooting stars** steps 1–4 as outlined on page 159.

2) Set your camera's drive mode to Continuous, rather than Single Shot.

3) Set the camera to Manual exposure mode, and depending on the base ISO of your camera, set the aperture to f/2.8 (ISO 100) or f/4 (ISO 200) and the shutter speed to 30 sec. If you use a higher ISO you will record fainter stars during each exposure, but increase the amount of noise in the final stacked image.

4) Set the intervalometer on your remote release to 31 seconds (this will give your camera one second to ready itself to fire the next shot after each exposure).

Tips

Turn off Long Exposure Noise Reduction before you begin shooting.

Experiment with longer exposures—if you are confident that your camera is capable of exposures longer than 30 seconds without a detrimental increase in noise, adjust the shutter speed and intervalometer on your remote release accordingly.

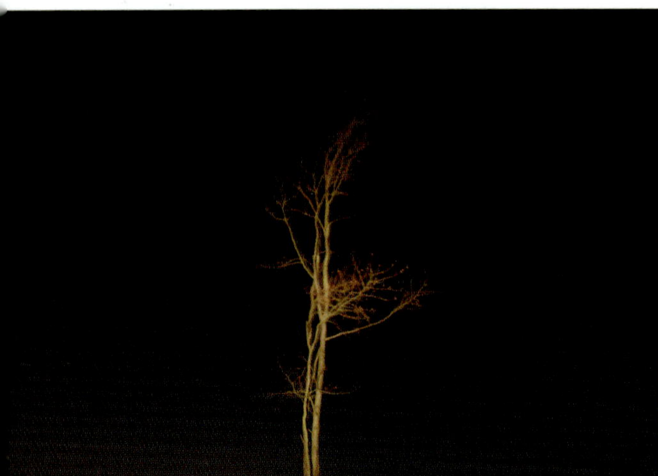

POLE STAR
The first shot from the sequence of 110 shots that were "stacked" to create the image on the previous page.

Canon EOS 7D, 10–22mm lens (at 12mm), 30 sec. at f/4, ISO 200

5) Set the number of shots required on your remote release. Two shots will equal one minute's worth of exposure, four shots would be two minutes, and so on.

6) Start exposing and wait until the sequence has completed.

Once you have your completed sequence imported onto your computer, run your chosen stacking software to assemble the final image.

Stacking software

There are currently two star trail stacking programs available online: StarStaX and Startrails. StarStaX is available for Windows, Mac, and Linux operating systems *(www.markus-enzweiler.de/software/software.html)*, while Startrails is Windows only *(www.startrails.de/html/software.html)*.

Both programs are freeware and work in a similar way. Start by exporting all the images that need stacking into a separate folder as JPEGs (if the images you originally shot are Raw files you'll need to convert them first). Once you've launched the star stacking software, navigate to the folder you've just created and select all the images. Click on the button that starts the stacking process and wait until the stacked image is generated. When it's ready, select your output folder, save the image, and exit the software.

Note

Startrails can be used to generate time-lapse videos from a sequence of JPEGs.

STARSTAX
Creating a stacked star trail using StarStaX.

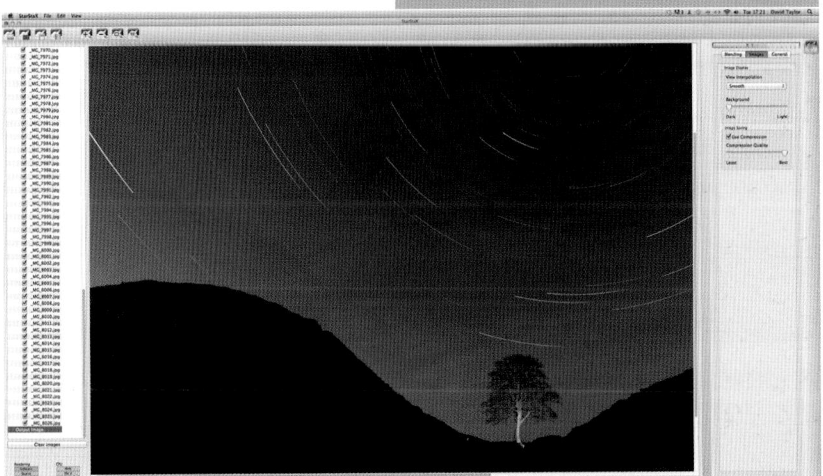

The moon

The moon, as with the stars, moves across the night sky. The distance it moves is approximately its own diameter every two minutes. This means that even an exposure of a second will result in an unsharp moon, and as with stars, the longer the focal length, the greater the potential for lack of sharpness. Fortunately, the moon is relatively bright, and with a reasonably fast film or medium ISO setting on your camera, it is possible to set a sufficiently fast shutter speed to avoid this problem.

There are many variables that affect the exposure settings you would use, including the height of the moon in the sky and the phase of the moon. When the moon is full and the sky is black, for example, try setting the ISO to 400 and the shutter speed and aperture to 1/1000 sec. and f/8 respectively. When the moon is half full (referred to as either the first or last quarter, depending on whether the moon is waxing or waning) reduce the shutter speed to 1/250 sec. When the moon is a thin crescent, the shutter speed should be slower still, and 1/60 sec. would be a good starting point.

However, these exposure settings are only approximate and it's a good idea to bracket. These settings will also only be correct for the moon, so any landscape details will only be exposed correctly if the ambient light is high enough to illuminate them sufficiently.

Note

Metering the entire night sky will tend to cause your exposure meter to overexpose. If your camera has a spot meter function, use this to determine the exposure from the moon, ignoring the sky around it.

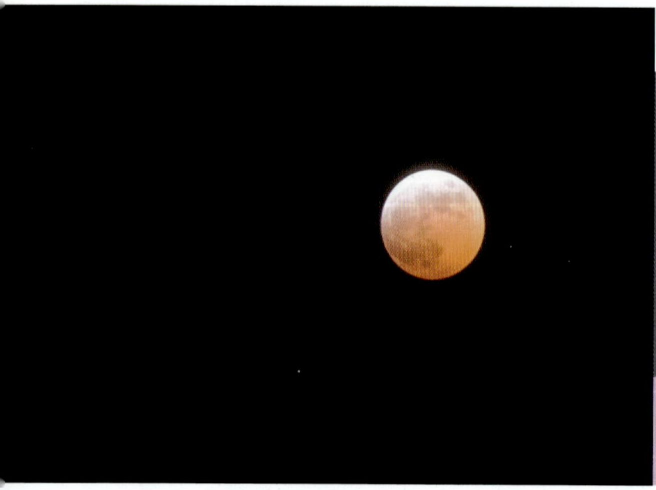

ECLIPSE
Lunar eclipses occur at least twice a year and are caused by the earth stopping light from the sun reaching the moon—this only occurs when the moon is full. To find out when lunar eclipses will occur visit eclipse.gsfc.nasa.gov/lunar.html

Canon EOS 5D, 400mm lens, 1/4 sec. at f/5.6, ISO 1250

Moon phases

Over the course of 28 days, the moon changes its appearance. At the start of the lunar cycle the moon is full: the whole face of the moon is lit and therefore visible. From full, the moon wanes, and mid-way through the 28-day cycle the moon is "new"—the face of the moon is unlit and invisible in the night sky. From new, the moon waxes, until on day 28 the moon is full once more and the cycle starts over.

During the different phases of the cycle the moon rises and sets at different times of the night and day, as detailed in the grid below. Photographing the moon during the times when it is visible during the day can be just as effective as shooting it at night, but in the days before the moon is full it rises as the sun is setting. This means that there will be sufficient ambient light for landscape details if you wish to include them in a composition with the moon. However, the moon is more interesting visually when waxing or waning as craters and other surface details along the shadow boundary are better defined.

Moon Phase		Rises	Sets
Full	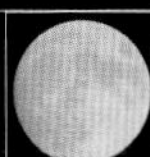	Sunset	Sunrise
Waning gibbous	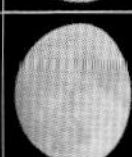	Post-sunset	Post-sunrise
Last quarter	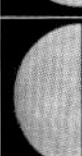	Midnight	Midday
Waning crescent	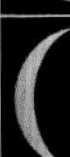	Pre-sunrise	Late-afternoon
New moon		Sunrise	Sunset
Waxing crescent		Post-sunrise	Post-sunset
First quarter	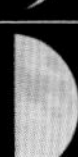	Midday	Midnight
Waxing gibbous	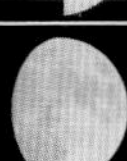	Late-afternoon	Pre-sunrise

Candles

Candles have a very attractive warm light that will give an image a romantic glow.

Warmth

With most forms of illumination, the first task is to adjust the white balance to produce a natural-looking image. Candles are different though, as it's the very warmth of the light that is appealing. Some experimentation is required, but I often leave the camera set to Daylight white balance to avoid cooling the warmth of the candlelight down (shooting Raw means this can be adjusted later if necessary).

Candlelight is a very weak light in comparison to even the lowest wattage household light. If you are using candlelight to illuminate another object in your image, the other object will need to be reasonably close to the candle to be illuminated adequately. It's a good idea to show the candle in the image if it's illuminating another object, but there's no reason you couldn't have other candles out of the image area to provide extra illumination.

Candlelight is a point light source, so contrast will be high, but in many ways this is no bad thing—the light is good for creating mood and atmosphere, and deep shadows only add to the effect. When metering, use your camera's spot meter to meter from the illuminated areas of your subject, or from the stem of the candle itself, just below the flame. The flame will probably cause clipping in the image's histogram, but some clipping will be unavoidable, especially if you want other areas of the image to be exposed adequately.

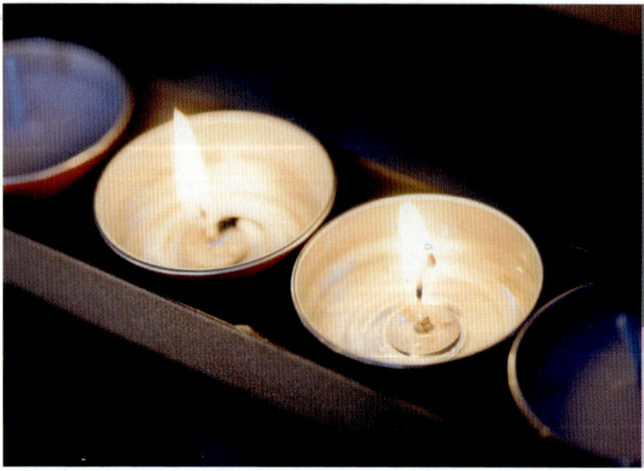

ALONE
Candles make attractive subjects in their own right. Fill the image space for maximum impact.

Canon EOS 5D, 100mm lens, 1/60 sec. at f/3.2, ISO 800

Camera: Canon EOS 7D
Lens: 70–200mm lens (at 100mm)
Exposure: 2 sec. at f/4
ISO: 100

Churches are a great place to photograph candles. Votive candles are often placed in front of painted panels, which can create an attractive image.

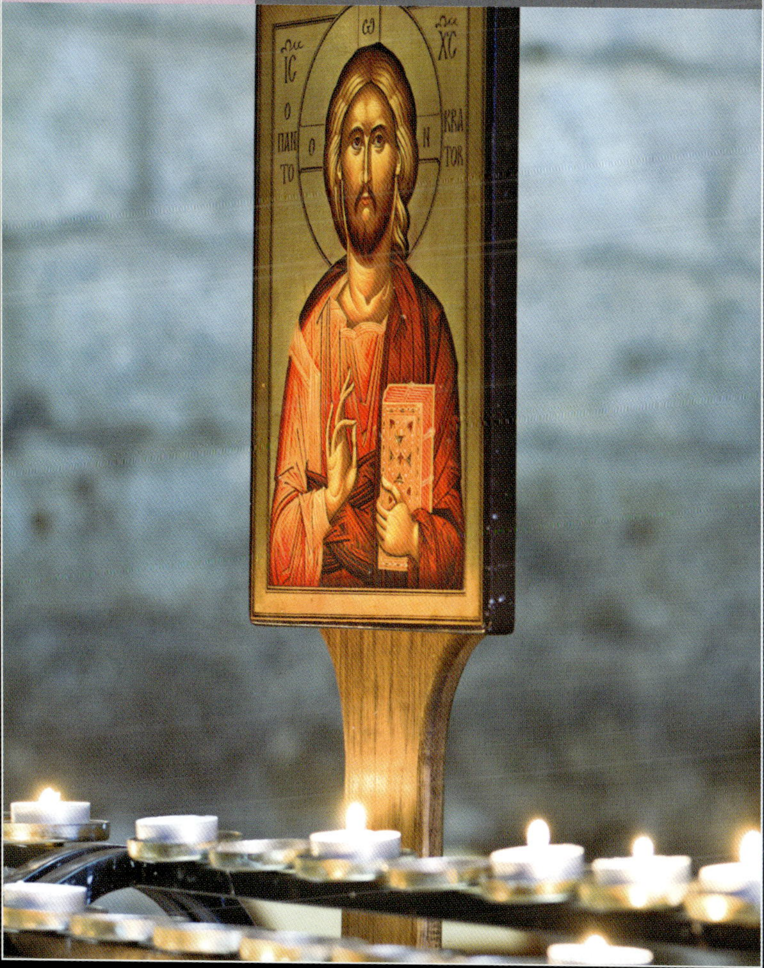

Bonfires and fireworks

Bonfires and fireworks are very photogenic subjects, and if there's a public holiday or anniversary there's bound to be one or the other—often both.

Flame

There's something pleasingly primitive about a roaring fire, particularly one outdoors on a frosty evening. There are several approaches to take when photographing bonfires. The first is close ups of the flames and later, the embers. Use a longer lens to fill the image frame without getting dangerously close. If you're handholding your camera, an image-stabilized lens is ideal, although if the fire is particularly large and bright it's often possible to use a relatively fast shutter speed. To capture the shape of the flames use a shutter speed between 1/250 sec. and 1/1000 sec., but if your camera is on a tripod, experiment with slower shutter speeds to create a more ethereal effect.

Another way to shoot bonfires is when there are people between you and the fire. Because of the contrast range, the people will be silhouetted against the flames, and this combination of people and fire is a good way to show the scale of the fire itself. Focus on the person, rather than the fire behind; it won't matter too much if the fire is out of focus as this will make for quite a striking image.

Your camera's light meter will probably be fooled by the differences in light levels between the fire and the background, so apply positive exposure compensation of 1.5–2 stops if necessary. If you're unsure, bracket and check the histogram on your camera. Finally, be aware that bonfires have a very warm color temperature. You could adjust the white balance, but personally I prefer to use a Daylight preset to preserve the warmth and then adjust the white balance afterward if necessary.

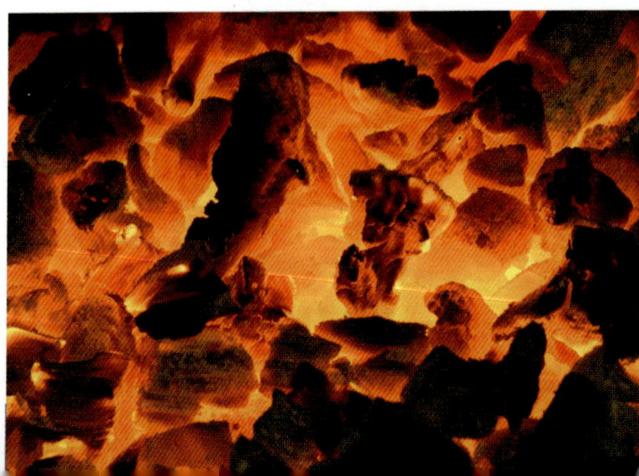

EMBERS
Once the fire (and the heat) has died down, getting in close to the embers can produce striking abstract images.

Canon EOS 5D, 100mm lens, 13 sec. at f/16, ISO 100

Camera: Canon EOS 7D
Lens: 17–40mm lens
(at 40mm)
Exposure: 1/800 sec. at f/4
ISO: 800

Fast shutter speeds are needed to freeze the flames and individual sparks.

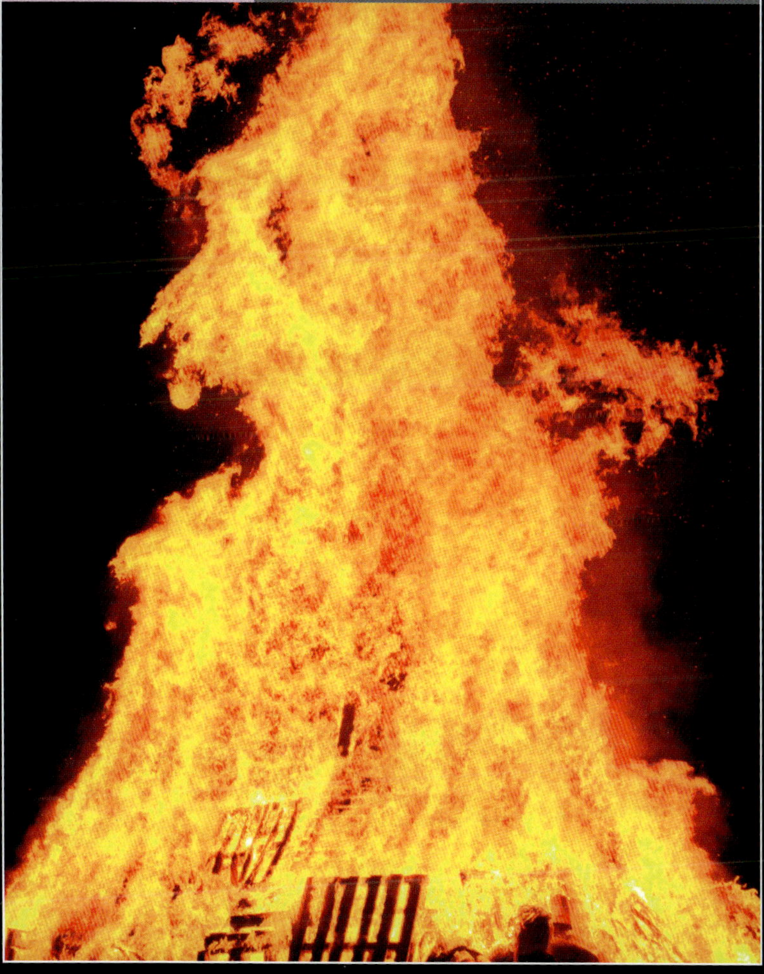

Fireworks

Firework displays are a popular photographic subject, although to get the best out of the opportunity it pays to prepare in advance. If you know the location of the display try to visit when it's light, to allow you time to look around for the best vantage point. This is often not the place where the fireworks will be set off, but the top of a hill or high building some distance from the display area. By gaining height you will be looking across at the fireworks rather than up at them. Keeping back from the main event area will also lessen the chances of you or your camera being knocked over by other spectators.

On the evening of the display, you will need to mount your camera on a tripod. A remote release is useful so that the shutter can be fired without the camera being touched, and it will

> ***Tip***
>
> *Switch to manual focus and focus at ∞.*

Canon EOS 1Ds MkII, 17–40mm lens (at 20mm), 1/2 sec. at f/13, ISO 800

ECLIPSE

I broke my own rules with this shot and set my camera and tripod up within the crowd of spectators. Fortunately I had an assistant who helped make sure that no one tripped over my tripod.

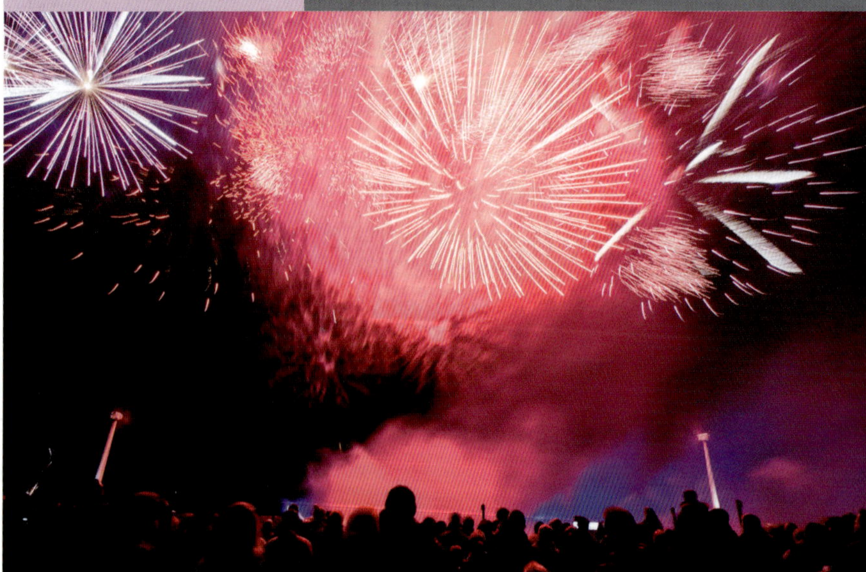

also allow you to watch the display without looking through the camera's viewfinder.

Choosing the right lens can be tricky. If there is any wind this can affect the way that the fireworks drift, so I usually start with a wide-angle lens to make sure that I'm capturing the entire display and then gradually zoom in over the course of the display for a tighter, more abstract view of the fireworks.

If the display is a large, organized event there will usually be a regular stream of fireworks, so after a while it's often possible to anticipate when to fire the shutter. The shutter speed you use will depend on the ISO setting, but generally fireworks are more effectively recorded with shutter speeds of 1 sec. or longer. So that you don't miss anything, switch off Long Exposure Noise Reduction—it's frustrating if you have to wait for your camera to process an image before you can shoot again! Displays often end in a noisy and colorful climax, so if you know the approximate length of the display, keep an eye on the time and be ready for the final moments.

Smaller displays are often more difficult to photograph as there are often longer gaps between individual fireworks. One solution is to set your camera to Bulb and lock the shutter open. After a firework has exploded carefully cover the front of the lens with a piece of black card and remove it when you hear the next one being fired. Using this method will also allow you to build up the number of fireworks recorded within the same image. After a minute or so, you can release the shutter and review your image.

Note

Many compact cameras, and some digital SLRs, have a "firework" mode. This sets the camera so that longer shutter speeds are used. The downside is that these modes typically force you to use JPEG rather than Raw.

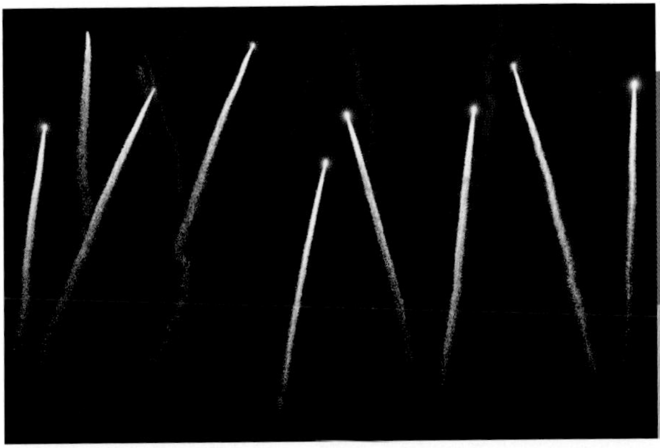

CLOSER
Once I'm confident that I know where fireworks will appear in the sky I often switch to a telephoto lens and record firework close-ups.

Canon EOS 1Ds MkII, 100mm lens, 1/50 sec. at f/11, ISO 800

Camera: Canon EOS 1Ds MkII
Lens: 200mm lens
Exposure: 1/15 sec. at f/7.1
ISO: 100

MOONRISE

This scene was shot at mid-summer on the day before the moon was full. This meant that there was still enough ambient light to record the scene with a reasonably fast shutter speed and for the castle to stand out against the dusk sky.

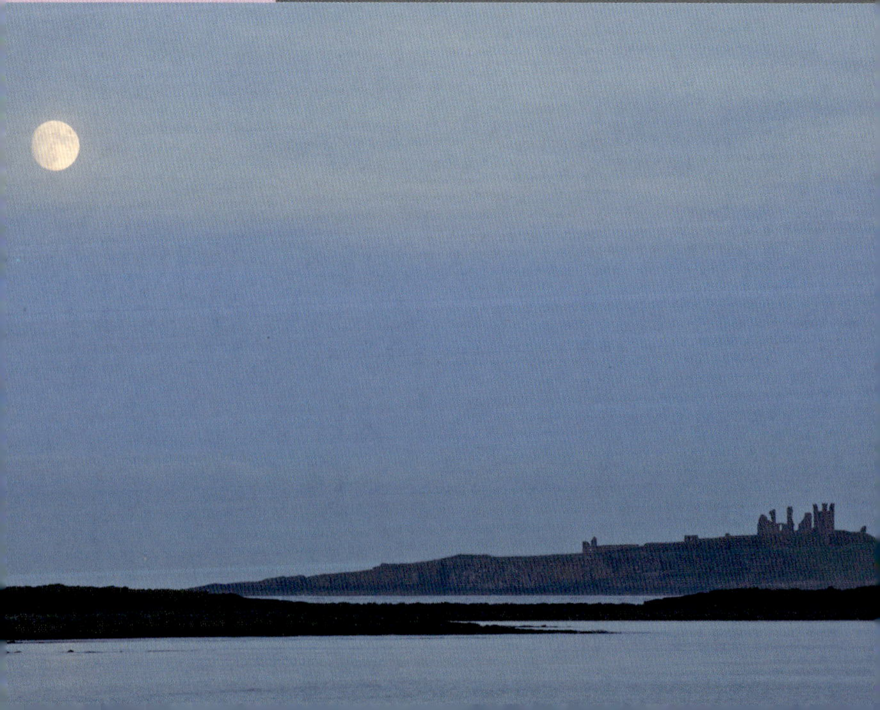

Camera: Canon EOS 1Ds MkII
Lens: 100mm lens
Exposure: 15 sec. at f/6.3
ISO: 100

HEAT

Flames are hot, so the further you are from them the safer you and your camera will be. For this image I used a telephoto lens so that I could fill the frame without getting too close to the flames.

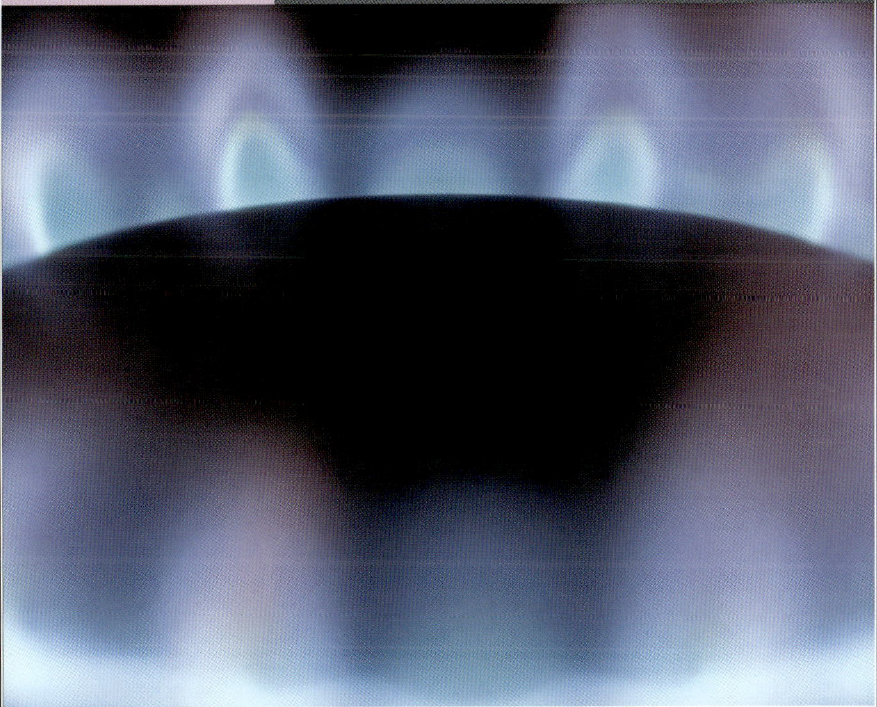

Silhouettes

When your subject is between your camera and the main light source, the result—if the exposure is set for the background—will be that your subject recorded as a silhouette.

Ideally, the subject for a silhouette should be a bold, easily-recognizable shape. Anything with a complex or ambiguous shape will require too much thought from anyone who looks at the resulting image later. Try to make sure there is empty space around your subject and that other elements of the scene don't intrude or overlap. If you're creating a silhouette of a person, a profile is easier to recognize than a person facing toward (or away from) the camera.

The focus should be set for the subject, but the exposure you use should be correct for the background. Use your camera's spot meter to measure from an area of the background that roughly corresponds to a midtone (in the image on the opposite page this was the blue area in the top right quarter of the sky). Compose your shot, fire a test shot, and review the histogram. A "standard" exposure for a silhouette would show clipping on the left, which is to be expected as silhouettes are generally close to black. If the histogram is clipped on the right, use your camera's exposure compensation controls and apply negative compensation.

Tips

If your camera doesn't have a spot meter, you can use your zoom lens to effectively "spot meter" from a particular area. Zoom in, excluding the part of the image that you want silhouetted, take a meter reading, and set that as the exposure. Zoom back out to frame your composition.

Use your subject to hide the light source if possible. If the light source is the sun, don't look at it directly through your camera lens.

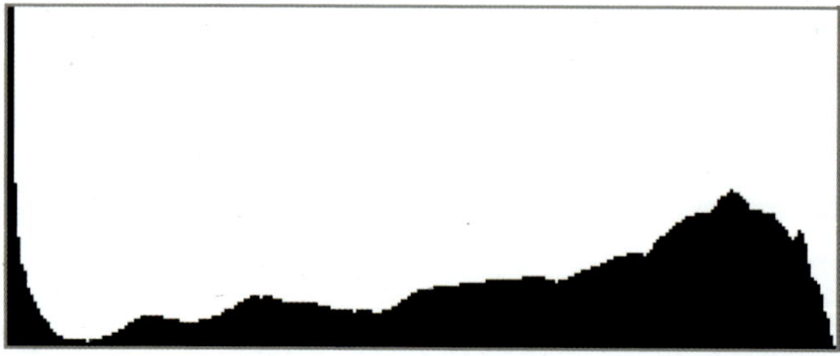

SKEWED
The histogram for the image on the opposite page. Note how the left edge is clipped.

Camera: Canon EOS 7D
Lens: 17–40mm lens (at 17mm)
Exposure: 1/15 sec. at f/16
ISO: 100

Silhouettes are most effective when your subject is easily recognizable, despite being stripped of its detail.

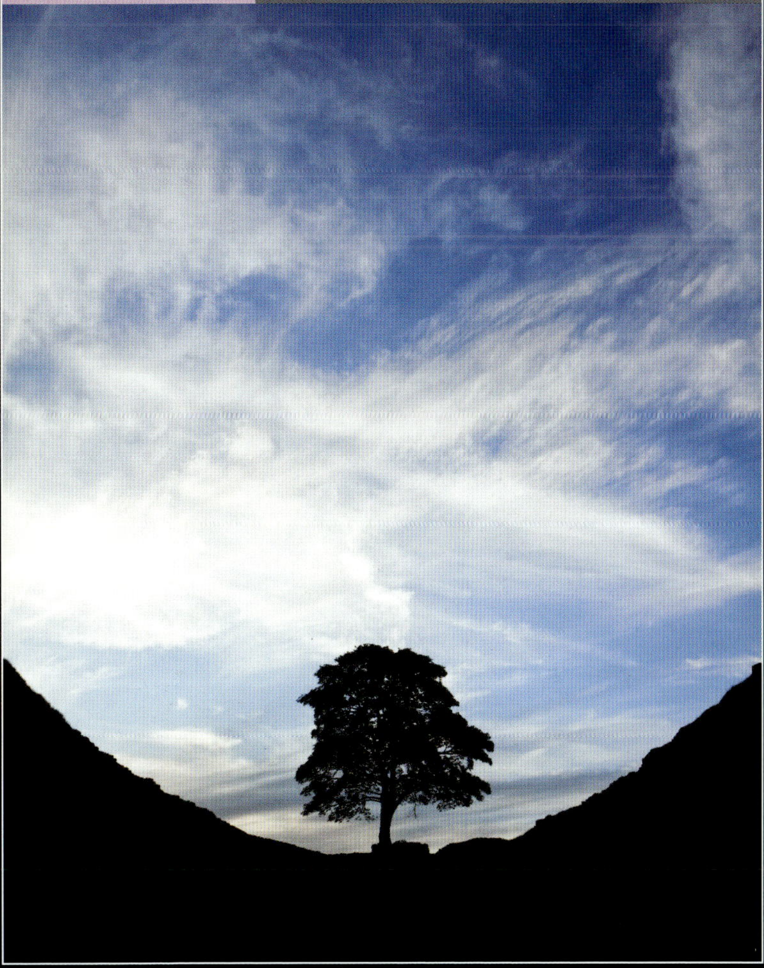

Painting with light

Not every photographic subject is conveniently floodlit, so sometimes you will have to provide your own light source. This can be in the form of a flash or even a handheld flashlight.

Painting with light is the technique of lighting a subject during a long exposure. This can be achieved either by using a handheld flash or with a suitably powerful flashlight.

It is worth noting that a camera flash and a flashlight have different color temperatures, with a flashlight being the warmer of the two. Which you use is partly down to esthetics, and partly down to practicality: flash works well when you are photographing larger subjects, as it's difficult to direct the light, whereas a flashlight is great for photographing more intimate subjects as you can light areas of a subject very specifically.

Painting with light: flash

What you need: Tripod, flash unit (preferably two), fully charged batteries for your camera and flash, remote release.

1) Arrive at your chosen location before dusk and select your composition. Your subject should be sufficiently close so that you can find your way between your camera and the subject quickly, but safely, once the shutter on your camera has been fired.

2) Attach the remote release to your camera and focus on the subject. If you use AF to do this, switch the lens to MF once focus has been achieved so that it doesn't shift.

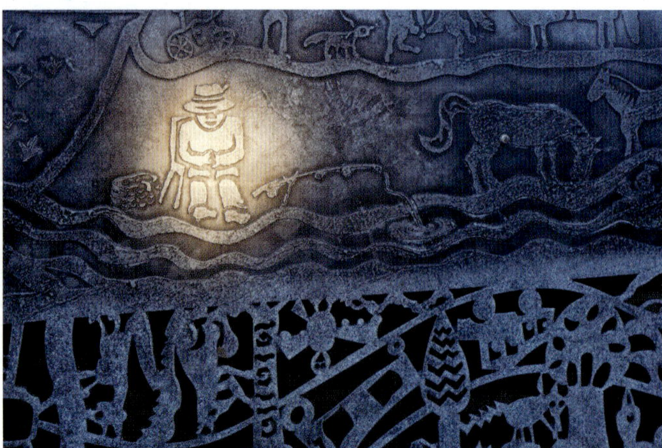

SMALL BRUSH STROKES
A flashlight can be used to pick out small details in your subject.

Canon EOS 1Ds MkII, 50mm, 1 min. at f/16, ISO 100

Camera: Canon EOS 7D
Lens: 10–22mm lens (at 14mm)
Exposure: 30 sec. at f/7.1
ISO: 100

A flashlight can be used to "paint" large areas of your image, as well as smaller sections.

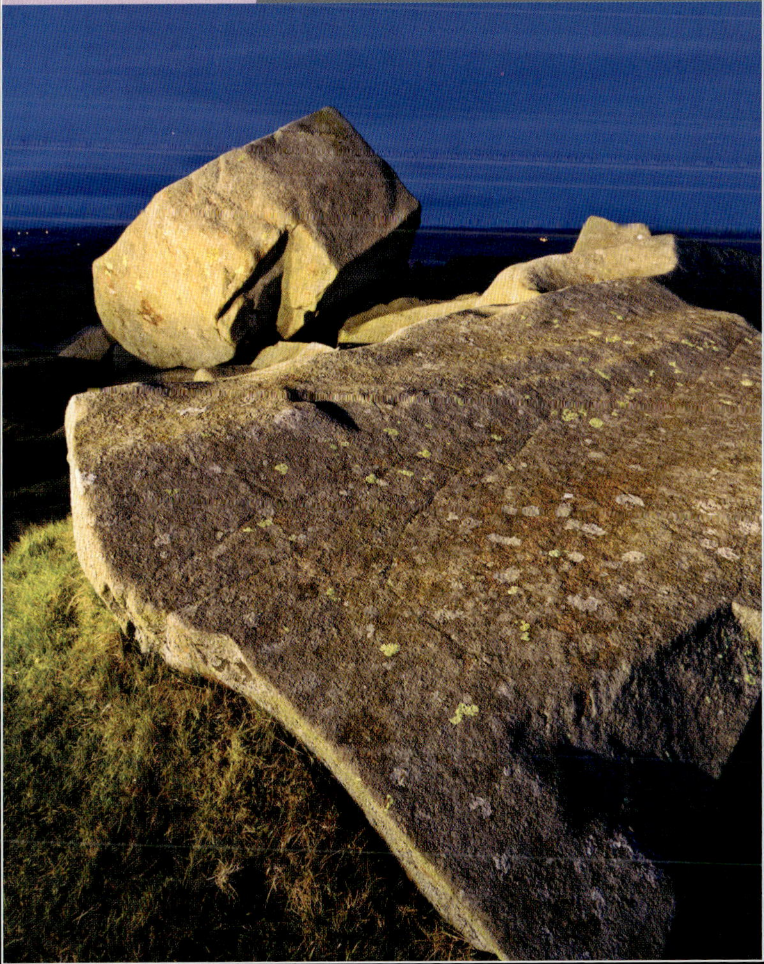

3) Set your camera to Bulb and the aperture to f/11. The ISO doesn't need to be high—the base ISO of your camera should be sufficient.

4) Wait until the ambient light levels are sufficiently low that the required shutter speed is roughly 2 minutes. Depending on whether you are facing east or west this is usually 30–40 minutes after sunset.

5) Lock the shutter open and walk quickly over to your subject, taking your flash(es) with you. Fire the flash using the test button, aiming it toward the subject. However, don't fire the flash when you are between it and the camera, as you'll be recorded as a silhouette!

6) Move around your subject, trying to "paint" evenly with your flash. If you have two flashes, alternate between them as this will give one time to recharge while you fire the other, allowing you to work more quickly.

7) Once you feel that 2–3 minutes is up, return to your camera and end the exposure. Review the image and check the histogram to see if the exposure looks good.

Note

The number of flashes that will be required will depend on the size of your subject. 30–60 flashes wouldn't be an excessive number for an average-sized building, so be prepared!

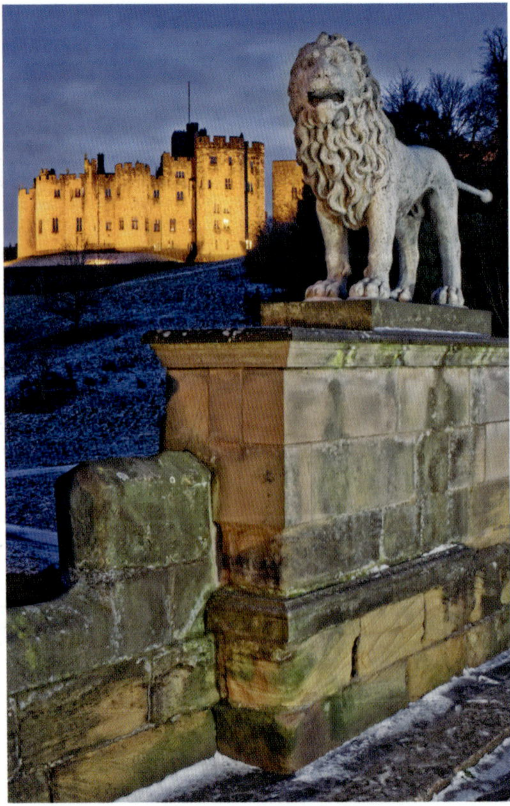

FLASHDANCE
This decorative bridge was completely unlit, so flash was used off-camera to illuminate it. Because the wall and lion were close to the camera it only required 20 flashes to light it evenly.

Canon EOS 1Ds MkII, 50mm lens, 1 min. at f/16, ISO 100

Painting with light: flashlight

What you need: Tripod, flashlight, fully charged batteries for both your camera and flashlight, remote release.

1) Follow steps 1–2 for **Painting with light: flash**, as described on page 176.

2) Once the ambient light levels are low, but there is still color in the sky, switch on your flashlight and shine the light on your subject. To determine the correct exposure, use your camera's spot metering facility to meter from the lit area.

3) Set the exposure, fire the shutter, and begin to move the light from your flashlight smoothly around your subject. You can stand next to the camera to do this, but this will light your subject from the front. For a more interesting lighting effect try moving away to either side of your camera and "painting" your subject at an angle relative to the camera.

4) Once the exposure is complete, review the image and check the histogram to see if the exposure looks good.

Note

When using a flashlight to paint with light, I usually set my camera to Manual so the camera won't alter the exposure as the ambient light levels change. I generally shoot a number of frames so that I can choose later which image has the most pleasing balance between the ambient light and the flashlight.

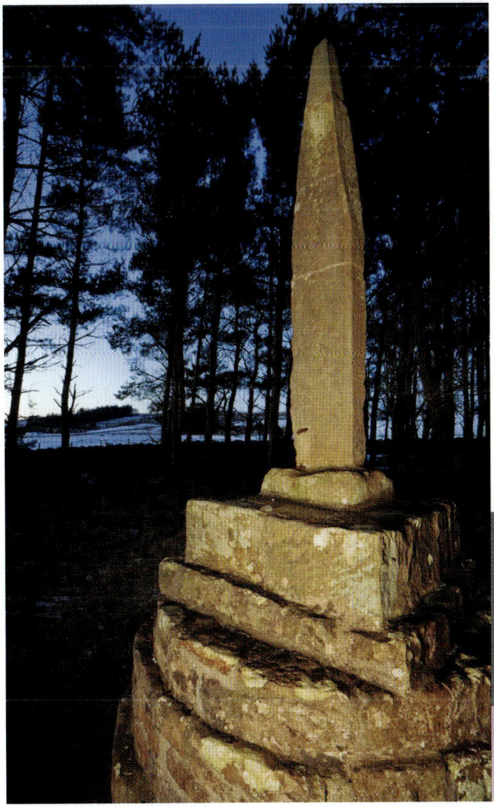

CLOSE TO

The closer you are to your subject, the less powerful your flashlight needs to be. This exposure was achieved with a small flashlight, as both it and the camera were only a few feet from the subject.

Canon EOS 1Ds MkII, 17–40mm lens (at 20mm), 1.5 min. at f/16, ISO 100

Panning

Panning is a technique that involves recording action shots in low light at slow shutter speeds, while keeping the subject relatively sharp.

When light levels are low, it's more difficult to achieve the shutter speed you need to freeze action. You could increase the ISO, but that would risk a corresponding increase in image noise. Panning describes the act of moving your camera, timing its movement to follow a subject, so the subject will remain sharp and the background will be blurred. This often creates a greater sense of speed than a "straight" shot with a fast shutter speed.

Shooting a panning shot

What you need: Lens (focal length dependant on how close you are to your subject).

1) Position yourself so that there is nothing between you and the point at which your subject will pass by. Think about the background—although it will be blurred, plain backgrounds will often work better than busy, colorful ones.

2) Switch the lens to Manual focus and focus where you think your subject will be.

Note

Panning requires practise and experimentation, so don't despair if you don't immediately perfect the technique.

WIDE-ANGLE LENS

As long as it's safe to get close to your chosen subject, wide-angle lenses will allow you to pan further during the exposure.

Hasselblad Xpan, 45mm lens, exposure details unrecorded, ISO 50 (Fuji Velvia)

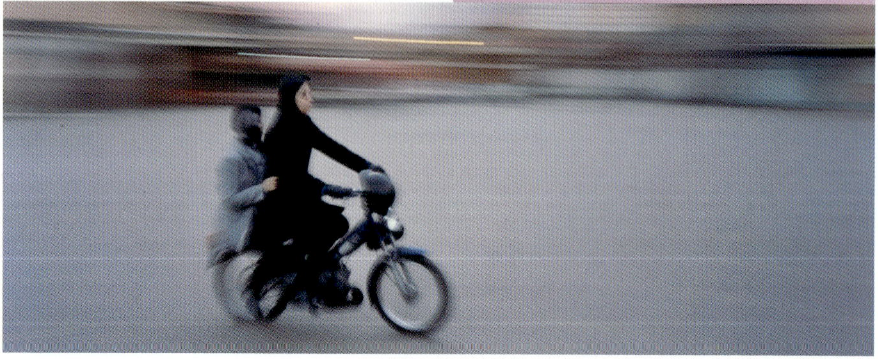

Alternatively if your camera has predictive focusing, keep the AF switched on and select the central focus point.

3) There is no correct shutter speed to use for a panning shot: use a higher shutter speed if possible for faster subjects, but it should still be slower than the shutter speed you would use to freeze movement.

4) As your subject approaches, follow the movement with your camera. If you're using predictive autofocus, press the shutter-release button down halfway to activate the AF system.

5) Press the shutter-release button down smoothly as your subject approaches the closest point to you, and then smoothly release it once the subject has passed. Continue to follow the movement of the subject with your camera as you do so.

Tip

Panning can be used in conjunction with slow sync flash. This will make the subject even sharper as the flash will freeze the movement at the point of firing. However, don't use flash if it might prove a dangerous distraction for your subject. Panning works best when the subject is moving parallel to you.

BLURRED
The slower the shutter speed you use, the more impressionistic the image will be.

Nikon D70, 100mm lens, 1/20 sec. at f/11, ISO 200

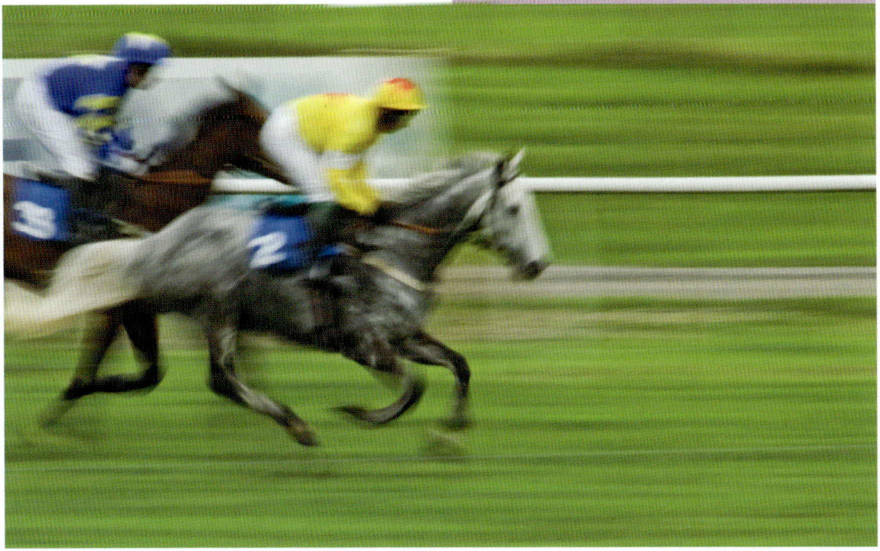

The abstract approach

You don't need to think literally when shooting in low light. Manipulating your camera or lens during an exposure can produce striking abstract images.

Zoom burst

Generally, once a composition has been chosen with a zoom lens the focal length is left well alone. However, turning the zoom ring during an exposure creates what is known as a "zoom burst." This has the visual effect of making your subject appear as though it is streaking toward the camera; the more the lens is zoomed during the exposure, the more exaggerated the effect. Low light is ideal for this technique, as longer shutter speeds give you more time to turn the zoom ring. Streetlamps can make great subjects, particularly if you can look down from a high building or hill at the scene.

Shooting a zoom burst

What you need: Tripod, remote release, zoom lens with wide focal length range.

1) Mount your camera on a tripod and compose your shot with the zoom at the widest

Tip

A related effect involves de-focusing your camera. Start with your camera in focus and then, during the exposure, smoothly turn the focus ring to minimum focus.

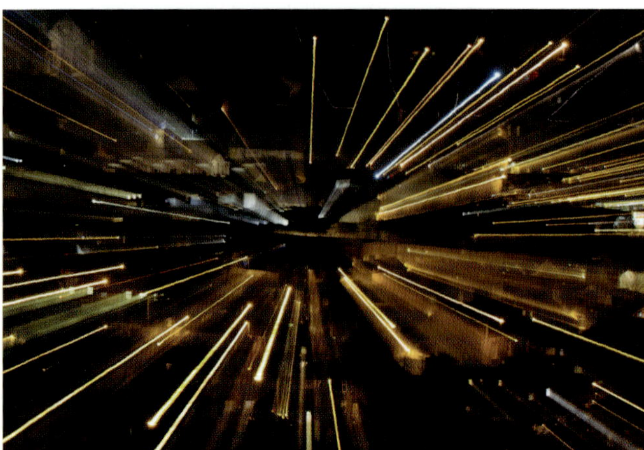

ZOOM

I prefer using longer zoom lenses to create a zoom burst, as the perspective is more compressed.

Canon EOS 7D, 70–200mm lens (zoomed from 70mm to 200mm), 5 sec. at f/5, ISO 100

end of its focal length range. Switch your lens to manual focus and focus at ∞.

2) Set the camera to Manual exposure and set the aperture and ISO to give you a shutter speed of 2–8 sec.

3) Trigger the shutter using the remote release. As you do, smoothly turn the zoom ring so you zoom into the scene. Try to time the turn from minimum to maximum zoom to match the length of the shutter speed (you may need to practise beforehand). Try not to knock the camera as you do this, as any movement in the camera will be recorded as a slight kink in the light trails.

4) Review the image on screen and reshoot if necessary.

Movement

A different, if equally abstract, effect can be achieved with any lens (prime or zoom) by moving the camera during a long exposure. Street lighting or any other point light source is ideal as a subject.

Shooting a panning abstract

What you need: Lens.

1) For this effect you need to handhold your camera. Switch your lens to manual focus and focus at ∞.

2) Switch the camera to Manual exposure and set the aperture and ISO to achieve a shutter speed in the region of 2–8 sec.

3) Fire the shutter. As the camera exposes, smoothly pan your camera. Try to time the extent of the panning to match the length of the shutter speed (it's worth practising this before you shoot).

4) Review the image on screen and reshoot if necessary.

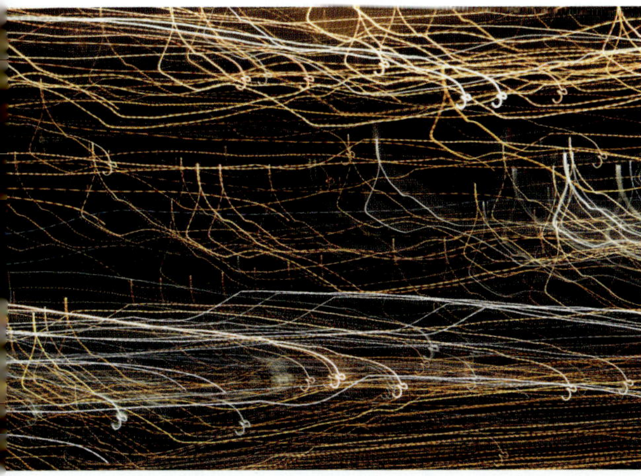

PANNING
Jiggling your camera around during the panning process produces an even wilder result.

Canon EOS 7D, 70–200mm lens (200mm), 6 sec. at f/4, ISO 100

Reeds

This image was shot approximately half an hour after sunset, so there was still color in the sky. The white balance was set to Daylight so that the blueness of the ambient light was maintained, and so that the flashlight used to illuminate the reeds in the foreground would appear warmer, creating an appealing color contrast.

Camera: Canon EOS 7D
Lens: 10–22mm lens (at 20mm)
Exposure: 30 sec. at f/13
ISO: 100

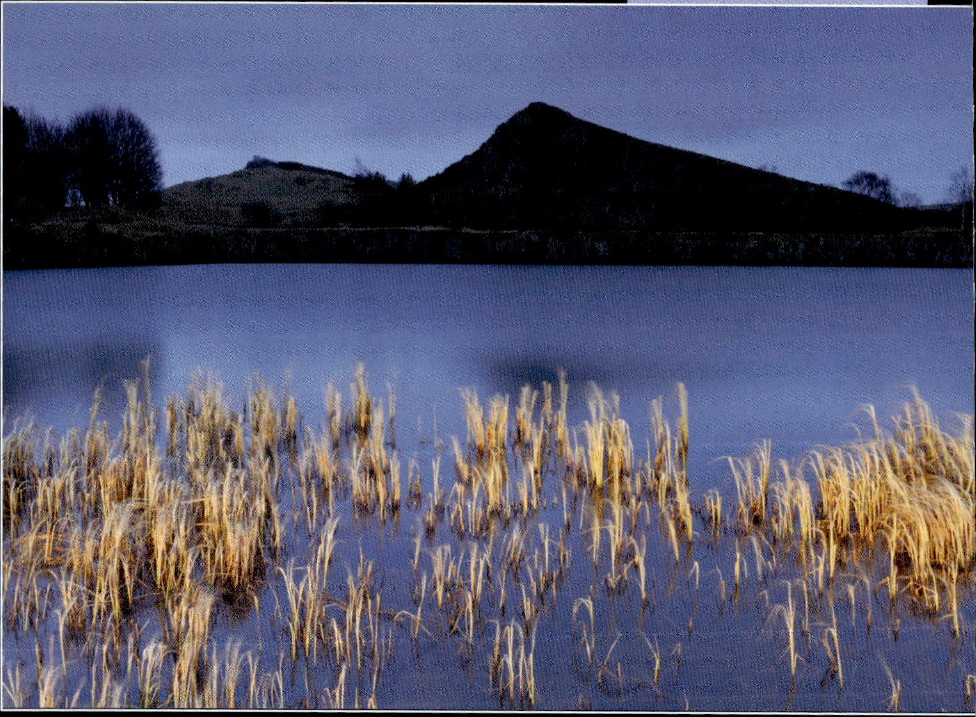

A colorful pre-sunrise or post-sunset sky makes an interesting backdrop for a silhouetted subject. Because the sky will still be relatively bright, it's often possible to use relatively fast shutter speeds and handhold the camera as I did here.

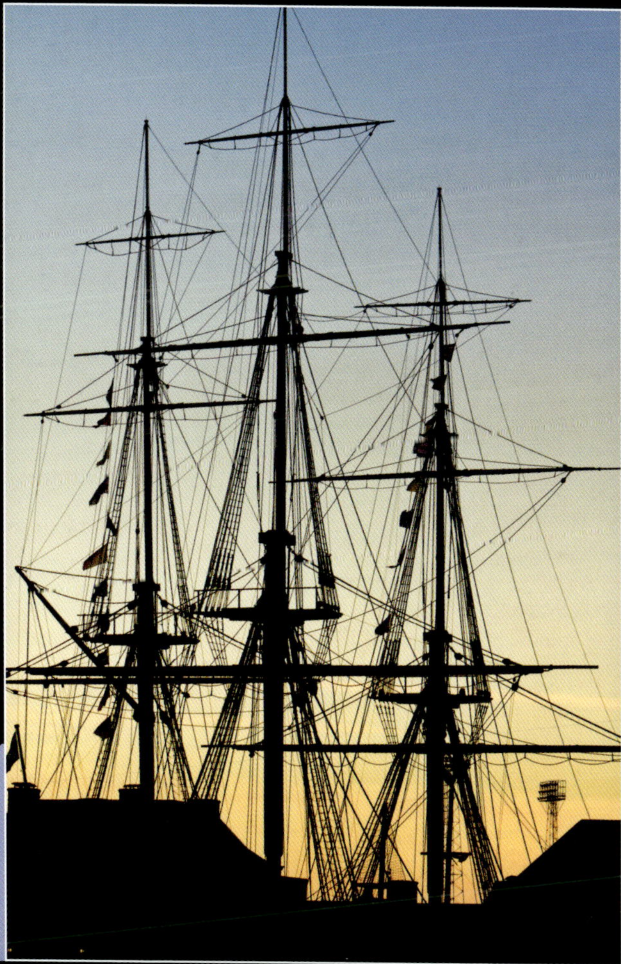

Camera: Canon EOS 7D
Lens: 70–200mm lens (at 100mm)
Exposure: 1/125 sec. at f/6.3
ISO: 100

Glossary

Aberration An imperfection in a photograph, usually caused by the optics of a lens.

AE (automatic exposure lock) A camera control that locks in the exposure value, allowing a scene to be recomposed.

Angle of view The area of a scene that a lens takes in, measured in degrees.

Aperture The opening in a camera lens through which light passes to expose the sensor. The relative size of the aperture is denoted by f-stops.

Autofocus (AF) A reliable through-the-lens focusing system allowing accurate focus without the user manually turning the lens.

Bracketing Taking a series of identical pictures, changing only the exposure, usually in ½- or ⅓-stop increments.

Buffer In-camera memory of a digital camera.

Center-weighted metering A metering pattern that determines the exposure of a photograph by placing importance on the light-meter reading at the center of the frame.

Chromatic aberration The inability of a lens to bring spectrum colors into focus at one point.

Codec A piece of software that is able to interpret and decode a digital file such as Raw.

Color temperature The color of a light source expressed in degrees Kelvin (K).

Compression The process by which digital files are reduced in size.

Contrast The range between the highlight and shadow areas of a photo, or a marked difference in illumination between colors or adjacent areas.

Depth of field (DoF) The amount of a photograph that appears acceptably sharp. This is controlled primarily by the aperture: the smaller the aperture, the greater the depth of field.

DPOF Digital Print Order Format.

Diopter Unit expressing the power of a lens.

dpi (dots per inch) Measure of the resolution of a printer or scanner. The more dots per inch, the higher the resolution.

Dynamic range The ability of the camera's sensor to capture a full range of shadows and highlights.

Evaluative metering A metering system whereby light reflected from several subject areas is calculated based on algorithms. Also known as Matrix or Multi-segment metering.

Exposure The amount of light allowed to hit the digital sensor, controlled by aperture, shutter speed, and ISO. Also, the act of taking a photograph, as in "making an exposure."

Exposure compensation A control that allows intentional over- or underexposure.

Extension tubes Hollow spacers that fit between the camera body and lens, typically used for close-up work. The tubes increase the focal length of the lens, magnifying the subject.

Fill-in flash Flash combined with daylight in an exposure. Used with naturally backlit or harshly side-lit or top-lit subjects to prevent silhouettes forming, or to add extra light to the shadow areas of a well-lit scene.

Filter A piece of colored or coated glass or plastic placed in front of the lens.

Focal length The distance, usually in millimeters, from the optical center point of a lens to its focal point.

fps (frames per second) A measure of the time needed for a digital camera to process one photograph and be ready to shoot the next.

f-stop Number assigned to a particular lens aperture. Wide apertures are denoted by small numbers (such as f/1.8 and f/2.8), while small apertures are denoted by large numbers (such as f/16 and f/22).

HDR (High Dynamic Range) A technique that increases the dynamic range of a photograph by merging several shots taken with different exposure settings.

Histogram A graph representing the distribution of tones in a photograph.

Hotshoe A light area with a loss of detail in the highlights. This is a common problem with flash photography.

Hotspot A light area with a loss of detail. A common problem in flash photography.

Incident-light reading Meter reading based on the light falling onto the subject.

Interpolation A method of increasing the file size of a digital photograph by adding pixels, thereby increasing its resolution.

ISO (International Organization for Standardization) The sensitivity of the digital sensor measured in terms equivalent to the ISO rating of a film.

JPEG (Joint Photographic Experts Group) JPEG compression can reduce file sizes to about 5% of their original size, but uses a lossy compression system that degrades image quality.

LCD (Liquid Crystal Display) The flat screen on a digital camera that allows the user to preview digital photographs.

Macro A term used to describe close focusing and the close-focusing ability of a lens.

Megapixel One million pixels is equal to one megapixel.

Memory card A removable storage device for digital cameras.

Mirror lock-up A function that allows the reflex mirror of an SLR to be raised and held in the "up" position prior to the exposure being made.

Noise Non image-forming interference visible in a digital image caused by stray electrical signals during exposure.

Opensource Software created by unpaid volunteers, which is often free to use.

PictBridge The industry standard for sending information directly from a camera to a printer, without having to connect to a computer.

Pixel Short for "picture element"—the smallest bits of information in a digital photo.

RAW The file format in which the raw data from the sensor is stored without permanent alteration being made.

Red-eye reduction The file format in which the raw data from the sensor is stored without permanent alteration being made.

Resolution The number of pixels used to capture or display a photo.

RGB (Red, Green, Blue) Computers and other digital devices understand color information as combinations of red, green, and blue.

Rule of thirds A rule of composition that places the key elements of a picture at points along imagined lines that divide the frame into thirds, both vertically and horizontally.

Shutter The mechanism that controls the amount of light reaching the sensor, by opening and closing.

SLR (Single Lens Reflex) A type of camera that allows the user to view the scene through the lens, using a reflex mirror.

Soft proofing Using software to mimic on screen how an image will look once output to another imaging device, such as a printer.

Spot metering A metering pattern that places importance on the intensity of light reflected by a very small portion of the scene.

Teleconverter A lens that is inserted between the camera body and the main lens, increasing the effective focal length.

Telephoto A lens with a large focal length and a narrow angle of view.

TTL (Through The Lens) A metering system that measures light passing through the camera's lens at the time of shooting.

USB (Universal Serial Bus) A data transfer standard, used by most cameras when connecting to a computer.

White balance A function that allows the correct color balance to be recorded for any given lighting situation.

Wide-angle lens A lens with a short focal length and consequently a wide angle of view.

Useful web sites

GENERAL

Digital Photography Review
Camera and lens review web site
www.dpreview.com

Flickr
Photo sharing web site with a large user base
www.flickr.com

David Taylor
Landscape and travel photography
www.davidtaylorphotography.co.uk

Luminous Landscape
Comprehensive online guide to photography, including HDR
www.luminous-landscape.com

EQUIPMENT

Adobe
Photoshop, Photoshop Elements, and Lightroom editing software
www.adobe.com

Apple
www.apple.com

Canon
www.canon.com

Nikon
www.nikon.com

Olympus
www.olympus-global.com

Panasonic
www.panasonic.com

Pentax
www.pentax.com

Sigma
www.sigmaphoto.com

Sony
www.sony.com

PHOTOGRAPHY PUBLICATIONS

Photography books & Expanded Camera Guides
www.ammonitepress.com

Black & White Photography magazine
Outdoor Photography magazine
www.thegmcgroup.com

Index